BABEL

The Cultural and Linguistic Barriers
Between Nations

Professor Henry Prais

BABEL

The Cultural and Linguistic Barriers Between Nations

edited by
RAINER KÖLMEL and JERRY PAYNE

ABERDEEN UNIVERSITY PRESS
Member of Maxwell Macmillan Pergamon Publishing Corporation

First published 1989
Aberdeen University Press

© The Contributors 1989

British Library Cataloguing in Publication Data

Babel: the cultural and linguistic barriers between nations.
1. Cultural relations. Role of language
I. Kölmel, Rainer   II. Payne, Jerry
303.4′82

ISBN 0 08 037969 9

Typeset from author-generated discs
and printed by AUP Glasgow/Aberdeen—a member of BPCC Ltd

Contents

Preface

The essays in this volume can only be a modest salute to a very remarkable person, Professor Henry Prais. How does one capture the excitement and vitality, the range, vision and sparkle of this dynamo of a man? We all have our ups and downs in life. We who have been privileged to get to know Henry Prais are fortunate that he survived the most searing experience of his young life in Nazi Germany in the 1930s. Thus when he came to Britain as a refugee he was already mature beyond his years. Perhaps it was this narrow escape that has given him such a spark and zest for life, and a care and concern for people which found their happiest expression in his work with students.

I recall very vividly one of the great highs in his life. He returned triumphantly one day from having bearded the then Principal of Heriot-Watt, Robin Smith. He had persuaded the Principal to let him expand the language service teaching courses which he conducted with his matchless enthusiasm into a fully fledged degree course, in Interpreting and Translating. It was a brilliant concept. Many of the essays in this volume take up the themes which Henry first nurtured in that new degree course. The rest is well known. The course has been an outstanding success, and the concept has been taken up in other institutions. He has proved a Prophet, leading the teachers of languages into a new Promised Land.

Of course Henry Prais has always been much more than a languages scholar, having the gift of tongues. In Britain the major force shaping his destiny was Glasgow, the city as well as the university. Glasgow, in all its rich variety and worldly-wise humanity and resilience, sat comfortably on him. He was a distinguished debater as well as student at Glasgow University, revelling in the impishness and jauntiness of student repartee. Happily, too, the Glasgow Boys and the Glasgow art scene nurtured his passion for the Arts in all their manifestations. His wife has shared in all these experiences, encouraging but also calming him in her gentle ways as the occasion demanded.

Colleagues as well as students have been enriched by this vast cultural awareness which Henry Prais displays, modestly but with immense erudition. I recall vividly a journey to the south which we undertook together in 1974, to sound out a subject sub-committee chairman of the University Grants Committee. Naturally, we got our priorities right, and visited the Turner exhibition in the Royal Academy en route. What better companion could one have for such a feast? One's horizons were extended, and sensibilities heightened.

Henry Prais made his talents freely available to societies and groups outside

the immediate university community, playing a full part in the artistic life of
Scotland. Yet in the end it is students who really matter to him. Eyes light up
when students recall his teaching, the enthusiasm, the subtle insights, and
the boyish sparkle.

Few men have had such an influence for good in cultivating the human
spirit and reminding us of the essential dignity of Man. So it is with a sense
of privilege at having been a colleague and friend, with affection and also
humility that I commend this volume of essays.

Tom Johnston

Introduction

The origins of this book require some explanation. It was conceived as a tribute to Henry Prais, the first holder of the Chair in the Languages Department of Heriot-Watt University in Edinburgh. Although Henry retired in 1980 and now lives with his wife Edith in Jerusalem, he maintains close contact with his former colleagues inside and outside the Department. We cannot say we were at all surprised by the positive response which greeted our proposal to bring out a *Festschrift* to mark his 70th birthday. The impact of his personality and intellectual vitality on those privileged to work with him was as lasting as was the diverse contribution he made to cultural and academic life between his arrival in Scotland from Germany in 1938 and his retirement.

Professionally, Henry will perhaps be best remembered for his role in establishing Heriot-Watt's degree in translating and interpreting. This was therefore our natural starting point when we came to the difficult task of devising a theme which would be both sufficiently broad to encompass the range of interests of potential contributors and sufficiently narrowly defined to prevent the *Festschrift* from becoming merely a collection of disparate articles. Translation, in the broadest sense, was also the theme of the inaugural lecture which Henry delivered in 1977. It was entitled *Reflections on the Tower of Babel*. In the lecture (which was never published—Henry's reluctance to commit himself in print was always a mystery to his friends), he never strayed far or long from a deliberation on the role of translation and the translator, which was appropriate to the context of the lecture. However, in typical fashion, he used the biblical theme as a spring board for a host of fascinating speculations and intellectual sallies, setting parameters wider even than those we believe to have been staked out by the varied contributions in this volume. For all the apparent eclecticism (the range covers literary, linguistic, pedagogical and historical themes) each article addresses issues whose origins can ultimately be traced to the post-Babel condition of disunity and disharmony in the world.

In his lecture Henry did not seriously dispute the (obvious) interpretation of the Babel story, namely as a mythical explanation for the existence of a multitude of languages and peoples. However, he went a great deal further, developing the idea of a pre-Babel world as 'a paradise of language', a 'verbal, real and conceptual harmonious unity' in which there was a 'direct and undistorted relationship between man and the world and the objects in it. Men did not only understand each other but they had an identical understanding of the world around them.' Like that other paradise myth which Henry loved to dissect (on one memorable occasion during a seminar on Kleist's *Über das Marionettentheater*) the story of Babel is circular. In other words, in diagnosing the essential problem it also reveals the possible remedy, in this case a longing

1

for a return to the primeval state, to 're-establish a common, harmonious and pure language', or, as Noel Thomas writes in the context of Elias Canetti's *Auto-da-fé* in this volume '... the fragmentation of language points to the possiblity of linguistic reintegration. The fall foreshadows redemption, healing and the bridging of the division.' The step from here to seeing translation as an 'act of restoration of that common pure language' was an easy one for Henry to take. Translation as a sort of divine task, a step towards repossessing a lost unity and reestablishing a common humanity. Sceptics might understandably be reluctant to be convinced that the work of the EC's translation service, for example, (an estimated 770,000 pages of translation produced in 1986 in the Commission alone!) is inspired by such lofty ideals, yet the end such means serve is that of lowering barriers between nations and promoting international understanding, however prosaic and commercial the immediate purpose may appear. Neither is this faith in the function of translation a naive one; the naive put their faith in the panaceas of Esperanto or machine-translation. Idealistic it might be, particularly in the Britain of the 1980s when cultural philistinism appears to rule the day. But Henry was also a realist and what he achieved in his *Reflections* was to put translation in the perspective it deserves, to accord it its proper status in the order of things.

Translation as a step towards re-establishing communication between the uncomprehending, translation seen then not as a mechanical exercise, not just as a transfer from the phonemes of one language into those of another but a higher-level process in which the translator assumes the role of go-between between cultures, a broker working for understanding between nations. This is the thread running through Albrecht Neubert's article. In it he develops his well-known theory of translation as 'mediation' and the translator as 'mediator'. His unashamed profession of internationalist faith is in tune with the new climate of openness in most of Europe.

The preference for using film subtitles as opposed to dubbing would suggest a rejection of the illusion which dubbing attempts to create; subtitles aim to promote verbal communication without suppressing the fact that cultural bridging is going on. Ian Mason examines the sort of problems facing the translator of cinema subtitles and provides an excellent illustration of the sort of constraints (in this case those of time and space) and often intractable problems that confront the translator in professional practice. There are as many forms of translation as there are forms of original composition. In identifying the difficulties Arabic native-speakers have in translating from particular types of English text Basil Hatim (who was born near the biblical Babel!) finds that certain compositional conventions commonplace in English texts represent a significant hurdle for those unfamiliar with the linguistic culture of the source text, further evidence of the link between linguistic and cultural barriers. His conclusion that the structure of counter-argumentative texts is 'culture-specific' is a measure perhaps of how deep post-Babel divisions have become. Anthony Stanforth's is another contribution which examines, this time at a microcosmic level, the way cultures come into linguistic contact. His article, which concentrates on the morphological adaptations made to

German loan material in British English, is part of a wider project to investigate the influence of German on English from both the cultural and linguistic points of view. Jim Halliday and Elena Crosbie provide a survey of Soviet 'lexical history' and examine the effects that changes under Mr Gorbachev have had on the political vocabulary of Russian. Finally, Margaret Lang demonstrates the vital role played by cohesive textual devices in the communicative process and how their use and reception can promote or hinder that process.

Turning to the professional dimensions of language, Hugh Keith considers the demands placed on practising translators on the basis of a survey he conducted amongst several large companies in Britain. Surprisingly perhaps, he finds that the most serious deficiency remarked on lay in the area of mother-tongue competence. If he is concerned with the bread and butter end of the market, Janet Altman, herself a practising interpreter, devotes her article to the elite of the 'mediating' profession, the conference interpreters. Like Hugh Keith she carries out an empirical survey, this time, however, among professional practitioners in Strasbourg. Mireille Poots, who has a long-standing and passionate concern for the foreign-language competence of engineers, combines an attack on British linguistic insularity with a heartfelt plea that the universities appreciate and adapt to the demands of a rapidly opening market in Europe, particularly in view of 1992 and the creation of the single market.

Alan Thompson's account of the history of the BBC's World Service itself serves as a bridge between the linguistic and national repercussions of Babel. Radio waves can cross frontiers more rapidly than any other medium of communication, unless of course the messages are suppressed by jamming (thankfully less prevalent in this era of *glasnost*). Although governments have always been quick to recognise the value and effectiveness of international broadcasting it has not always served to lessen confusion and promote the sort of harmony and unity alluded to by Henry Prais in his lecture on Babel. One nation's truth will continue to be another's propaganda. David Harron is a second-year student of French and Spanish in the Department of Languages at Heriot-Watt. His account of the present state of the national debate in Scotland and of the options available to those seeking a new political expression of Scottish distinctiveness is therefore a particularly appropriate addition to this volume. His interest and expertise in an academic area not specifically related to his language studies is something which Henry Prais would heartily approve of. Jerry Payne looks at the historical background to a problem that continues to beset Hungarian nation-building. More than in other European cultures language has played a decisive role in defining the Hungarian national identity. Rainer Kölmel shows how national barriers were abandoned and Babel reversed in war-time Glasgow. When refugees from Nazi oppression (among them Henry Prais) and radical and enlightened Glaswegian citizens came together they created a lasting cosmopolitan tradition in the European City of Culture. Andy Hunter identifies a cultural barrier of a different kind. In his historical survey of cultural debates and movements in France from the Second Republic to the Popular Front he shows that class and class consciousness prevented the emergence of a unified national culture.

Racialism is a heightened, perverted form of nationalism. Hamish Ritchie, in the first of three articles on literary themes, picks the work of a writer unknown outside Germany; Artur Dinter's rabid anti-semitism in fiction preempted the factual anti-semitism in the twelve years of Nazi rule. Elias Canetti, whose novel *Auto-da-Fé* is the subject of Noel Thomas's contribution, was a refugee from racial oppression. In his article Noel Thomas quotes a passage from an essay by Canetti which appears to be depressing confirmation of the persisting effect of Babel on the human condition: 'I realized that there is no greater illusion than the view that language is a means of communication between people. Rarely does anything penetrate into the mind of another person, and when this does take place then it is something incorrect.' The leitmotif in Karin McPherson's essay on the GDR writer Christa Wolf's latest novel *Störfall* also involves the limitations of language. In her view the book should be read not only as 'the severance of self from language' but also in a more optimistic vein, implicit also in the Babel myth, as a 'search for a possible continuation ... a future for language and words'.

Stewart Paton, co-founder of the Department of Languages at Heriot-Watt University, reflects on the residential literary study weekends which were central to Henry Prais's idea of what the role of literature in an applied languages course should be. The study and discussion of the literature of unfamiliar cultures (whether read in the original or in translation) was seen as being of 'vital importance in widening cultural horizons and refining perceptions of what is genuinely different'.

Translation as Mediation

Albrecht Neubert

Research and teaching have at all times responded, more or less directly, to the needs of society. Of course, the history of science and in fact of all academic disciplines bears witness to seemingly opposite motivations, with scholars maintaining their quest for truth about objective reality on the one hand and the thrust of facts and their complex relationships in their own right on the other hand.

The rise of translation studies in the course of the past fifty or so years is, I think, a telling example of a concerted response to the enormous proliferation of 'bilingually mediated communication' (*zweisprachig vermittelte Kommunikation*) encompassing practically all walks of life. There is no doubt that translation and interpreting have been around since speakers of different languages have been unable to communicate directly. And there have always been writers and translators, philosophers and scholars who have expressed their ideas, their confidence and their misgivings about how good or how bad, how reliable or how disappointing, or at any rate how diverse translations can be. But it was not until the middle of this century that individual statements about translations turned into a fully-fledged body of thought devoted to systematizing, from many different angles, what constitutes the linguistic activity which has given us the label the 'century of translation'. Simultaneously, in conjunction with the appearance of innumerable books and articles there has sprung up an equally large number of training centres purporting to deliver the manpower society needs to achieve communication across languages and across countries and cultures. More and more conferences are taking place where research on translation is presented and discussed and applications of the results to the teaching of translation are hotly debated. Thus the study of translation and, in particular, the academic institutions where the practice of translation is taught do not exist in an intellectual ivory tower. They serve social needs as well as they can, whether everybody is aware of it or not.

Yet it is also a fact that many scholars divest themselves of any responsibility for making a contribution to better teaching methods. In fact they study translation in the same disinterested way linguistic scientists look at language. In the true spirit of socially disinterested Chomskyan 'Reflection on Language' they take it as a unique subject matter, viz. the result of a special kind of 'language faculty'. 'Stimulated by appropriate and continuing experience, (this) language faculty creates a grammar that generates sentences' which are *both identical with and* different from the *formal and semantic properties* of the source and the target languages. The translator can be said to exploit his *knowledge of* the two languages generated by those two grammars. He 'proceed(s) to use the (one) language that he now knows' substituting it for

5

the one used by someone else but which happens to be one that he also knows (cf. Chomsky 1975, 36). Translation, then, is an outgrowth of our normal 'cognitive capacity' (ibid. 3-35) to 'quite effortlessly make use of an intricate structure of specific rules and guiding principles to convey (our) thoughts and feelings to others, arousing in them novel ideas and subtle perceptions and judgements' (ibid., 4).

What translation adds to this capacity is that it enhances this already extraordinary intellectual achievement by accomplishing it on the basis of a tacit understanding of an 'abnormal' communicative situation in terms of an unavoidable 'normality'. Namely, 'normal', i.e. monolingual, speakers/ writers communicate in a language that is not the same as the one in which the translator has to excel in recreating *their source-language expressed* 'thoughts and ideas' with the aim of arousing in his *target-language* readers 'novel ideas and subtle perceptions and judgements'. Normally, that is, in monolingual communication, the 'thoughts and ideas' of the language user are not supposed to clash with 'the novel ideas and subtle perceptions and judgements' they are meant to arouse. They correspond with each other.

In bilingually mediated communication, however, with the input in a language contrasting with the language of the output a further decisive complication has to be taken into account: The 'thoughts and ideas' to be conveyed are not those of the person who conveys them, and the 'novel ideas and subtle perceptions and judgements' are not aroused by the 'quite effortless use of an intricate structure of specific rules and guiding principles' in the same recipient who shares the original sender's 'cognitive capacity'.

The *thoughts and ideas* and the *medium* in which they are expressed are markedly set apart from the *perceptions and judgements* and the new *medium* in which they surface after the act of translation. Translation, by definition, breaks up communication by placing the *mediator* between the intending speaker/writer and the intended addressee.

It is precisely this complex involvement of bilingually mediated communication in the most diverse kinds of situations that makes the study of translation *per se* so problematic if it is carried out without recourse to the constraints to which it is subjected in real life situations. Whereas the 'language faculty' of the ordinary language user can be conceived of as exhibiting universal properties shared by all human beings, and in fact it may be treated as a human universal, the *translation faculty* is anything but universal. On the contrary, it can be said to be highly unusual, even quite abnormal, considering the fact that the likelihood of successfully repeating something that has already been said or written before (and to a particular addressee) is invariably bound up with failure or, at least, certain losses of information.

Describing and explaining translation in a social vacuum, therefore, runs the risk of barking up the wrong tree. Of course, one can engage in the quite illuminating pastime of establishing *equivalence relations*, which point out in a fairly systematic and perhaps also quite comprehensive way how grammatical constructions and lexical items of a source language can be matched by target structures and words. Yet it must never be overlooked that what one ends up with are only *potential equivalences*. More often than not actual translations will be quite unlike those 'expected' renderings. Above all, they will never draw from any isolated grammar or lexicon 'modules'. In plain words, the study of translation is not a branch of contrastive linguistics.

Theoretical concerns as well as practical applications, if they are meant to reflect the reality of translation, cannot abstract from the *mediated quality* of this kind of language use. Unless he treats it as the basic feature of research the theorist cannot hope to focus on the features that distinguish translation from all other forms of verbal communication. Unless they turn it into a key aim both the practitioner and the teacher are bound to miss out one of the most important enabling factors of translatability. In actual fact, mediation is perhaps the missing link that can bring together the endeavours of theoretical and applied translation studies. It can inspire research and, equally, orient teaching. It can do so because it singles out the uniqeness of the translation process and because it characterizes the main trait of the translator's personality.

An awareness of the translator's role as a mediator can also explain the often-quoted advice that the translator should step into the original writer's shoes and act out the sender's part on the stage provided by the target language. I think this amounts to asking for the impossible. Equally, the translator cannot pretend to be identical with the target language addressee. His sophistication is knowing two languages when the others are quite happy to be conversant with either the one or the other. His lot is an almost schizophrenic language faculty split up into two hemispheres. And he can only escape this *di-lemma* by taking up the task of the mediator.

Embracing the mediator's job, I think, puts the translator in a position that allows him to cope with the 'highly unnatural situation' mentioned above. *Translation is mediation.* Instead of making him an omnipotent author-figure or a self-styled evaluator of the original text who bestows upon his audience what he alone deems proper based on his *personal* understanding of the source, the mediator's function gives him the modesty and discretion needed to bridge the communicative gap between the sender and his audience. Contrary to the individualist stance, so often propagated in modern theorizations about the translator as decision-taker (cf. Kelletat's (1986) witty repartee), I follow Gemar (1988, 65)

> 'Plus modestement, je crois plutôt que le traducteur est un *médiateur* (my emphasis—A.N.) entre le texte de départ et le destinataire du texte d'arrivée, qu'il soit désigné ou anonyme, dans lequel je reconnais la société tout entire, voire l'humaine condition'.

Mediation, then, is a concept of great explanatory power as well as of far-reaching descriptive potential. But how can we hope to integrate it into translation study as well as into translation teaching without being dazzled by its evidently axiomatic quality? The translator as mediator, so what? If, as I pointed out above, translation is mediation what does this qualification actually specify about translation? Is it not but a tautology, as perhaps already seemed to be the case in our definition of translation as *bilingually mediated communication?* What is the concrete nature of translational mediation? How can we break up this all-inclusive concept into more manageable components or features?

Mediation, evidently, applies to various aspects of the translation process as well as the translation product. Thus I speak of the *mediated process* and the *mediated product*. Both are the work of the translator as *mediating agent*. He acts according to *mediating strategy* with the aim of achieving a *mediating effect*. And all this occurs in a *mediating situation*. Further, the original becomes a *mediated text* just as the author may be looked upon as a *mediated sender*. As for the receiving end, mediated/ing aspects of translation, the recipient of the translation, *for whom* the mediation is effected, is not at all involved in any mediated/ing activity. Although what the recipient actually gets is something mediated, he himself is neither 'mediating' or 'mediated'. Reading a novel in translation or seeing a translated play on the stage or a dubbed film on TV, perusing a travel brochure or consulting an instruction manual both in translation, listening to an interpreter doing speeches or dialogue etc. may not give us first-hand information, since it is mediated, but the actual amount or degree of mediation involved cannot normally be judged by the addressee. Apart from occasional lapses in the surface structure of the translation the target speaker, precisely because of his monolingual 'language faculty', is unable to perceive any mediation phenomena. Similarly, the source text writer, whom I, perhaps somewhat prematurely, called the 'mediated sender' is not really involved in the mediation process either, unless the 'original' was produced with the sole and express intention that it was to be translated, which is certainly the exception to the rule.

It turns out that mediation as such, translational mediation, pertains primarily to the translator, the mediator par excellence. Whatever he comes into contact with gets drawn into the mediational mechanism. The constitutive feature of mediation is what I would like to call, for want of a better term, its *double* or *doubling* character. Whatever is perceived by the translator in the source text is 'doubled' in his mind, that is, becomes a candidate for being substituted by newly generated 'language material' as a result of his 'target language faculty'. Words and sentences, structures and overall designs of the original, when they strike the eye or ear of the translator, are continually being subjected to a subtle negotiation process that matches potential target material with the incoming segments and combinations with the aim of testing it with regard to its suitability as material for the outcoming text. All the time the translator's source and target language faculties are at work, sometimes at play. It is an unending mediating process, which occurs on practically all levels of language, or rather on all levels of the two languages. Actually, there is rarely ever a direct link between the same levels of the source and target languages, such as between source grammar and target grammar or between source lexis and target lexis. At least, the matching process most commonly flips up and down the linguistic levels making sure that other levels help mediating where non-correspondence on the same level is the rule.

There is, however, a feature or complex of features of the source text that is of much greater importance than the many multi-levelled items and arrangements which bother the translator's mediating faculties. It is something which underlies the various surface elements or something those linguistic signs and sign relations help build up in the mind of the translator seeking to understand what he has read or heard and getting ready to carry it over into his new medium. This decisive feature is the *meaning* of the source text expressed sequentially as well as globally. It is the main object of mediation. Everything in the original aims at conveying meaning or meanings. It is here that the practitioner, the scholar, the teacher, and the student of translation all have to show their mettle. It is also here that the mediating nature of translation finds its deepest justification. Without the mediation of meaning there would be no translation.

Why is this so? As early as 1965 Catford, in the true Firthian tradition, pointed out in *A Linguistic Theory of Translation* that 'meaning is a property of a language. A source language text has an SL meaning and a target language text has a TL meaning—a Russian text, for instance, has a Russian meaning (as well as Russian phonology/graphology, grammar and lexis), and an equivalent English text has an English meaning' (Catford, 1965, 35).

More recent investigations into the nature of linguistic meaning, to be sure, have discovered many more aspects of semantic structure but they have not really gone back on the fundamental notion that meaning is language-specific, or rather that it is specific for a particular language. Barwise and Perry, for instance, in their seminal book on modern semantic research *Situations and Attitudes* make the point succinctly:

'(...) the meaning of a human language consists of an intricate relation M between utterance events and other aspects of objective reality, a relation entirely determined by the way the linguistic community uses the language. To know the language is to be able to exploit this relation, in tandem with other available resources, to give and receive information about the world'. (Barwise and Perry, 1983, 17).

Translators, then, with their two language faculties, in principle, have two sets of meanings at their disposal which they can deploy, at least in the abstract. Yet it follows from the logic of semantics that the meaning relationships they have internalized as their knowledge of the source language contrasts significantly with the substance of meaning relationships they have in store as their knowledge of the target language. When they set about their mediating job what they actually do is *negotiate meanings*.

But is this not a vain effort since, as we have seen, meanings between languages cannot be identical? What really is it then that they negotiate? What is it that translators manage to put across? In point of fact translations offer not identical meanings but something I would term *mediated meanings*.

What are mediated meanings? Evidently, mediation affects the semantic core of the original text as well as transforming its surface features. Mediation may be likened to breaking the semantic code of the source and recoding its meaning(s) by means of the semantic conventions of the target language.

What actually gets transferred is a 'function of sequences of source signs'. These signs are, so to speak, 'variables' of this function. They are variables that have been selected by the author of the source text from among the stock of signs available in the (source) language. The signs picked out by the translator for the target version are then the variables that relate to the original function. Or to put it differently, this function is assigned new signs in the target text.

Thus, it is the *semantic function* that is shared by both the source and the target signs. When we claim that a translated piece of text is *equivalent* to a segment of the original we mean precisely this 'functional identity'. The relation of *equivalence* is, of course, a basic ingredient of *translatability*. For any text of part of text to be translatable it should be said to have a potential target language counterpart whose semantic function is substitutable for the semantic function of the source. The translator—and this is the *first phase* of his mediating activity—starts from the meanings of the original and identifies their semantic functions, the functional roles these meanings play in a specific text. Then he takes this semantic functionality as his guiding principle to search for target signs and constructions which might be suitable candidates for the job of carrying a semantic load that is acceptable as a *functional equivalent*. Finding functional equivalents is the *second phase* of the mediation process.

The translator as mediator, then, *mediates source meanings* by interpreting their *semantic functions* with regard to their matching potential by way of *target meanings*. Thus functional equivalence is established not between meanings but between semantic functions. And it is the mediator who 'does the trick', which consists of making language-specific (source) meanings amenable to translation by 'extracting' language-unspecific semantic function and converting them again in terms of adequate (target) meanings.

One can simplify this somewhat complicated procedure by calling the semantic functions of meanings *functional values*. Another term, which stresses the embeddedness of the values to be exchanged between the members of the two *communicative* communities of source and target language users, is *communicative value* (Neubert 1985, 138). Both terms stand for what we get when we *mediate meanings*. And it is about how the translator can get hold of what they refer to in the text that translation is all about. They make sure that texts are translatable.

Functional values are not invariably attached to the signs of a particular language. They are a property of signs in context. In fact, they are largely conditioned by the text in which they, in turn, help to attain its unique textual profile. At least, it is within a text that they make their concrete appearance. They arise as constituent parts of texts and their distribution contributes significantly to the functional/communicative value of a text, that is, both of the whole text and its integral parts (subtexts and chunks). Very often, however, one can already identify functional values within sentences. In fact, a sentence, that is its functional value, is a function of the communicative value of its grammatical and lexical components. Sentences, seen in this light, are in fact *text sentences*. Above, I claimed that we translate not words and constructions but their functional values. Let me now qualify this definition by saying that we can only *translate text sentences*. This contains our credo of translation as mediation in a nutshell. Sentences as fully integrated parts of texts are the proper stuff of translation. They point forward and backward all the time and have to be perceived by the translator as flexible units whose functional value is intricately interwoven with the complex pattern of adjacent sentences. When the translator is holding his 'doubly sensitive' lens (remember the 'doubling' character of his translator's language faculty!) over a text sentence he is intensely conscious of what he did with the previous sentences and he has to take into account what the rest of the text has in score for him. Tackling the 'default sentence' is pre-empted by preceding translational choices and equally pre-empts all follow-up moves. It is quite true that what happens in the act of translation is the extremely elusive matching process occurring simultaneously at a number of lexical and grammatical points *within* a sentence. But while the translator is in the midst of this puzzle he brings to bear an enormous amount ouf *outside* or *extrasentential* information. Without this textual backup (and of course also his linguistic and encyclopedic knowledge) the functional value of any single sentence would be beyond his reach.

I can only hope that my theorizing about the mediator's job of the translator has not clouded the practical issues to be derived from this approach. My only justification is that the challenge to the translator, to his skill and responsibility, is such that he must be able to base his efforts on firm theoretical ground. How easy is it for the expert in any field, for whom the translator does his work, to sneer at the non-expert nature of his endeavours. The concept of *mediation* is, I think, ideally suited to highlight the unique expertise of the translator in his own right. When it figures so prominently in translation studies then I tend to believe this is an indication of at least two things that, in all modesty, speak well for our profession:

First, it marks a decisive step in the science of translation towards a clear-cut characterization of what constitutes the translator's role and what sets it off against all other kinds of verbal activity.

Second, it serves as a useful orientation for the teaching of prospective translators as well as a guideline for practising translators to take their bearings in the daily struggle against the 'untranslatable'.

Bearing this in mind one should not find it too difficult to see the two strands of translation studies distinguished at the outset in a new perspective. Theoretical and applied studies have more in common than is often thought (and deplored). The one has to clear the ground for the other. And the latter justifies the former. Theory without practice is empty. Practice without theory is blind. When mediation is effected something theoretically founded is practically carried out. What translation studies describe and explain is actually performed as a practical assignment.

Finally, mediation also sheds new light on the *ethos* of the translator. His place between the author and his audience, between the original and his product, in effect, his reliability is not that of the copier or imitator nor can it be that of the original writer. In acting out the role of the mediator he introduces an entirely new quality into communication. Writing and speaking in the name of others and for others is *mediated communication*. If the use of language is a distinctly human trait, translation is perhaps a just as typically human phenomenon. In fact, without multilingually mediated communication mankind would not have evolved the way it has over the ages. Translation being one of the oldest professions, it has contributed immensely to building up, exchanging and reviving the achievements of human knowledge and the treasures of the world's cultures among all peoples. When we speak about the vast stock of facts, ideas, hypotheses, conjectures, and myths we have amassed about the world we can be sure that the overwhelming number of documents and books, actually almost everything laid down on paper, has at various stages been transmitted through translations. Translators have seen to it that whole eras have come down to succeeding generations and that vastly divergent cultures could cross-fertilize each other.

What is quite evident with regard to the role of translations in the course of the unfolding and widening of our knowledge over the ages becomes even more obvious if we think of the almost limitless mediation between different languages that has been going on in modern times. In our 'information society', with the printed and spoken media churning out their products at an ever growing speed, the amount of translated material among texts distributed and/or propagated is tremendous. Mediating processes are involved everywhere and at all stages of information transfer. Although the person of the translator and, in particular, his name very rarely stand in the limelight his mediating function is constantly called upon and his activities are modestly, yet nevertheless decisively going on in the background. Mediators are servants. They hold the torch so that both parties, who would be in the dark without them, can communicate. But they themselves remain in the dark, and their ethos demands it that they are happy about it. Deep in their minds they can be and, in fact, they are extremely proud about their triumph as mediators. They achieve something that even the most powerful or influential person, the greatest writer and the most effective communicator—all in their native languages—are unable to do. They do it and the others get the praise. But they know that without them the world would be a much poorer place to live in.

References

Barwise, J and Perry, J, *Situations and Attitudes*. Cambridge, Mass., 1983
Catford, J C, *A Linguistic Theory of Translation*. London, 1965
Chomsky, N, *Reflections on Language*. London, 1975
Gemar, J-C, 'Pour une méthode générale de la traduction: traduire par l'interprétation du texte.' In: *Bulletin of the Canadian Association of Applied Linguistics*. Vol. 10, No 1., 1988
Neubert, A, *Text and Translation. Übersetzungswissenschaftliche Beiträge 8*. Leipzig, 1985

Speaker Meaning and Reader Meaning: Preserving Coherence in Screen Translating

Ian Mason

1. Mass communication and translation

It is probably true to say that most people have relatively little awareness of the effects of translation on their non-professional everyday life. Most translated documents, for example, are not destined for a mass readership: scientific and technical papers, EEC directives, international contracts and so on are all specialised by their very nature. Popular fiction is translated in such a way as to minimise the intrusion of the fact of translation: readers are invited to proceed as if the original had been composed in their own tongue. The same is largely true of press quotations from foreign statesmen. There is, however, one area of activity where translating tends to impinge upon receivers' consciousness in a way that cannot be ignored. The cinema and television are media of mass communication in which it is frequently necessary to resort to translators, whose intervention is generally apparent to viewers. The three common modes of translating employed are, of course, dubbing, voice-over translation and subtitling. A dubbed version may, with the aid of lip-synchronisation and voice-matching, be successful in preserving the cinematic illusion: characters on screen appear to be expressing themselves in the target language. But unless a top-quality job is done (as in the case of feature films which are commercially viable in more than one country), the results of the dubbing process will be apparent to the viewer and may even detract from the successful commmunication of meaning. The voice-over translation, on the other hand, does not seek to maintain the pretence and the viewer is left to imagine that person(s) seen on screen are expressing themselves in the words heard. Even more so in the case of subtitling, the viewer is presented with the fact of translation: those on screen are both seen and heard to be speaking another language and subtitles are offered as a guide to how communication is proceeding.

Thus, in the case of cinema and television fiction, translation tends to interfere with the cinematic illusion, to act as an obstacle to viewers participating fully in the construction of a fictional world. At the same time, it is of course thanks to the translator that meaning is relayed, that access is provided to works of fiction produced in another language. How do translators recreate in the target language (TL) a communication process which is reflected in the source-language (SL) dialogue between characters on screen? To what extent can the barriers to cross-linguistic and cross-cultural communication be overcome? What is the nature of these barriers and what areas of meaning get lost in the process? These are some of the questions to which we shall seek tentative answers in this article; tentative, because there is a need for far more systematic empirical study of the process of translating for the screen than has been achieved so far. Thanks to advances made in discourse analysis, text linguistics and conversation analysis, a new framework now exists for translation studies. There is scope for the study of screen translating as an instance of cross-cultural communication. It is the aim of this article to make a small contribution to that area from the perspective of discourse studies.

2. Contextual constraints on subtitling

The literature on translating for the cinema is relatively small in volume and concentrated in its scope. It provides an account of the ground rules for subtitling and examples of the kinds of problems encountered. Vöge (1977) and Minchinton (1987) evaluate the relative advantages of subtitling and dubbing; Titford (1982) describes the physical constraints involved in subtitling; Fawcett (1983) also alludes to these and observes the difficulties inherent in coping with colloquial use of language. We do not intend to go over this ground again in any detail. In short, these studies tend to confirm the intuitive judgement that the considerable contextual constraints on subtitling create particular kinds of difficulties. They are, broadly speaking, of three kinds:

(1) The shift in mode from speech to writing requires that certain features of speech (non-standard dialect, emphatic devices, code-switching, turn-taking) be represented in the target text (TT) in written form.
(2) The physical constraints of available space (generally up to 33, or in some cases 40, typewriter spaces per line; no more than two lines on screen) and the speed of sound-track dialogue are the factors which govern the medium ('channel') in which meaning is to be conveyed.
(3) The reduction of the source text (ST) as a consequence of (2) above means that the translator has to reassess coherence strategies in order to maximise the retrievability of intended meaning from a more concise TL version. In straightforward communication, the normal redundancy of speech gives hearers more than one chance of picking up intended meaning; in subtitling, the redundancy is inevitably reduced and chances of retrieving lost meaning are therefore fewer.

Points (1) and (3) in particular can be related to three dimensions of context which govern the structure and texture of discourse (on these and following notions, see Hatim and Mason 1990):

A *communicative* dimension accounts for factors relating to language users (dialect, idiolect) and to language use (field, mode, tenor of discourse). In the mode of translating we are considering, the transfer from speech to writing of dialectal features and of the interpersonal relationship of participants in discourse, as reflected in the speech they use (tenor), imposes additional constraints on the translator.

The *pragmatic* dimension involves the use of language to achieve some effect, to steer the occasion towards one's own communicative goals; in short, it involves *language as action*. In the case of screen translating, relevant considerations here are perceiving and preserving the *sequence of speech acts* (cf Ferrara 1980) in such a way as to relay the dynamics of communication (how is Speaker A steering the discourse in his or her own direction? How does Speaker B respond to perceived threats, insinuations, etc?). The temporal succession of subtitles on screen is, of course, quite different from the linear sequence of connected written dialogue in that the reader's eye cannot dart backwards and forwards in recapitulation and anticipation: the sequence of speech acts has to be perceived as it occurs (as in the case of spoken text). Moreover, any implicatures present in ST dialogue must be relayed and judgement exercised as to the degree of inferencing required of TL viewers/ readers to retrieve these.

Finally, there is a *semiotic* dimension of context, within which the subtitle behaves as a sign. Iconically, it possesses an independence which is not displayed by an equivalent portion of ST; the segmentation to which discourse is subjected in translation isolates the subtitle from preceding and following text. As signs, then, these entities interact (i) with the moving image, (ii) with the continuous ST soundtrack and (iii) with preceding and following subtitles. Coherence is upheld when this three-fold interaction is successfully preserved.

In the light of this, we can see that the mechanisms involved in the decoding of subtitles by cinema and television audiences are quite complex. In communication, meaning is something which is negotiated between speakers and hearers; it is not a succession of predetermined notions, conveniently packaged for consumption. Consequently, it has become common to talk of hearer meaning as well as of speaker meaning. In other words, speakers intend to communicate meaning and deploy their linguistic resources accordingly; hearers construct a mental model of what, for their purposes, they believe speakers' meaning to be, based on the linguistic and pragmatic evidence available to them. A fundamental assumption underlying this hypothesis is that hearers (and readers) do not have direct access to speaker meaning: they proceed to interpret on the basis of their contextual awareness and the incoming sequence of language signals.

Another important notion in recent theories of communication is that of *relevance* (Sperber and Wilson 1986). Speakers manage their discourse in the light of what they deem to be relevant to the current situation—and in particular to the needs of their interlocutors—while hearers search the incoming message for evidence of relevance to the current context. Governing this aspect of communication is the inevitable trade-off between speakers' desire to communicate their meaning as fully (effectively) as possible and their awareness of hearers' limited attention span (hence the need to be economical or efficient). The physical constraints involved in subtitling are bound to intrude in this process and, to some extent, to upset the delicate balance which is negotiated between producers and receivers of texts.

One other factor needs to be taken into consideration. So far, we have been using the terms 'speaker' and 'hearer' indiscriminately to refer to (1) participants in dialogue on screen and (2) the interaction between speakers on screen and the hearers/readers in the television or cinema audience. But the two processes are not identical in terms of the type of communication which is going on. A distinction needs to be made between participants and non-participants in discourse. Bell (1984) points out the importance of this distinction and further refines our model of communication by listing four different kinds of possible audience for any speech event. The *addressee* is someone whose presence is ratified by the speaker and who is being directly addressed; the *auditor* is not being directly addressed but is a ratified participant in (receiver of) the communication; the *overhearer* is not a ratified participant but his or her presence is known to co-communicants; finally, the *eavesdropper* is an overhearer whose presence is not known to co-communicants. Within this framework, we can say that the cinema audience constitute eavesdroppers on the screen dialogue which exists within a fictional world. The characters on screen behave as if they are not overheard and are unaware of any audience. Nevertheless, screen dialogue is not natural dialogue; any comparison of a screenplay with a transcribed sequence of naturally occurring conversation will demonstrate the point. The natural ellipsis between interlocutors who are familiar with each others' state of knowledge (or at least make assumptions about it) is quite striking whereas, in scripted dialogue, reference is more explicit, there are fewer false starts, hesitations, incomplete utterances and so on. In reality then, a script-writer is communicating meaning to an audience—but indirectly, via the written-to-be-spoken dialogue of figures on screen. In this sense, the cinema/TV audience may be considered as auditors in Bell's terms. In this essay, we are principally interested in how the *fictional* communication of meaning between characters on screen is relayed to a cinema or television audience by means of subtitling; in our analysis of speaker and hearer meaning, we enter the fictional world of the film, in which real communication is assumed to be taking place.

3. A Case Study—The Data

To illustrate the problems of subtitling as translation and to try out, to a limited extent, the model of communication outlined above, we have chosen to analyse two short sequences from an episode of the French television drama series *Châteauvallon*. The series was screened on British television by Channel Four in two separate versions, one dubbed and the other subtitled. Each episode was repeated, with subtitles, a few days after the dubbed version had been screened, thus affording a rare opportunity to compare the two modes of translating in action and to assess the effect of each on communication.

Furthermore, it is probably true to say that it is in the nature of the discourse of 'soap operas' that it reflects, at a fairly basic level, the prevailing cultural attitudes, beliefs, 'myths' of the society which gives rise to them. In this sense, the translatability of such discourse constitutes a test of the barriers between cultures, a gauge of the extent to which the discourse of one culture can be expressed in the language of another. At the same time, of course, there is a sense in which the 'soap opera' represents a universal genre within Western cultures. The popularity of *Neighbours* in Britain or, say, *Dallas* in France bears witness to the transferability of the cultural values portrayed. But within the conventions of the genre, there is cultural specificity too. And at a time when programmes of this kind are increasingly being offered to television audiences beyond their country of origin and when subtitling is becoming more and more common as a mode of translation, it seems worthwhile to consider some of the barriers imposed by the constraints under which it operates.

Let us now attempt to summarise, in a rough and ready fashion, the unfolding of the action in each of the two sequences. They were chosen because they are striking examples of 'discourse at work' beyond the level of the actual words spoken. In each one, the interlocutors are keen to gain the upper hand in conversation, to prevail upon each other and achieve a communicative goal—changing their interlocutor's behaviour or demonstrating their own superiority. Consequently, the following synopsis of Sequences I and II concentrates on the pragmatics of the exchanges, on rhetorical purposes and rhetorical effects. The onus on the translator in sequences such as these is then a heavy one: in addition to propositional meaning, indications of the power dynamics of the exchange need to be relayed wherever possible, all within the narrow confines of written subtitles of limited length.

In Sequence I, Quentin, (Speaker A), the mayor of a French town who is standing for re-election, is being advised by his agent (Speaker B) to campaign in a more aggressive style. Quentin resists this, claiming first of all that his opponent, Armand Berg, (who also happens to be the brother of Quentin's ex-wife) is a 'nice guy', then that he is a mere amateur at politics. The agent rejects both these arguments and gains the upper hand by implying that Quentin may lose the election. Quentin is now on the defensive, denying that his unpopularity as mayor will cause an upset but then admitting that he could not bear to lose the first round of the election. The agent senses that the exchange is going his way and moves straight to his goal: he tells Quentin to smear Armand Berg by linking his name to that of his cousin, Philippe Berg, who is being prosecuted for corruption. Quentin refuses point blank— but signals his relative weakness in the exchange by adopting a pleading discourse. Sensing his superiority, the agent threatens to walk out; Quentin calls him back. Confident now that his candidate will prove compliant, the agent goes onto the attack; he accuses Quentin of weakness and of lacking resolve since his wife left him. This reference to his personal affairs wounds Quentin and, as the sequence ends, he protests loudly at the intrusion. But the impression is clearly given that he will no longer resist his agent's plan.

In Sequence II, Quentin encounters his electoral opponent Armand Berg (Speaker C) at the local market. Both imply that the other is present at the market purely for the purpose of electioneering. Quentin partly cedes this point but turns it to his advantage by suggesting that as a candidate he must listen to his voters. Berg parries this by turning it into a joke. His opponent now moves onto the attack: he compliments Berg on his sense of humour and also on his nerve at daring to stand for election in Châteauvallon. Berg, puzzled, tries to elicit from the other what he is getting at. Quentin keeps the advantage by giving no more than veiled hints of what he is alluding to.

Challenged again, he mentions Berg's cousin, Philippe Berg, the presumed criminal. Berg is by now aware that he is under attack; he parries the blow by passing off his relationship with his cousin as of no electoral significance and then counter-attacks by pointing out that Quentin had appointed the same Philippe Berg as his assistant at the town hall: a deliberate choice rather than a mere family tie. Quentin is defeated by this argument and signals his submission by the weak admission: 'Ah j'ai toujours eu un penchant pour les Berg, que voulez-vous?' (Oh well, I suppose I've always had a soft spot for the Bergs).

What both of these sequences have in common is that they are dialogues in which a power struggle is being played out, each ending with the tacit submission of one participant to the other. Unlike other sequences where the camera is the primary narrator, in neither I nor II does the moving image narrate the unfolding of this struggle in the same way as does the dialogue. There are some visual clues—the election agent sits on the desk behind which Quentin is sitting, thus reinforcing his dominance; at the market, Berg, having made his point, moves off, showing his disinterest in prolonging the exchange; at all points, facial expressions constitute important paralinguistic evidence in support of our interpretation of what is going on. But, as auditors, we rely on the dialogue itself for our primary evidence of the evolution of the exchange.

It is not, of course, the subtitler's task even to attempt to represent all of the linguistically encoded meaning in the ST. Subtitles are intended to be a summary of ST discourse and meaning is to be retrieved by a process of matching this summary with visual perception of the action on screen, including paralinguistic features, body language, etc. In this article, however, we are not attempting to assess or criticise a particular set of translations. We assume that, for the most part, the TT subtitles are competent and that any alternative renderings which might be offered would effect only minor improvements to the coherence of the dialogue. As stated earlier, our interest is rather in the barriers to understanding which are an inherent part of translated discourse, the nature of the inevitable loss in translation. In the analysis which follows, we hope to show that it is frequently not the propositional content but rather the illocutionary force which is not relayed from ST to TT.

4. Analysis: Preserving Coherence in Translation

4.1 Speech acts

The subtitle often corresponds to the boundaries of a speech act in the ST and it is interesting to observe the inevitable shifts in illocutionary force (i.e. that part of the meaning of an utterance which has to do with the speaker's intentions) between ST and TT. Two examples from the sequences being analysed will illustrate the point. In the first, Speaker B is insinuating that Armand Berg can be smeared with his cousin's bad name (*NB: In the examples*

quoted, the ST appears on the left, with subtitles on the right, in one or two lines
as they appear on screen):

B: Alors, Berg Philippe, Berg Armand,   Berg Philippe, Berg Armand:
    même magouille, même combat   caught in the same web of intrigue

The discourse of the committed political slogan is apparent to any auditor of
ST, leading to an interpretation that the element in question is intended as
an ironic gloss on the smear campaign that could be set in motion. The
subtitler's difficulties can be judged by the extra length of the subtitle line (34
spaces) and the near impossibility of achieving similar illocutionary force. In
this instance, equivalence has been sought from the discourse of political
journalism ('caught in a web of intrigue'), thus retaining the allusion to a
smear campaign.

The other example is the closing element of Sequence II, cited earlier:

A: Ah, j'ai toujours eu un penchant   I've always been fond of the Bergs,
    pour les Berg, que voulez-vous?   what can I do...

The difficulty of finding a token-for-token equivalent for the French expression
que voulez-vous is a recognised one. But in this case, it is the illocutionary
force (resignation, self-exoneration) which is difficult to render in a succinct
way. The subtitle, in attempting to convey the sense, opens up an alternative
interpretation along the lines of: 'What can I do about the Bergs?' (cf the
translation offered at the end of the synopsis of Sequence II above). In fact,
what the two examples show is that, when brevity is required, it is the transfer
of illocutionary force which is often the barrier to successful retrieval of
intended meaning.

Let us now consider not isolated speech acts but the ways in which these
combine in sequences, as evidence of the way the communicative transaction
is developing. Ideally, such an analysis should cover long sequences of
dialogue, observing the process of inferencing and the preservation of coherence in sustained discourse. For the sake of brevity, however, we have singled
out short sequences which illustrate the general point at issue. Responding
to a provocative statement by Speaker B that the candidate's sentimental
problems are not relevant to the election campaign, the latter protests:

B: Est-ce bien à l'ordre du jour   Do you really think your love life
    tes... problèmes de coeur?   is relevant now?

A: On est pas des bêtes, non?   Well, we're not beasts.

Here, an appeal by Speaker A to his addressee's emotions seems to have
turned into a peremptory statement. The tag question *...non?* in French has
become *well* in English, an item frequently used to convey disagreement or
to emphasise a statement. The receiver of the TT subtitle can infer that A's
move is an attempt to close off a topic and an instruction to B to move to a
new one. Yet in the ST, A's appeal expects a reaction and B's next move:

B: Ne sousestime pas le frère, hein?	Don't underestimate the brother.

is interpretable as a direct response which could be glossed as: 'your sentimental problems are irrelevant to the matter in hand; moreover, they are responsible for your overlooking the threat posed by your ex-wife's brother's candidature'. The problem for the subtitler is then to be seen as one of relaying the sequence of speech acts, despite the separation in time of subtitles on screen. In the dubbed version, the corresponding dialogue, transcribed below, gives an indication of how the sequence may be better preserved in the spoken mode:

B: D'you think your love problems are really relevant right now?

A: Well... we're not machines, you know

B: Don't underestimate the brother.

Another significant speech act sequence is that which follows the election agent's threat to walk out at the end of Sequence I:

B: Bon, ben alors démerde-toi, hein si tu veux être battu... après tout	Well, sort your own mess out then, if you want to be beaten
A: Ecoute, tu pourrais m'épargner ce genre de phrase, quand même	I can do without that kind of talk
B: Non, parce que mon problème, c'est de te réveiller (...)	You can't. I'm trying to shake you up

A lot happens in this short section of dialogue. As suggested in our synopsis of the action, B threatens to walk out (he moves to the door) and his first utterance above is intended to be seen as a conversation-final move. A, however, eager to maintain contact, seeks an excuse to re-open the dialogue: he reproaches B for his defeatist talk. As a conversational move, this demands a response and, in turn, offers B an excuse for not carrying out his threat. But B's response is a straightforward rejection of the substance of A's appeal. B's discourse is now that of authority, reinforcing his dominance of A; the walk-out gambit has succeeded. The subtitles seek to reflect this sequence of events. They do not misrepresent the propositional content of ST. But the relatively disjointed nature of the TT speech acts and the abruptness of utterance allows the auditor to infer a subtly different power dynamic, one in which there is a simple assertion/counter-assertion pattern between A and B: 'I can...' 'You can't'. For evidence of B's rhetorical victory over A, the TT auditor is therefore mainly reliant on the moving image.

4.2 Mode-shift

Our second category of problems apparent in the sequences being analysed pertains to the shift of mode from speech to writing which occurs when films are subtitled. The difficulty of representing spoken colloquialisms in writing has already been mentioned and is discussed elsewhere (Fawcett 1983). Another relevant factor is that some features of spoken expression are retrievable by the TL audience from the ST itself. Emotions such as anger can be detected from voice volume, emphatic devices and so on. Thus, Speaker A's exasperation at the end of Sequence I is apparent as much from his emphasis of final mute 'e's as from the subtitle:

A: Ah merde! merde! Arrête   Stop talking about Florence, for God's
     de me parler de Florence!   sake!

However, there is one feature of speech which is not so easy to convey in the written mode—or indeed at all, in English. It is the use of word order to convey emphasis, salience, contrast and so on. There are numerous examples in Sequences I and II where fronting or disjunction of topic is not represented in subtitles—and indeed, could not be represented without producing a longer, less easily readable (and therefore unacceptable) version. Disjunctive elements in the following examples are italicised:

Il nous a rabiboché 2 ou 3 fois,   He often patched things up
sa soeur et moi   between his sister and myself

Est-ce bien à l'ordre du jour   Do you really think your love-life
tes problèmes de coeur?   is relevant now?

mais *le courage*, euh, de quel   but what sort of courage do you mean?
courage voulez-vous parler?

Oui ... mais *ça*, il faudra en   You'll have to convince the voters of
convaincre les électeurs   that

par contre *ses collaborateurs*   ... you do choose your colleagues
et ses amis, on les choisit (...)   and friends

With the exception of the emphatic 'do' in the last example above, the salience of ST discourse elements is not represented in TT. The loss in each individual instance seems slight. But the cumulative effect is to hinder retrieval of the dynamics of what is going on. Rhetorical devices such as these are conveyors of meaning in a wider sense, pointing as they do to the underlying thrust of discourse.

4.3 Down-toners and boosters

Our third category is no doubt the most significant one. It pertains to the inevitable omission in subtitling of whichever ST elements are seen as of least communicative importance. Once again, it must be stressed that this is in the nature of the exercise; the translation is intended as an abridged guide to ST discourse, and not as a full translation. But we are here examining the nature of these omissions, the significance of what gets lost in translation.

Modality and affective meaning are conveyed by the use of all kinds of short expressions which serve to reinforce or attenuate the force of what is being said. Holmes (1983) uses the terms down-toners and boosters to refer to this phenomenon: we can tone down the aggressiveness of an assertion by the addition of all kinds of attenuating items : 'well', 'perhaps', 'you know', etc. Conversely, we can strengthen the force of an utterance in the same way: 'surely', 'really', etc. Moreover, in conversation, the same tokens ('well', 'actually') can be used as both down-toners and boosters. The ways in which we accommodate to our interlocutors, by modifying the force of our utterances to suit what we deem to be 'polite' or appropriate to the immediate communicative situation, are accounted for within the theory of politeness developed by Brown and Levinson (1987). The application of their hypothesis and findings to the field of (spoken) translation studies is a fascinating area of research still to be carried out. There is not space here to give a resume of politeness theory, nor to apply it in any meaningful way to our data. Merely, we hope to show how there is inevitable but *systematic* loss in subtitling of indicators of interlocutors accommodating to each other's 'face-wants' (Brown and Levinson 1987) and negotiating with each other the development of meaning within the dialogue. One of the samples quoted earlier provides a good illustration of what we have in mind:

A: Ecoute, tu pourrais m'épargner   I can do without that kind of talk
       ce genre de phrase, quand même

We can identify at least four elements in this utterance which show accommodation at work. In addition to the down-toners *écoute* ('listen') and *quand même* ('all the same'), there is the attenuation signalled in the use of the conditional tense, *pourrais*, and in the use of the modal verb *pouvoir* itself. Speaker A is apparently recognising both the relative weakness of his position and the need not to antagonise Speaker B further (the latter is poised by the door, ready to walk out of the discussion). For a French addressee or auditor, an utterance shorn of these prominent politeness features would appear pointedly direct and face-threatening:

Epargne-moi ce genre de phrase   (Spare me that kind of talk)

In comparison with the actual ST utterance, the subtitle (*I can do without ...*) is liable to be interpreted as peremptory and direct. The omitted items in the ST, while relatively devoid of content in terms of propositional meaning, are strong pointers to the interpersonal meaning of the exchange.

The dubbed script for this whole exchange is quite different:

B: Right then. Sort it out yourself. If you want to lose... it's your funeral

A: Oh come on, you don't have to make those kind of comments

B: No, because my problem is to wake you up (...)

There is more room in the dubbed version for the usual politeness features and the interpersonal attitudes and power dynamic are relayed quite successfully. On the other hand, the constraint of matching lip movements is probably responsible for the less-than-fully coherent 'No' in B's second turn. The contrast between the two modes of translating (brevity in subtitles, lip movement in dubbing) is clearly illustrated in this example.

Our two Sequences abound with down-toners and boosters such as these. Two further examples will suffice to give an idea of the extent of the phenomenon. When the election agent advises Quentin to take his opponent seriously, the reply is:

A:	Mais non... c'est un amateur, va	He's an amateur

The item *va*, which is both persuasive and dismissive, together with *mais non*, function as powerful boosters, both absent from the subtitle. Secondly, when the agent suggests the smear campaign, Quentin's reaction is:

A:	Ah non, non, écoute, non... non ça serait dégueulasse, hein, pas d'amalgame, s'il te plaît	No, that would be dirty. Let's not confuse issues

The unavoidable brevity of the subtitle leaves the impression that Quentin's reaction is clear and confident; but in the ST, the extra items point to his disarray, a sign which is not missed by his interlocutor, who goes on to exploit it. Again, the dubbed version is able to reflect the true position:

Ah no. Oh, now look here, no, that would be disgusting, don't start mixing, will you, please

In all, out of a total of 37 conversational turns in Sequences I and II, we counted 47 interpersonal features of this kind, functioning either as down-toners or as boosters. Prominent among the indicators in the ST were:

> *hein, oui,oui, même, non?, sûrement, va, tu sais, tu vois, alors là, quand même, ben, écoute, après tout, bien entendu, que voulez-vous, enfin, peut-être, ah bon, j'sais pas,* etc.

In the dubbed version, on the other hand, whatever the comparative quality of the translation, there is room for a more systematic representation of this important feature of meaning. Naturally, no thorough evaluation can be made without considering the quality of both dubbed and subtitled versions. Other subtitlers would no doubt have opted for other solutions and many of the subtitles given above as examples could be improved. In this paper, however, our main concern is with those observable features which may be related to the process of subtitling itself.

5. Conclusion

A consistent trend emerges from our analysis of Sequences I and II, illustrated especially in the examples quoted in sections 4.1 and 4.3 above. The trend, we suggest, is inherent in the nature of subtitling and the constraints under which it operates. Cumulatively, the absence of the politeness features which we have discussed cannot fail to convey a different idea of the personality of the characters on screen and of their attitudes towards each other. Items which, taken in isolation, appear to be of relatively little significance turn out to be powerful indicators of rhetorical purpose and the dynamics of inter-action. It is interesting to note that a similar tendency to overlook these features has been observed in the work of non-professional liaison interpreters—where the constraints on the translator are of a somewhat different nature (Knapp-Potthoff and Knapp 1987). In that study, it is further noted that it is in any case difficult to translate such features without over-playing them. Achieving *equivalence of discoursal effect* in the culture of the TL is indeed a daunting objective for any translator. What is peculiar to subtitling as a mode of translating is that it brings these problems to the fore, allowing us to single out an important obstacle to cross-cultural communication.

References

Bell, A, 'Language style as audience design'. *Language in Society* 13, 1984: 145-204
Brown, P and S Levinson, *Politeness*, C.U.P. 1987.
Fawcett, P, 'Translation modes and constraints', *Incorporated Linguist* 22 (4) 1983: 186-190
Ferrara, A, 'Appropriateness conditions for entire sequences of speech acts', *Journal of Pragmatics* 4, 1980: 321-340
Hatim, B and I Mason, *Discourse and the Translator*. London: Longman. 1990
Holmes, J, 'Speaking English with the appropriate degree of conviction', in *Learning and Teaching Languages for Communication*, C Brumfit (ed). London: CILT 1983
Knapp-Potthoff, A and K Knapp, 'The Man (or woman) in the middle: Discoursal aspects of non-professional interpreting' in K Knapp, W Enninger, A Knapp-Potthoff (eds) *Analyzing Intercultural Communication*, Berlin: de Gruyter. 1987
Minchinton, J, 'Fitting Titles', *Sight and Sound* 56 (4): 279-282. 1987
Sperber, D and D Wilson, *Relevance: Communication and Cognition*. Oxford: Basil Blackwell. 1986
Titford, C, 'Subtitling, constrained translation', *Lebende Sprachen* 27 (3) 1982: 113-116
Vöge, H, 'The translation of films: subtitling versus dubbing', *Babel* 23 (3) 1977: 120-125

Argumentative Style Across Cultures: Linguistic Form as the Realization of Rhetorical Function

Basil Hatim

Overview

I adopt the position that there are two basic forms of argumentation: through-argumentation and counter-argumentation. A through-argumentative text is characterized by extensive substantiation of an initial thesis. A counter-argumentative text, on the other hand, involves the rebuttal of a cited thesis.

In counter-argumentation, the text form which we shall focus on in this paper, two debating positions are made to confront each other: that which presents the 'thesis cited to be opposed', and that which states the 'counter-claim'. In terms of text structure, counter-arguments usually display the following sequence of elements: cited thesis → counter-claim → substantiation of counter-claim → conclusion. The genre[1] Letter to the Editor, for example, uses this text format extensively:

Text A

So Ron Brand (Letters, April 29) fears that 'urban scholars' suffer happy indoctrination from the television screen to which they are constantly glued at home and at school.	CITED THESIS
While I have yet to see a school where the students spend all their time watching television, what worries me more is his assumption that watching television is necessarily a passive pastime in which no learning can take place.	COUNTER-CLAIM
Many studies of how people watch television have shown this to be a skilled and active process; it is merely the concrete and common-sense nature of these skills which means that they are devalued in and out of schools. (...)	SUB-STANTIATION

The Guardian May 4, 1989

In this type of argumentation, evaluative discourse predominates, realized by devices of cohesion such as those which convey emphasis (recurrence, parallelism, etc.), as well as highly marked word order, heavy use of modality, etc. In Text A, for example, a high degree of evaluativeness is manifested by the discourse signals *so, fears*, marked word order in *while I have...*, *what worries me more is ...*, and emphatic devices such as *yet, merely.*

Of the various elements in a counter-argumentative text, we shall in this paper restrict our attention to the text-initial 'opponent's thesis' and the way it is presented. Citing the claim of one's opponent for the purposes of subsequently rebutting such a claim is, we believe, culture-specific. Not all linguistic communities see the need to structure their counter-arguments in a way which includes an explicit citation of the opponent's views. And of those communities which do structure their counter-arguments in this way, not all approach the matter with the same degree of detachment or involvement.

It may be argued that these cultural peculiarities betray certain subtle attitudes to the notion of truth. But instead of focusing our discussion on questions relating to the philosophy of language, our interest in this paper lies primarily in seeing how the rhetorical function 'representing the views of one's opponent', and the attitude to 'truth' implicit in such a stance, ultimately find expression in linguistic form. Specifically, with the training of translators in mind, we approach this text-linguistic phenomenon as a practical problem likely to confront those who find certain rhetorical conventions in the languages from which they work to be generally alien, if not at times utterly disturbing. We are here concerned with translators who for all kinds of socio-cultural reasons cannot readily relate to the conventional opaqueness with which opponents are represented in argumentation in certain European languages. In the discussion which follows, this tendency is illustrated from English, a language which is particularly prone to 'indirection'[2] of this kind.

Counter-argumentation as a Text Type

Rebuttal is a universally established form of counter-argumentation. However, in terms of the mechanisms involved (i.e. text structure and texture), different languages handle rebuttals differently. The general tendency in Arabic, for example, is to let the text hinge on the point of view of the person putting forward the rebuttal, with the position of the opponent occupying a secondary place. In English, on the other hand, the counter-argumentative procedure of making a point is less direct. In fact, the hallmark of this mode of argumentation in English is the 'statement' of the opponent's position with which the text is initiated, followed by the counter-claim and a substantiation of such a claim.

But, as we shall argue, the statement of the opponent's position in English counter-argumentative texts is rarely, if ever, a straight-forward representation of the opponent's views. Gaps are deliberately and subtly left in the citation to undermine the opponent's stance. Thus, while at one level the opponent's position appears to be fairly represented and appropriately endorsed, this is done in such a way as to highlight those points which weaken his or her position and prepare for subsequent opposition. This is true even when the opponent is quoted verbatim as in Text A above (cf. the function of *so, fears*). In this type of text it is the opposition which is the ultimate goal of the text producer. The device, sometimes referred to in studies of rhetoric as 'the straw man gambit', is illustrated in Text B below:

Text B

Tomorrow's meeting of OPEC is a different affair.   INITIAL THESIS

Certainly, it is formally about prices and about Saudi Arabia's determination to keep them down.	CITED THESIS I
Certainly it will also have immediate implications for the price of petrol, especially for Britain, which recently lowered its price of North Sea oil and may now have to raise it again.	CITED THESIS II
But this meeting ... is not primarily about selling arrangements. It is primarily about the future of the organization itself. (...)	COUNTER-CLAIM

Times editorial

Text B begins with a topic sentence. Two options are at the disposal of the text producer for the development of the argument: (a) embarking on an extensive substantiation of the thesis stated (Through-argument); (b) citing an opponent (real or imagined) as a prelude to the making of a counter-claim which is then to be substantiated. The producer of Text B has obviously opted for the latter strategy. The argument is structured in such a way as to give what appears at first sight to be a fair hearing to the opposition but is in fact slanted to diminish the views cited: 'there are those who argue that tomorrow's meeting of OPEC is about prices, etc.' In fact, the opponent's position is not only acknowledged but apparently endorsed by the use of the emphatic device *certainly*.

On closer reading of these initial elements within the text, however, two things become clear immediately:

(1) Semantic gaps are introduced at crucial points in the citation of the opponent's argument. These gaps are normally produced by the use of qualifications, the main purpose of which is to restrict the categorical nature of the statements made (e.g. *formally*, *immediate*, etc. in Text B).

(2) As it is not in the interest of the 'arguer' to emphasize the entire 'cited thesis', the use of emphasizers such as *certainly* can only be adequately explained in terms of a restriction of their scope of emphasis to the semantic gaps referred to in (1) and nothing else. That is, what is being emphasized in the introduction of Text B is not the notion that 'tomorrow's OPEC meeting is about prices' but the notion that it is so 'only formally'.

The problem which interests us here is this peculiar use of emphasis, together with the deliberate manipulation of 'gapping' in the manner illustrated by *formally* and *immediate* in Text B. These peculiarities, which we take to be typical of English counter-argumentative style, are a major source of difficulty for text receivers not familiar with the rhetorical conventions involved. The difficulty for an Arab translator, for example, lies in perceiving the intended meaning and recognizing the gaps. When Text B was given as an on-sight translation assignment to a group of Arab post-graduate students, the majority perceived it as a Through-argument. To them, the use of *certainly* signalled the substantiation:

Text C

> Tomorrow's meeting of OPEC is a different affair since/because it certainly is about prices...

Perhaps the students were not sufficiently familiar with the 'concessive' value of 'certainly' and that may have resulted in a semantic gap in their awareness of the way the device was used in English. But the real difficulty may be attributed to a number of more general causes. At a very general level, Arabic tends to favour more direct forms of argumentation than that of the 'counter-argumentative' mode. While this observation awaits further research and a more definitive statistical statement, our own research into the matter indicates a predilection in Arabic for what we have referred to as 'through-argumentation'. At least in present-day rhetorical practice, the general tendency in Arabic seems to favour a situation in which the arguer's own views are foregrounded with the opponent's position left very much in the background.

This tendency may be related to a number of deep-rooted socio-cultural factors having to do with 'distance' (detachment or involvement) and the nature of the ensuing relationship between addresser and addressee. As Text B above shows, counter-argumentation is a more detached form of making a point. In texts of this type, the text producer assumes a higher degree of doubt on the part of the text receiver concerning the validity of the claims to be made by the text produced. That is, had the producer of Text B above opted for the more direct 'through-argumentation' format and thus embarked on the substantiation of the initial thesis, he or she would have had to take for granted audience endorsement of the views put forward later, an assumption which the rhetorical conventions of Arabic seem to generally encourage. The counter-argumentative format opted for, however, takes into account an element of uncertainty on the part of a large segment of the audience, an assumption which is invariably made in the Western rhetorical tradition even if the evidence for the existence of such opposing views is not readily available. This stems from a general need to accommodate the text receiver's presumed doubts.

Counter-argumentation in Arabic

At the present stage of research, one can only speculate on the reasons for the tendency in Arabic to adopt a more direct through-argumentative format. These would seem to be closely bound up with solidarity, politeness, face-saving and other related pragmatic phenomena. They may even be political or simply reflect the fact that those in authority would not tolerate having their position overtly opposed. The counter-argument in Text B above makes a concession to a belief entertained by an adversary, thereby recognizing part of an audience likely to hold views counter to those advocated subsequently in the text. A through-argument, on the other hand, would normally be based on the premise that the entire audience is prepared to accept the stance adopted in the text. In texts of this type, such an assumption would render unnecessary the need even to acknowledge the existence of any opposition.

But it is wrong to assume that counter-argumentation is completely alien to Arabic. Old manuals of Arabic style discuss this form of argumentation and recommend it to students of rhetoric. In his book on the criticism of prose, Ibn Qudama, a fourteenth century Arab rhetorician, suggests that...

> 'In effective argumentation, the argument builds on initial premises which are accepted by the opponent.
>
> Ibn Qudama (1982 edition)

Nevertheless, two basic features distinguish present-day Arabic counter-argumentation from English and can probably account for the difficulties faced by the Arab reader. To start with, Arabic does not extend the use of devices such as *min al muakkad* (*'certainly'*) to include this kind of 'counter-argumentative' meaning illustrated by Text B above. In fact, the use of *min al muakkad* text-initially would relay precisely the opposite effect to that produced by the use of 'certainly' in a parallel English text. In Arabic, *min al muakkad* is meant 'sincerely' and the emphasis relayed is genuine. To produce an equivalent effect to that aimed at in a text such as Text B above, more explicit semantic marking is needed. Consider Text D (a literal translation from Arabic) which illustrates the way emphatic devices are used text-initially in Arabic:

Text D

> Of course, the economic policy to be applied differs substantially according to the kind of gap determining the rate of investment; therefore it is of vital importance to determine the kind of constraint to economic growth. (...)

The intention of the producer of Text D is to argue a point through. The function of signals such as *of course* is genuinely emphatic and may here be glossed as 'we categorically believe that...'. To translate this text idiomatically, more explicit signals will have to be employed in the English translation (e.g. *There is no question but that...*).

The second feature of counter-argumentative text initiators in Arabic has to do with the explicitness of syntactic marking. It is customary for Arabic counter-argumentative texts to begin with explicit signals of the intentionality involved (e.g. the use of the SVC nominal structure; VSC verbal structures are used only when the verbal element is semantically empty).[3] This word order variability may be contrasted with the fixity of the SVC surface format in English. It is this surface fixity, however, which is at the heart of the problem for readers from a different linguistic background. Seemingly fixed word order arrangement in English masks subtle variation in meaning. Within the surface SVC format, two text initiating functions may be distinguished:

(a) Oral Health care does not have the makings of a dramatic issue, and its

effect on the economies of nations is insignificant. Yet very few people manage
to avoid oral disease. (...)

World Health Forum (1984)

(b) Viruses and many bacteria cause disease by damaging or killing the cells
they infect; consequently, a vaccine aims to prevent infection of these cells by
the virus or bacterium. (...)

World Health Forum (1988)

Sentences (a) and (b) are the initial elements of two different texts. Sentence
(a) ushers in argumentation in which the initial citation of the thesis is later
followed by opposition. Sentence (b), on the other hand, is the scene-setter of
a non-evaluative expository text which is followed by the various aspects of
the 'scene set' presented through detached analysis. It is only text context
and aspects of text constitution such as structure and texture which could
resolve the ambiguity surrounding what sentences such as (a) and (b) actually
mean and help the receiver of the above text samples to appreciate the text
types involved.

The Translation of Counter-arguments

It might perhaps be argued that, in translating counter-arguments in general,
it is not crucial to perceive the intended meaning of devices such as the initial
'certainly', 'of course', etc. In terms of the end-product, we are told, the
consequences of not appreciating the subtlety of these devices are rarely
detrimental. After all, what is in a word! Thus, it is suggested, the translator
will be guided by the way the source text is structured and this should enable
him or her to revise initial misconceptions once he or she encounters the
statement of the opposition ('But', 'However', etc) and the substantiation
which follows.[4]

This view is erroneous. Misunderstanding of text function is frequently
caused by very minor misreadings. This is true even when working from
English into other related European languages where problems of explicit
semantic and syntactic marking outlined above do not even surface. In
working into a language such as Arabic, however, the problem of not appreciating text function can be very serious indeed. Two aspects of misconstruing
text function may be distinguished. Firstly, rendering items such as 'certainly'
uncritically as *min al muakkad* will encourage the translator to deal with what
is really a thesis cited to be opposed as a statement of conviction. The translator
will misconstrue important source language clues pointing in the direction
of 'gaps' intended to undermine the opponent's position. Secondly, and far
more seriously, the translator, having initiated the discourse with what in
Arabic would be a through-argument signal, may fall into the trap of carrying
on as if he or she were constructing a through-argument. There is even
the danger that the signal for the opposition (But..., However...) would be
overlooked simply because such a text element would not be expected.

In working into English from a language such as Arabic, on the other
hand, confusing counter-arguments for through-arguments (or vice versa)

can most certainly lead to very serious deviations. Here, the Arabic *min al muakkad* ('certainly') which typically initiates a through-argument gets uncritically rendered as 'certainly' which would normally usher in a counter-argument when used text-initially in English. English receivers of such texts will immediately be struck by the conspicuous absence of any semantic gaps or other syntactic devices used to relay 'the straw man gambit' effect. Moreover, the absence of a coherent opposition will also be noticeable. In short, what is originally a through-argument will be misleadingly presented as a counter-argument. Translators sensitive to textual phenomena such as these would not opt for an item like *certainly* (which leads the reader to expect the wrong kind of text) but would instead choose a wording which unambiguously invites the reader to expect a through-argument (e.g. *there is absolutely no doubt that...*).

Translating vs Composing

So far, we have identified two basic argumentative text forms: counter-arguments and through-arguments. The basic difference between these two forms lies in the text-initial elements. Counter-arguments are initiated with a 'thesis cited to be opposed' while through-arguments are initiated with a 'thesis cited to be argued through and defended'. The purpose of the English-Arabic contrastive text linguistic outline presented above has been to underline the seriousness of errors made in translation as a result of the inability to appreciate the device known as 'the straw man gambit' in English counter-argumentation.

But how is one to account for the existence of counter-arguments in Arabic which as we have just explained do exist, albeit rarely? To answer this question we need to establish a distinction not typically made in translation studies between 'translating' and 'composing'. There will be certain forms, styles, etc. which will be accepted in translating but which would not come naturally in composing. The tendency becomes more pronounced the higher the level of text organization one is dealing with. From a translating point of view, except for the difficulties outlined above, counter-arguments may appear in Arabic as counter-arguments. It is almost as if a corpus of translated texts has built up this text type over the years.

Strictly from a composing point of view, however, it is safe to conclude pending further research that counter-arguments occur far less frequently in Arabic than they do in English. That is, given a situation in which an arguer takes exception to something his or her opponent has suggested, the resulting argument in Arabic would invariably be presented in the form of a thesis supporting the arguer's own position, followed by a substantiation (through-argumentation), rather than as a thesis representing the opposition followed by a counter-claim (counter-argumentation). Our rudimentary research into this aspect of contrastive rhetoric suggests that this trend persists in modern standard Arabic despite the fact that old style manuals discuss and recommend counter-argumentation as an effective persuasive device in the rhetoric of Arabic. Apart from the small group of text users influenced by

Western rhetorical form, there is only a small minority of literate Arabs who follow the style of argumentation recommended in ancient literary tradition.

Notes

1 For definitions of 'text', 'genre' and 'discourse', see G Kress (1985) *Linguistic Processes in Sociocultural Practice* (ECS806 Sociocultural Aspects of Language and Education), Deakin University, Vic.
2 The term 'indirection' is used here in the sense of 'implicitness' of meaning; see M Stubbs (1982) *Discourse Analysis.* London: Blackwells
3 This argument is pursued in detail in B Hatim (1989) 'Text Linguistics in the Didactics of Translation', *International Review of Applied Linguistics.* Heidelberg: Julius Groos Verlag
4 These arguments are examined in detail from a translation perspective in B. Hatim and I Mason (1990) *Discourse and the Translator.* London: Longman

The Morphological Assimilation of German Loan-words in English

Anthony W Stanforth

1. Introduction and Corpus

1.1

Loan-word studies have traditionally concentrated on the borrowing of lexis as a reflex of cultural contact. This essentially diachronic approach links the development of the vocabulary with extra-linguistic causes and frequently forms part of quantitative assessments of the influence a particular language has on another. Less attention has been paid to the processes of assimilation which the borrowed material undergoes in the new environment of the host language. Such assimilation occurs on the phonetic/phonemic, the graphemic, the semantic and the morphological levels.

It is the last of these that will concern us in the present article, which forms part of a wider project to investigate the influence of the German language (NHG) on English from both the cultural and the linguistic points of view. While this influence is but one of the many that has contributed to the development of the English language and while it is not, in quantitative terms, especially strong,[1] German has nevertheless made a significant contribution to the vocabulary of English, especially in certain areas of technical vocabulary such as chemistry and metallurgy, and has not hitherto been examined in depth. This is in contrast to the considerable attention that has been paid to the steady flow of Anglicisms (both American and British) into German during this century.

1.2

The corpus underlying the project consists of a collection of 1160 items, drawn from the following sources:

1: the *Oxford English Dictionary* (1933 edition) (=*OED*)
2: the 1933 Supplement to the *OED* (=*OEDS*)
3: 318 items, not included in (1) & (2), taken from the British press between 1968 and 1988.

Between 1972 and 1986 a further Supplement to the *OED* was published (=*OEDNS*), and at the time of writing the 2nd edition of the *OED* has appeared (=*OED2*), incorporating the 1933 volumes, the 1933 and the 1972-86 Supplements, as well as even more recent material. German borrowings contained in the post-1933 volumes have not as yet been systematically excerpted and are therefore not included in the statistics that follow.

1.3

Of the 1160 items in the corpus, 879 (76%) are loan-words (e.g. *kindergarten*). The remaining 281 (24%) items are made up of loan-blends (e.g. *house-frau*)—24 items (2%), loan-translations (e.g. *chain-smoker*)—199 items (17%) and semantic loans (e.g. *staff*)—58 items (5%). The loan-translations and semantic loans express German concepts by means of English morphemes and are therefore not relevant in the present context. The loan-blends, however, will need to be considered along with the loan-words.

1.4

The 879 loan-words in our corpus can be subdivided into two categories, the first comprising loans formed by German material, the second made up of German coinings based on Latin or Greek roots (e.g. *homoeopathy*, *inertia*). These account for 165 items, or 19% of the loan-words. The international character of such words masks their German provenance and they, like the loan-translations and semantic loans, may be disregarded in the present context.

2. Form-classes

2.1

Taking the loan-words formed from German material (714 items) and the loan-blends (24 items) together we can assign the material to the following form-classes: 702 nouns; 15 verbs; 16 adjectives; 2 adverbs; 2 pronouns; 3 particles; 4 affixes. Six of the verb forms are also used substantivally, and have therefore been counted under both heads. It can be seen that substantival loans predominate overwhelmingly. The pronouns (*du, Sie*), adverbs (*sehr schmetternd, schnell*) and the particles (*ja, nein, bitte*) occur only as quoted forms and will not be further discussed.

2.2

The morphological assimilation of this material will be examined with reference firstly to inflection, secondly to word-formation (compounding, affixation, derivation and clipping).

3. Inflection

In the majority of cases the German language borrowings, once accepted and listed by English dictionaries, have been fully assimilated morphologically. Vestigial German inflection is more likely to be encountered during the earliest stages of the assimilation process. To investigate these the earliest examples cited in the *OED* were potentially useful; however, the material collected between 1968 and 1988 provides greater evidence of the assimilation process, since these items had at the time of collection not yet found acceptance in the standard language. This material comprises 318 items, of which 177 have now been recognized by the *OEDNS*. It should be added that in the majority of cases the citations did not contain inflected forms; among such as did occur, noun plurals predominated.

3.1 Noun inflection

3.1.1 Plural marking   The English plural in -(*e*)*s*, as the normal marker of noun plurality, is very quickly used with German loan-words. Once accepted into the language they are handled by the user as 'native' nouns, as the following passage illustrates:

> 'Beerenausleses fetch high prices, but the price-gap between these and Ausleses is exaggerated. There are no greater German wines than the finest Ausleses, only sweeter ones.'[2]

Virtually all the German nouns included in the *OED* material capable of forming a plural do so by adding -(*e*)*s*. One exception is *lied*, whose plural *lieder* was borrowed intact. The highly specific sense of this musical term has helped to fix and preserve the plural form. It is, therefore, necessary to distinguish between German plurals borrowed as such, and German nouns needing to be marked for plurality once part of English.

The newer, non-*OED* material, throws up more instances of German plurals, as well as English and German plural forms in variation. The German plural markers in question are:

ϕ: *dichter und denker; fallschirmjäger; gastarbeiter; kartofellpuffer; rippchen.*

Here the context shows the plural sense. The zero-morpheme plural marker does not contrast with English morphology (*sheep—sheep*).

ϕ + umlaut: *wandervögel.* The remarks above apply.

e: (die freien) berufe; berufsverbote; fachbereiche; (die goldenen zwanziger) jahre; kantonalfeste; lehrstücke; sachwerte; schottenpreise; wanderjahre.

en: anlagen; bauern schnitten; bummelstudenten; Bundeswehrhochschulen; fachhochschulen; fraktionen; genossen; gesamthochschulen; kneipen; korporationen; lederhosen, pensionen; pickelhauben; schützen; (technische) hochschulen; wohngemeinschaften; zwischenprüfungen.

er: länder.

This last term joins *lieder* as a second -*er* plural, and as in the case of *lieder* it was borrowed as a plural form. The *OEDNS* has examples of *Lands* dated 1920 and 1950 which appear to be loan-words rather than loan-translations, but today only the German plural is encountered.

The non-*OED* material reveals various instances of the German plural marking system causing problems. Thus, in the following sentences, singular forms are used in the plural: 'Fine examples can be bought ... [for] a fiver or so—up to nearly £20 for great *trockenbeerenauslese*'—*Obs.* 25-11-73—(but note the assimilated plural of *auslese* quoted above); 'Dr. Hagan points to the close relationship between industry and the technical Fachhochschule, roughly analogous to polytechnics'—*THES* 9-6-89.[3]

Variation between English and German plural markers is evidenced in the cases of *festschrift; glockenspiel* and *schloss*. Thus, for *festschrift* we may compare the following examples:

> 'This book assembles Tyson's major articles on Mozart, previously scattered through journals and festschrifts.' (*TLS* 29-1-88);

> 'This topic [historiography] used simply to provide relaxation for eminent historians while waiting for the *Festschriften* to roll in ...' (*TLS* 14-3-86).

It would be tempting but incautious to claim that in this case the German plural reflects an earlier stage of assimilation, and that it is only a matter of time before *festschrifts* will be the only plural form. The term *festschrift* has been in the English language since 1901, and both plural forms are well attested.[4] The occurrence of the plural in -*en* here reflects the attitude of the writer, the user of the term, towards the loan. The author has chosen to use the German term, with italics and the German plural, regardless (and surely not ignorant) of the fact that a more assimilated variant was available. The co-occurrence of the English and German plurals reveals more about the stylistic value of, and the user's attitude towards, the foreign form than about the sequencing or timing of assimilation.

A similar observation may be made in the other two cases: a reviewer of 'The Magic Flute' in the *THES* refers to the 'childish humour of the *glockenspiele*' (*THES* 16-6-78), while *The New Oxford Companion to Music*[5] uses the English plural; and two citations from the *Observer* show alternative plurals for *schloss*: 'The Circus plus Mrs. Cleese rampant among the *schlösser*' (30-9-73) and 'The doctor in the Daimler would then have to start making sure such schlosses [=nursing homes, British context] have a sight better facilities' (8-4-73). In these last two examples it is even more obvious that the selection of the plural form is dictated by stylistic considerations.

3.1.2 Genitive   The German genitive singular -*s* is not attested. The English construction with *of* does not require the noun to inflect, and any German noun automatically adopts the English case inflection system on entry into the language (e.g. 'the disgruntled officers of the *Bundesnachrichtendienst*'—*Obs.* 12-5-74) even prior to its adoption, translation, or, where appropriate, use in non-German contexts. Where the genitive -*s* appears, this reflects native English usage rather than any German influence ('A stylish, if not powerful, heroic singer, he had the *heldentenor's* common difficulty with cantabile line ...'—*Obs.* 6-5-73).

3.2 Adjectival inflection

3.2.1   As we have seen, the majority of German loans in English are nouns; only 16 adjectives are attested in the corpus:

> *echt; ersatz; gemütlich; hitzefrei; klein; lumpen; machbar; paritätisch; rechtskonservativ; temperamentvoll; verboten; völkisch*; and four names in adjectival form (see below, 4.3.1).

Additionally, five occur as part of borrowed noun phrases (NPs): *the alte herren, Deutsche Mark; Deutsche [sic] tafelwein, grünen hügel* and *ungetreuen geschäftsführung.*

Of these 21 items, *echt, ersatz, lumpen* and *verboten* are well integrated into the English language. Their earliest datings are 1916, 1875, 1948 and 1912 respectively (*OEDNS*), and by now they occur regularly in non-German contexts. As fully assimilated loan-words they do not show any German inflection: 'no *verboten* topics'—JAI Press announcement for a book on psychiatry, 1982. *Lumpen* has only become an adjective after entering the language, and will be discussed below (3.4.1) as an example of form class shift and of clipping (4.4).

Gemütlich and *temperamentvoll* have no closely equivalent terms in English and are occasionally used in non-German contexts: 'Tokyo's best known singers, boys as well as girls, are more cuddly than corrupting. They appear in relentlessly *gemütlich* television pop shows' (*Obs.* 15-4-73); 'Then there is the case of his *temperamentvoll* stepson, Hamlet, ...' (*Obs.* 11-3-73).

Völkisch is only used in National Socialist contexts: '... a fanatical and at times hysterically unbalanced *völkisch* enthusiasm which swept Hitler into power in 1933' (*THES*, 7-3-86).

The remaining adjectives (apart from the names) are either quotations ('Helmut Schmidt's favourite words are *Machbar [sic]* ("do-able") and *Flasche* ("numbskull")'—*Obs.* 19-5-74), or else nonce borrowings to impart 'local colour' (*hitzefrei; klein; paritätisch* and *rechtskonservativ).*

This last item, however, provides a rare example of German adjective inflection: 'And should not the *rechtskonservative* appeal of Strauss and Dregger be analysed in relation to the decline of the NPD?' (*THES* 20-1-78). This appeared in a scholarly review of Geoffrey Pridham's book *Christian Democracy in Western Germany*, and reveals its author's familiarity with and care for German inflection. It is an exception and again illustrates the importance of the role of the user when assessing morphological assimilation.

A second example of adjectival inflection highlights the pitfalls of retaining an ending: 'Ludwig Rosenberg ... became leader of the *Deutsche* TUC ...' (*Obs.* 18-3-73).

Adjectival inflection also occurs in the five noun phrases noted above. Of these *Deutsche Marks* is obviously the most significant and best known. The problem of coping with the adjectival ending within NPs is seen in the fact that, apart from the abbreviations *D-Mark* and *DM*, three variants regularly occur: *Deutsche Mark, Deutschemark* and *Deutschmark.*

That difficulty is attested, too, in the use of the phrase *alte herren* ('He also says the *alte Herren*, the club "old boys", are out of touch ...'—*Obs.* 8-10-72), where the shift from English to German morphology occurs within the NP, leading to a technically incorrect adjective ending, and the genitive and accusative cases defeat the writer of '... so wasn't the big bank guilty of *ungetreuen Geschäftsführung*, even if they weren't guilty of *Urkundenfälschung?* And the outside auditors certified all the *Urkundenfälschung* and the *ungetreuen Geschäftsführung* ...' (*Obs.* 11-3-73).

Ignorance of the foreign system can also easily lead to transcription errors: 'Germany classifies its wines Tafelwein, Deutsche [*sic*] Tafelwein ...' (*Obs.* 4-10-74). In the last of the borrowed phrases, however, the writer, who, judging by the context, probably knew German, smoothly clears the hurdle: '[Wieland Wagner's and Götz Friedrich's] changes disturbed the reassuring sense of ritual so dear to opera-goers but nowhere so powerfully active as on the "grünen Hügel", Bayreuth's holy green hill' (*Sunday Times*, 7-8-77).

Despite the occasional appearance of inflected forms (whether or not correct) in noun phrases, German adjectival inflection has had no influence on English. Where it occurs it will be dealt with in an ad hoc fashion and will only rarely be reflected in dictionary entries, such as in cases where NPs (e.g. *Deutsche Mark*) appear.

3.2.2 Substantial adjectives   In our material there is only one case of a German substantival adjective. This is *beamter*, which is used twice in the same text and is correctly inflected: 'Whenever a *Beamter* is first employed ...'; 'many other groups in Germany have the status of civil servants, or rather, *Beamte*' (*THES*, 17-7-77). Unlike the adjectives used attributively and discussed above, a writer using a German substantival adjective in English is obliged to choose an ending—the word cannot simply be left uninflected. The examples quoted here indicate the writer's ability to manipulate the German inflection, but this need hardly surprise us, since that writer is Ralf Dahrendorf.

3.3 Verb morphology

The fifteen verbs in our material may be grouped into three categories.

3.3.1   The first is made up of verbs taken directly from German:

> *to abseil:* 'At the end of the day ... we would abseil (that is, slide by easy stages using a harness) down to our bivouac for the night'—*Obs.* 13-1-74.) The verb no longer needs glossing, and occurs in all tenses (e.g. *abseiled*);
>
> *to gallicize:* 'to treat (unfermented grapejuice) with water and sugar, so as to increase the quantity of the wine produced' (*OED*). The term derives from the name of the originator of the process, a Dr. L. Gall of Trier. To this was added the suffix *-isieren*, and the resulting form, when

borrowed, produced the 'blundered' (*OED*) adaptation *gallicise*. To be fair, there is also a correct form *to gallize*;

to stroll: (*OED* 1603) < NHG *strolchen*;

to yodel: (*OED*, earliest citation 1830).

3.3.2 The second comprises German material contained in Yiddish expressions:

to schlep: 'to drag, lag behind, stall';[6]

to schmaltz: 'to add "corn", pathos, mawkishness':[7] 'I usually dislike schmaltzed biopics, especially about artists and composers'—*Radio Times* 7-9-79;

to spiel: 'to patter' (US origin, ex German; possibly Yiddish, but not in Rosten; see *OEDNS*).

3.3.3 The third consists of verbs formed from German material *after* it has entered English:

to blitz: < *blitz* subst. < *blitzkrieg* < NHG *Blitzkrieg*;[8]

to deckle: the noun *deckle* (< NHG *Deckel*) denotes a frame used in paper-making. Paper with a rough, uncut edge has a so-called *deckle-edge*. From this is derived a past part. used adjectivally—*deckled*. (See *OED* & *OEDS*);

to halt: < *to make halt* < NHG *Halt machen*;[9]

to hex: 'to bewitch', via Pennsylvania Dutch (see *OEDNS*);

to kraut out: a verbal derivative of the US slang term for a German occurs in the following: 'One woman was so disgusted with her Stuttgart hosts because they wouldn't slow down to her speed of German that she went home after three days, complaining that she was all krauted out.' (*Obs.* 1-12-74);

to schuss: this skiing term, borrowed as a subst., can now also occur as a verb, e.g. '... 28 skied sedately down the shortish Klosters run, while 32 schussed 12 miles down the Kublis ...' (*The Times*, 4-2-74);

to strafe: originally borrowed in the phrase *Gott strafe England* (*OED*) and now referring to shooting from low-flying aircraft;

to waltz: verb from subst. *waltz* < NHG *Walzer*.

Whatever the route into English taken by these terms, the result, as far as inflection is concerned, is the same: German endings are dropped and they are conjugated according to the English system.

3.4 Form class shifts

Once the German term has been borrowed, it may change its form class. Movement between form classes is relatively common in English, facilitated by its restricted systems of inflection.

3.4.1 Substantives used attributively Following the English possibility of using nouns in an adjectival function a number of the German nouns in our material are attested defining other nouns:

> *abseiling*: 'their———skills' (*THES* 7-3-86);
> *bildungsroman*: 'the———formula' (*Obs.* 22-4-73);
> *blitzkrieg*: 'with———speed' (*Obs.* 15-4-73);
> *jugendstil*: 'Visconti's———treatment of "Der Rosenkavalier"' (*Obs.* 24-9-72);
> *kitsch*: 'two unutterably———rooms' (*Obs.* 9-9-73);
> *lumpen*: 'this tragic———world' (*Obs.* 2-9-73);
> *spiesser*: 'this———ideology' (*THES* 9-6-78).

3.4.2 The following verbs have been derived from German nouns after entering English: *to blitz*; *to deckle*; *to halt*; *krauted* (*out*); *to schmaltz*; *to schuss*; *to waltz*, and have been treated under 3.3.

3.4.3 Two verbal forms appear as nouns.

The first, a German past part. *gedeckt* (usually spelled *gedackt*) 'an organ flue-stop having its pipes stopped at the top' (*OEDNS*);

the other, a noun derived from the Yiddish verb *to schlep—schlep* 'a "drag", a drip, a jerk';[10] it also occurs in the form *schlepper*. A slightly kinder definition of *schlepper* appeared in *Radio Times* (24-4-76) a propos of the US TV character Rhoda: 'Across the country she is known as a New Yorker, an ordinary working girl, a schlepper...'

3.4.4 Finally, two German adjectives which have become nouns in English:

bunter (first attested 1874) 'new red sandstone' has been clipped from *bunter sandstein* (first attested 1830—*OED*) and

schottische, which was shortened from the phrase *der schottische Tanz*. Here the adjective remained, its inflection intact: to confuse matters still further it then acquired a spurious French pronunciation. According to the *OED* the dance was introduced to England in 1848. Its first example is dated 1849 (*OEDNS*).

4. Word Formation

4.1 Compounding

4.1.1 Loan blends   Loan blends combine German and English morphemes, one element of a compound being borrowed, the other translated (e.g. *house-frau*; *sitzbath*). There are 24 examples in the corpus and they thus represent a very small proportion (2%) of the total borrowings (see above, 1.2). It would seem that the need to switch within a word from a foreign to a native morpheme or *vice-versa* inhibits recourse to this method of borrowing.[11] It may also be noted that the English element bears in most cases a strong formal similarity to the German (e.g. *house-/haus-*; *-singer/-sänger*), encouraging the translation from German to English.

There are 14 items with the pattern German+English (or in one case French) morpheme(s): *balm-cricket*; *bauern omelette*; *cornel tree*; *eigenvalue*; *erlking*; *feldspar*; *felstone*; *fugleman*; *grunstone*; *mawseed*; *minnesinger*; *spiegel-iron*; *spindletree*; *sitzbath*.

The ten loan-blends which exhibit the German element in final position are: *apple-strudel*; *beefburger*; *gray-wacke*; *houndsfoot* (<NHG *Hunds-fott* or Dutch *hondsvot*[12]); *housefrau*; *pitchblende*; *ravendruck*; *spitzkrieg* (journalese/nonce creation); *veldtschmerz* (journalese/nonce creation); *wiseacre* (MHG *wîzage* via Dutch[13]).

Of this latter group, none exhibit any evidence of German inflection, i.e. the compound has been fully assimilated into the inflection system of English. In addition to occurring as one compound word, hyphenation and in two cases spacing are introduced.

4.1.2 Other compounds   While the loan-blends are the result of a fusion of German and English morphemes to reproduce the original term in the host language, i.e. they are a mixture of importation and substitution[14] during the borrowing process, once a loan-word is accepted into English it is able to enter into compound formations in the same way as 'native' material. A large proportion of the German loans in our corpus are also attested in compounds, and it would not be in any sense revealing to list them here. Rather, we may limit ourselves to indicating a few especially frequent items, as well as drawing attention to German loans that have proved particularly productive in this regard:

> *angst*: *angst-prone*, and especially *angst-ridden*;
> *blitz*: *blitz-babies*;
> *glance-ore*: probably the oldest German loan in English (1458);[15]
> *homburg-hatted*;
> *kitsch*: *counter-kitsch, kitsch-merchant, porno-kitsch*;
> *lumpen*: *lumpen-avant-garde, lumpen-based, lumpen-bourgeoisie, lumpen-intelligentsia, lumpen-militariat, lumpen-peasantry*;
> *pretzel-stick*;
> *waltz-song*.

The most usual method of writing such compounds is by use of hyphenation. However, the hyphen is not invariably used: when it is omitted we tend to find two-word phrases rather than the unbroken units that are so characteristic of German. This is particularly noticeable in the case of the clipping *lumpen*, leading to its increasing use in an adjectival function. (See above, 3.4.1 under form class shifts and below, 4.4.)

4.2 Affixation

In addition to being compounded, borrowed material may also be combined with English affixes.

4.2.1 Prefixation   An example is provided the word *Nazi*, which a frequency count based on 65 weekly issues of the *Observer* in 1972-73 showed to be the commonest German loan-word used in the paper at that time.[16] This word regularly attracts the following prefixes: *anti-, neo-, pro-, proto-*.

Of especial interest in this section is the prefix *ur-*, since this would appear to be the sole German prefix to have been borrowed into and fully assimilated in English.[17] It now occurs freely in contexts where there is no German reference whatever: '... current taste prefers the open cynicism of W.C. Fields and the Marx brothers to Chaplin's simplistic ur-hippy belief in generalised love as a cure-all' (*Obs.* 11-11-73).

Other examples are: *ur-author*; *ur-Garnett*; *ur-Stalin*; *ur-Whitehouse*; *ur-woman*.

Clearly, this prefix fills a niche; it was borrowed as part of the following words: *urpflanze, ursprache, urtext*. The *OEDS* and *OEDNS* contain further items. It is, however, possible that *ur-* was helped in its transition from prefix borrowed together with a German term (e.g. *ursprache*) to an independent existence by its use in literary scholarship combined with the name of a text. Thus the *OED* shows an early (1901) example to be *ur-Hamlet*.

It may be noted that *echt*, treated above (3.2.1) as an adjective, also exhibits a tendency towards becoming a prefix: *echt-lyrical*; *echt-Coleridge*; *echt-English* (*OEDNS*).

4.2.2 Suffixation   Suffixation, too, is freely available to the borrowed material (e.g. *Gestapo-like*), and needs no further comment.

Despite the existence of the English suffix *-ism* our material shows one writer (Maurice Richardson) choosing to use German *-ismus*, presumably to lend an ironic, 'learned' aura to his words: '... he [Sir Harold Acton] retains a natural youthful affinity to some of the more extravagent forms of Sitwellismus, of which Osbert was ever the most energetic proponent.' (*Obs.* 16-6-74).

Just as we found one highly productive German prefix, so too we may record a German suffix which has taken on a new existence in English. This is *-fest*, whose route into British English very likely led via American. The earliest examples in the *OEDNS* are American, where the word was introduced by the German immigrant population (especially in *saengerfest*); it is discussed by Eichhoff in his examination of Germanisms in *Time*, who points to the additional possibility that the word, especially where it is used independently as a free morpheme, might represent a clipping of *festival*.[18] Nevertheless, the presence of the German suffix in German-American formations and the subsequent popularity of the morpheme as a suffix rather than free-standing lead us to count it as an example of a German suffix that has reached British English by a roundabout route.

Examples in our material are:

> *McLuhanfest* (*Obs*. 1-2-70);
> *filmfest* (*Radio Times* 17-11-73);
> *popfest* ('Reigate's open air popfest'—*Punch* 6-9-72);
> *rockfest* (*Obs*. 18-8-74);
> *schmaltzfest* ('... make a special effort to be in for this Warner Brothers Shakespeare schmaltzfest'—*Radio Times* 7-9-72);
> *talkfest* ('They are condemned by some as simply staging "talkfests" for small groups of academicians.'—*THES* 3-12-76).

The term has been reinforced in Scotland by the establishment of Glasgow's *Mayfest* as a permanent feature of the cultural calendar.

4.3 Derivation

Just as German loans in English are readily available for compounding and affixation, so also are they subjected to the same derivational processes as other words in the language.

4.3.1 Proper nouns

The usual suffix to form an adjective from a proper nouns is *-ian*: thus *Beethovenian, Brahmsian, Brechtian, Hitlerian, Wagnerian*. The polysyllabic names require a shift of word stress to the syllable preceding the ending.

German names ending in *-e* produce the variant *-ean*: *Goethean, Nietschean, Rilkean*.

Franz Kafka's name, ending in *-a*, poses problems; the usual adjective is *Kafkaesque*, though *Kafkaish* and *Kafkan* are attested (*OEDNS*).

The loaned name *Mitteleuropa* turns into a loan-blend when used adjectivally, e.g.: 'Pursued by Peter Ustinov's *mittel-European* analyst (God?) ...' (*Obs*. 29-10-72).

When proper nouns are made into adjectives by the suffixation of *-ian* the resulting form is then ripe for further affixation, e.g. *post-Freudian* etc.

4.3.2 Common nouns

The full range of derivational suffixes are available and occur widely in the corpus. There seems to be no inhibiting effect caused by mixing relatively unassimilated forms (e.g. *herrenvolk*) with English suffixes (*herrenvolkism*) such as we assumed to explain the paucity of loan-blends. In the case of the latter, two alternatives, either complete importation or complete translation were available. With derivation no such options exist, and

since derivation occurs *after* borrowing, the speed with which phonetic/
phonemic assimilation takes place minimises any problems of transition
from German to English morphemes. *Kitsch* quickly spawns *kitschy, kitschness*;
putsch produces *putschist, Nazi Nazism, langlauf langlaufing* and *langlaufers*.

4.4 Clipping

A further method of word-formation that plays a part in the assimilation of
German borrowings in English is clipping. We have already seen this process
at work in the case of *bunter* (3.4.4) where the noun defined by the adjective
bunter (*sandstein*) is dropped, causing the adjective to change form-class.

On entering the English language German *Hochheimer* became *hockamore*
and was subsequently clipped to *hock*, widening at the same time its semantic
range;

NHG *Lagerbier* was originally borrowed as *lager beer* (*OED*), but then clipped
to *lager*;

the fabric *Drillich* became first *drilling*, then was shortened to *drill*, though
Carr points to the possibility of Low German Origin—*drell*—for this form;[19]

and *Walzer* was clipped to *waltz*, possibly to avoid confusion with the *nomen
agentis*.

The loan-word *lumpenproletariat*, besides producing several variants as noted
above (4.1.2), has also been clipped to produce a noun *lumpen* ('The outlaw
and the lumpen will make the revolution ...'—*OEDNS*); this is frequently used
attributively (see above, 3.4.1) and may by now be regarded as an adjective:
e.g. 'Lumpen Tories go unwillingly to the polls' (*Obs.* 17-2-24); '... the desperate people of the streets. Yet it is this tragic lumpen world ... that we see
in these pages' (*Obs.* 2-9-73).

The productive pseudo-loan *blitz*, too, is the product of clipping. *Lightning
warfare* was translated into German as *Blitzkrieg*, and borrowed back into
English as *blitzkrieg*, then clipped to produce a term with a far wider semantic
range than the full form.

5. Conclusion

5.1

Any assessment of the morphological assimilation of German material in
English will be informed by the following factors:

    1: borrowing from NHG represents a quantitatively minor element of
       the English vocabulary;
    2: English has always borrowed freely from other languages;
    3: the relative simplicity of English morphology means that foreign
       material can be readily absorbed;

4: such assimilation is further helped, in the case of German loans, by broad similarities in the morphological structure of both languages;

5: while the assimilation of English material in German requires an *additive* morphological adaptation process—i.e. there is a need to supply grammatical gender for nouns, case, gender and number inflection for articles and adjectives, case and plural marking for nouns,—the movement in the opposite direction involves a *subtractive* process: gender is neutralised, articles and adjectives are uninflected, only the genitive singular case can be shown, and plural markers are generally reduced to the -*s*/-*es* system.

5.2

The result is that German loans are very quickly and easily assimilated into English. We have seen that there is very little evidence of a transitional stage showing residual German inflection patterns. What evidence we have of adjectival inflection is either frozen in loan phrases or is glimpsed fleetingly in nonce usage. There is no chance of German inflection patterns contributing to the already established systems of English inflection. Morphological systems are far more resistant to influence from other languages than the lexis. Even the massive influence of English on German has had insignificant influence on the morphology of NHG.[20]

5.3

Such examples of a morphological contribution from German as we did find are:

1: German plural markers borrowed with a particlar word and fully lexicalised as part of that word (e.g. *lieder*); and

2: the adoption of the productive affixes *ur-* and *-fest*.

Notes

1   Manfred Scheler quotes a figure of 0.5%, based on Finkenstaedt, Leisi and Wolff, *A Chronological English Dictionary* (Heidelberg, 1970), in *Der englische Wortschatz*. Berlin: Erich Schmidt Verlag (1977) p 72.

2   Johnson, H. *The World Atlas of Wine*. London: Mitchell Beazley (2nd edn 1977) p 41.

3   In this article German words (i.e. before borrowing) are cited in italics with initial capital, German loan-words (i.e. after borrowing) are cited in italics without initial capital. However, when they occur within exemplifying quotations they are reproduced exactly as in the source. The non-*OED* material cited here was taken mainly from *The Observer* (abbreviated *Obs.*), *The Times Literary Supplement* (abbreviated *TLS*) and *The Times Higher Education Supplement* (abbreviated *THES*). Other sources are named in full.

4   The earliest dating for both plurals is 1931 (*OEDS*).

5   Oxford (1983). Vol. 1, p 769.

6   See Rosten, L, *The Joys of Yiddish*. New York: Pocket Books (1970), p 350.

7   Rosten, p 356.

8   On the development of *blitzkrieg* in English see Stanforth, A, 'Schein- und Rück-
    entlehnungen aus dem Deutschen im Britisch-Englischen', in *Neuere Forschungen
    in Linguistik und Philologie* (=ZDL Beihefte N.F. 13), 1975, pp 114-29.

9   See Carr, C T, *The German Influence on the English Vocabulary* (=*S.P.E. Tract* 42).
    Oxford 1934, p 43.

10 See Rosten, p 350.

11 See Stanforth, A, 'Deutsche Lehnübersetzungen im Deutschen', in Feldbusch,
    E (ed.) *Ergebnisse und Aufgaben der Germanistik am Ende des 20. Jahrhunderts.*
    Hildesheim: Olms-Weidmann (1989), pp 130-38.

12 Carr, p 51.

13 Carr, p 43.

14 See Haugen, E, 'The analysis of linguistic borrowing'. *Language*, vol. 26, 1950,
    p 212.

15 Carr, p 39.

16 Stanforth, A, 'An assessment of the frequency of Germanisms in *The Observer*'.
    ZDL, vol. 43, 1976, pp 291-96.

17 A nonce-borrowing *pipi-* occurs in a reported comment by Stefan Heym ('I call
    it pipi-Stalinism'—*Obs.* 13-8-72), but it remains an isolated example.

18 Eichhoff, J, 'Deutsches Lehngut und seine Funktion in der amerikanischen
    Pressesprache'. *Jahrbuch für Amerikastudien*, vol. 17, 1972, p 170.

19 Carr, p 48.

20 See Cartensen, B, *Englische Einflüsse auf die deutsche Sprache nach 1945*. Heidel-
    berg: Winter (1965) p 68.

Political Realities and Political Lexis in the USSR

Jim Halliday and Elena V Crosbie

The history of the twentieth century has been overshadowed by the interplay between two dark and titanic forces. It has been argued that Fascism came to predominate in Germany because of Stalin's determination not to support the German socialists. Stalin and Hitler certainly learned from each other's methods in establishing and maintaining a totalitarian system. Fascism was crushed as a method of government, within Europe at least, and Soviet communism has been gradually weaning itself away from the Stalinist model ever since the dictator's death.[1] This tendency has become greatly accelerated since Mikhail Gorbachev acceeded to power (although it would be worth heeding Academician Sakharov's recent warnings that Gorbachev has taken all the main positions of power into his hands by undemocratic means). The process of mutation in the Soviet Union has recently become so extensive that it is possible that the changes which have been taking place since 1985 will result in a society which, when viewed against the background of Russian history, will be relatively liberal. We were privileged to be Professor Prais's colleagues for many years, and it seemed appropriate to include in a volume dedicated to Henry, whose life like that of so many others has been shaped by the traumas of European history, to include a study of the relationship between political reality in the USSR and the language of politics.

Although the British Prime Minister would vigorously deny it, all societies are teleologically motivated: even John F. Kennedy appealed to his countrymen to think not of what America could do for them, but of what they could do for America. But in few cases has the teleological dimension been so clear cut as in the Soviet Union from its earliest beginnings. The population has been constantly exhorted to sacrifice present satisfactions in order to further the greater good of society in the longer term. All possible resources were harnessed in the drive for forced industrialisation. The arts, too, were compelled to promote Stalin's policies. The predominance of the future became one of the overriding images in the Soviet political scheme. It was against this supremacy that Pasternak's Yuri Zhivago rebelled: although he was initially excited by the idea of the Revolution excising society's ills in a kind of radical surgery, he came to feel that life is not a substance, a material to be re-made—it is too transient to be put aside in the name of an ideal tomorrow.

All such hostility to the new regime eventually came to be crushed or, at least, deprived of a voice. The language, too, was pressed into service and came to reflect the changes taking place in the country. It did this not, in the main, by borrowing from other languages as in the pre-Revolutionary period, but by drawing upon the language's intrinsic resources to assign new meanings to existing words.[2] Examples include прослойка ('stratum'); смычка ('link' [between town and country]); ударник ('shock worker'); передовой ('progressive', 'vanguard'); перековаться ('to be [politically] re-educated'); перегиб ('violation of the correct line, harmful extremism'). New collocations were formed, many with quasi-military connotations: генеральная ('the general line'); передний край ('leading area' [of economic development']); дом отдыха ('rest-home'); отдел кадров ('personnel department'); служба быта ('service sector').

The tendency for these terms to be replaced by abbreviations has been frequently commented upon. Thus, районный центр ('district [administrative] centre') becomes райцентр; народный комиссар ('people's commissar') is reduced to нарком; ликвидация безграмотности ('the elimination of illiteracy') is shortened to ликбез and исполнительный комитет ('executive committee') to исполком.

In an even more active class of abbreviated words formed from compounds, the first element was truncated while the second component remained intact: продовольственный налог ('taxation in kind')—продналог; революционный трибунал ('revolutionary tribunal')—ревтрибунал; районный совет ('district council')—райсовет. This tendency was remarked upon by Alexander Solzhenitsyn in his novella *Matryona's House*, when the narrator muses on the name of the small village he is goes to settle in after his release from the camps—'Torfoprodukt' ('Peat Product'): 'Торфопродукт? Ах, Тургенев не знал, что можно по-русски составить такое!' ['Torfoprodukt! Ah, Turgenev did not know such words could be made up in Russian!'].

Also endemic to Soviet life were acronyms, such as *USSR*, *RSFSR* (the Russian Federation), ЧК (the Cheka, the secret police), вуз ('higher educational institution'), НЭП (NEP—the New Economic Policy), загс ('registry office'), etc.

Although Mikhail Gorbachev describes his reforms as 'revolutionary', the language of the reform process displays the main features that have been characteristic in the formation of the political lexis in the Soviet period (with the exception of the first few years of the industrialisation of the 1930s. Most of the lexis of *perestroika* has been derived by attaching new meanings to long-exisisting Russian words. Moreover, *perestroika* itself is quintessentially paradoxical. It is an attempt, from above, to exhort people to be more democratic. At the same time, when the 'grass roots' respond with democratic initiatives of their own, the repressive system tends to swing back into action. To that extent, therefore, a policy whose cornerstone is демократизация общества ('the democratisation of society') can be regarded as yet another in the long series of hortatory campaigns the Soviet population has been exposed to since 1917, even if it has been embarked upon with the best of intentions.

Indeed, the more cynical commentators have tended to look on concepts like 'democratisation' as weasel words, designed to enable the authorities to selectively devolve power to interest groups while retaining overall control. 'Glasnost, democracy, initiative, reconstruction, involvement, legal and human rights, all these are also a way of *not* saying freedom', asserts Anthony Barnett.[3] Another approach would be to say that these words are not intended to substitute for 'freedom', but are put forward as ways of ultimately achieving freedom. 'Democratisation' is a pointer to a means, rather than to an end which, in the Soviet view at least, has already been achieved. Nevertheless, to an outsider it is a term which appears to make little sense. In what way can it be superior to 'democracy', a word that is difficult to define, but which we instinctively apprehend. 'Democratisation' has the feeling of something less, of being not a synonym for democracy, but an attenuation of it.

Language is by its nature 'coded'. Nowhere is this seen more clearly than in the field of politics. While there is a part of the political lexis which is universal in its applicability, there is a segment of it which is country-specific and only has real meaning for the inhabitants of a particular territory. Given the nature of Soviet history, it is fair to say that the USSR is a state which has more 'discrete' political features than shared ones with the other countries of the developed world. One might therefore anticipate that the country-specific area of Soviet political lexis would be substantial. It is this very factor which accounts for the difficulty translators have in finding valid equivalents for many Russian political, economic and socio-cultural terms. The lexis depends to a large degree upon what Tzvetan Todorov refers to as the 'shared collective memory' to convey its meaning.[4] If the collective experiences of two peoples are very different, the translation even if extremely competently carried out may not convey to the target audience a fraction of the meaning it has for people belonging to the linguistic culture it emanated from.

There is, of course, the further possibility that since the translator does not always share in the collective memory of the people whose language he works with, there may be lacunae in his cultural 'baggage'. An interesting example can be found in Mikhail Bulgakov's story *The Heart of a Dog*, in the English version by Michael Glenny, one of the most skilful, renowned and most experienced translators from Russian. The hero, Sharikov,—a dog who has been turned by an operation into a man,—has obtained a job as a cat-catcher. Asked what is to be done with all the dead cats, he replies in the language of the proletariat: 'На польты пойдут—из них белок будут делать на рабочий кредит[5] ['They will be turned into squirrel fur coats which the workers can buy on their special hire-purchase scheme.'] Michael Glenny's translation, however, reads: 'They go to a laboratory, where they make them into proteins for the workers'.[6] Instead of the standard Russian word for 'overcoat' (пальто), which is an indeclinable neuter noun, Sharikov uses the colloquial variant 'польты' in the plural.The confusion between the Genitive Plural of 'squirrel' белка (белок) and the Nominative Singular белóк ('protein') has led the translator to an intelligent guess, given the food-shortages and malnutrition of the post-Revolutionary period. Here is an instance of how, when syntax and stress by themselves do not provide sufficient information, knowledge of the collective memory would be of assistance. This is, naturally, an even more serious problem for the translator of texts pertaining to even earlier historical periods.

The reader of a translation is in a position close to the man who finds a letter in the street. Although the words are very clear, 'he will still not be able to understand it fully, for he does not know the imnmediate circumstances concerning the person who wrote it or the person to whom it is addressed'.[7]

A further feature of the Soviet political lexis that the discrete nature of the regime might lead us to anticipate is a high level of euphemistic usage, since euphemism is a prominent aspect of the collective memory. The members of a linguistic community have no need to always designate certain concepts or events fully—indeed, there may be strong reasons for not doing so. Euphemism in the political lexis may be divided into two main types. In the first instance, there is the normal usage of the word, which refers to the avoidance of unpleasant truths or realities by substituting milder or weaker expressions. Thus, in the Stalin years, the term высшая мера наказания ('the supreme measure of punishment') was preferred to the older word казнь ('execution'), which was reserved for pre-Revolutionary contexts or descriptions of capitalist judicial systems. The term 'supreme penalty' was no doubt felt to be more neutral or perhaps even more humane than 'execution'; it also attenuated the impact of the scale of the repressions. An interesting twist to this is that 'supreme penalty' itself was generally abbreviated in common parlance to вышка, with a typical Russian diminutive ending, which made it sound almost homely.

The second type of euphemism in the political lexis overlaps with ellipsis, and occurs when there is no particular requirement to avoid facing up to unpalatable facts, but when it would be too complicated to refer to them explicitly each time. Expressions like обновление общества ('renewal of society'), for example, can be compared to the tip of an iceberg, at whose base lies a whole debate about the kind of socialist society that has been and should be constructed in the USSR; about whether the Stalinist system was an aberration or fundamentally correct in the institutions it created (but not about the means it used to achieve them—that is not on the agenda); about the admission after years of complacency that the country's economy and physical and social infrastructure are in a critical state; and finally, about the methods to be used to put things to rights and the timescale of the reforms. It is plainly more economical to refer to these notions (which are themselves a thumbnail sketch of the kind of issues at stake) by means of a form of shorthand than to spell them out. There is another reason why this would in any case be impossible: although the political consciousness of society may be collective, it is not necessarily homogeneous, and terms such as 'renewal' evoke wildly differing responses and interpretations.

The word застой, for example, has the generic meaning of 'stagnation', whereas its current discursive meaning in the collocation период застоя ('the period of stagnation') and cognate expressions such as застойные явления (literally, 'phenomena of stagnation') have the syntagmatic meaning 'almost anything to do with the Brezhnev period, especially if it is pejorative.' Formal translations in this case—or even descriptive ones—convey little of the implicit content of these expressions. Although their use in the media is intended to be negative, there may well be people for whom 'the period of stagnation' amounts to 'the good old days'.

By eliding over the full damage the Brezhnev period did to the country, there is always the risk that its seriousness (or the CPSU's responsibility for it) is thereby reduced. While this may have been the case in the initial, more tentative period of *perestroika*, the attack on Brezhnev and his cohorts in the media has intensified over time. One could speak, therefore, of the element of elision coming to predominate over euphemism as such.

The opposite has happened in the case of дедовщина, which is a colloquial word used to refer to bullying in the army, a subject which previously was completely taboo. Дедовщина is a compound of the diminutive дед (from дедушка, 'grandfather') and the pejorative suffix -щин-. Early in 1988, some of the more liberal publications such as *Ogonek*, *Moscow News* and the Leningrad youth magazine *Znamya* carried a disturbing series of reports on the the custom where conscripts serving their second year in the army (деды) would organise cruel initiation rituals for the new recruits, and would bully or maltreat them. This word appears to have had too unsettling an effect on the families of boys already serving in the army or approaching the age of conscription, for after a few months it came to be replaced by the less emotional (and more 'official') term внеуставные отношения ('relations not sanctioned by military statute'). From this it is clear that the direction of motivation of euphemism in the political vocabulary is variable.

The clearest examples of ellipsis in the lexis of politics are the two key words, *perestroika* and *glasnost'*, two of the fairly small number of Russian words that have been absorbed directly into English, and into other European languages. Part of the reason why they have been transliterated rather than translated like, for example, 'collective farm' is that they are simultaneously specific terms, and yet somewhat nebulous in their meaning. Although journalists and others initially spoke of 'restructuring' and 'openness', they quickly came to feel that these terms somehow failed to do justice to the original notions. The tendency now is for the Russian words to be used, followed by a qualification in English. The French, too, appear to be using *la transparence* for *glasnost'* less frequently. In any case, this was not a very satisfactory rendition for, as Nella Bielski has pointed out,[8] *la transparence* is based on seeing through, rather than speaking out, which is implied by the Russian term (*glasnost'* is derived from Old Russian *glas*, 'voice'). Even other Slavonic languages have difficulty in handling these terms. Yugoslav journalists tried out 14 substitute words for *perestroika*, but none of them proved to be adequate, and now the Russian term is used in transliteration in Serbo-Croat as well.[9] The Estonians, on the other hand, have found an eminently suitable equivalent: they use a term which means 'rearranging the furniture'.

It is hardly surprising that journalists and translators have trouble with *perestroika*—Mikhail Gorbachev in his book on the new political thinking[10] devotes six substantial paragraphs to the delineation of the notion. As Professor Dennis Ward pointed out,[11] Gorbachev was not trying to *define* the word, but to explain what he means by a whole set of complex measures. Nevertheless, his description of what *perestroika* amounts to includes points which are very specific and eminently realisable, and others which are so sweeping that they are essentially utopian. There are good reasons why a term with a wide semantic field should be used. It allows freedom of manoeuvre, and enables the debate and the reform programme to proceed on the broadest possible front and to evolve in unforeseen directions. *Perestroika* is a convenient way of encapsulating a wide-ranging and disparate idea in a concise and generally understood fashion.

Inevitably, as the policy of reform becomes institutionalised and becomes, to some extent, the new orthodoxy, so the lexis associated with it begins to lose its initial impact. It becomes 'desemanticised' and devalued through frequent usage; the lexemes turn, in effect, into cliches. The word застой ('stagnation'), which was briefly mentioned above, has itself become so stagnant that Soviet journalists have been substituting for it стагнация, a transliteration of the English word 'stagnation'.[12] If the word *perestroika* has become institutionalised, *glasnost'* has become re-institutionalised for a second time. Apart from being a term much used by Soviet dissidents in the 1960s and early 1970s, it was one of the dominant concepts in Russian politics of the middle years of the last century.

The parallels between its present use and its meaning at that time are striking. Although Nicolas I was advised to introduce *glasnost'* as a means of containing discontent, it became what would now be known as a buzz-word some fifteen years later, after Russia's humiliating defeat in the Crimean War. The country then faced—as it does now—intractable social, political and economic problems. One of the methods Alexander II favoured for tackling them was the fostering of a body of public opinion with which the autocracy could conduct a dialogue to create the necessary climate of support for the reforms it was contemplating, against the wishes of many members of the nobility and the land-owning classes. The dialogue that was envisaged was one in which certain limits established by the authorities would not be exceeded. It would enable the progressive and conservative elements in the bureaucracy to express the conflict of ideas between each other and with the views of the Tsar and his advisers. The more enlightened bureaucrats even as early as the 1840s saw *glasnost'* in a less constricting framework than this. They regarded its main function as serving as a check upon arbitrariness and corruption both in the bureaucracy and in society. W. Bruce Lincoln summarises their attitude to the practical application of *glasnost'* as 'a means to permit men who supported the cause of change as they envisaged it to participate in a broader discussion of a possible transformation of Russia.'[13]

Deciding whether Mikhail Sergeyevich Gorbachev rates as an enlightened bureaucrat or as a liberal Tsar is perhaps not so easy; what is apparent are the points of contact between *glasnost'* 130 years ago and at the present time, when the leader of the Soviet Union has called for the 'revolutionary renewal of society'. One of the criticisms of *glasnost'* in its present reincarnation is precisely that it too is selected: only those who support the currently adopted model of change have been given a real opportunity to speak out. While there has been some limited scope for those who hold reservations about reform to express them,[14] the debate has been definitely skewed against those who are fundamentally opposed to change. In so far as their views are ever put at all, they are generally summarized in articles criticising the 'forces of inertia'. This is unfair and undemocratic.

In the last century, as the notion of *glasnost'* took root, the numbers of those who wished to see it extended far beyond its initial, restrictive manifestation gradually increased. Equally, opponents who viewed *glasnost'* as a potential threat to the stability of government ranged themselves against it. The dichotomy inherent in the process was articulated by Alexander himself in 1857, when he insisted that the censorship must continue to exercise 'a judicious vigilance over the press', but that this should not 'inhibit thinking'.[15] The formulation that was ultimately accepted was that elaborated by O.A. Przheslavskii, a member of the Main Censorship Administration. *Glasnost'*, as he outlined it, would be essentially a part of government policy, whereby public opinion would place itself at the service of the autocracy in a manner defined by the autocracy. As Lincoln points out, 'Glasnost, as it came to be defined by 1865, became an effective weapon in the hands of state officials against the sort of glasnost to which men like Tsie, Herzen and Dolgorukov had aspired less than a decade earlier.'[16]

Here the parallels end. It is true that the Soviet version of *glasnost'* is, like its forerunner, a policy resorted to by a government conscious that only with the support of the general public can it emerge from the morass of problems that confront it. But, Gorbachev's *glasnost'* has already, in just three years, opened the Pandora's box so wide that it would be difficult to screw the lid back on as tightly as before. Journals which had become so dull and predictable that they were quite unreadable have, under new liberal editorships, won back readers in their millions, so much so that for a brief period restrictions had to be placed on subscriptions to them. The resulting outcry from a public that could not bear to be deprived of their favourite reading material was so great that Mr. Gorbachev intervened personally to ensure that sufficient supplies of paper could be found.[17] And, just as in Alexander's day, many people have not been content to accept an emasculated version of *glasnost'*: they have been pushing back the frontiers of 'openness' at every opportunity. This tendency has been greatest in the Baltic republics, which poses severe problems for the government. Things have already gone so far, however, that it is no longer a matter of using state *glasnost'* against a different sort of officially forbidden *glasnost'*, but of continually re-drawing the boundaries of acceptable compromise.

The crucial question, however, is not whether it would be *difficult* to close the lid on Pandora's box, but whether it would be *possible*. This is where the issue of гарантии ('guarantees') comes in to its own. Gorbachev is well aware that so far only the most reckless people, or those who are desperate because their plight is already unendurable, or those who are beyond the pale and therefore have nothing to lose, are willing to speak out: the majority prefer to keep their heads under the parapet until they can be sure of the course events will take. The others will not be drawn into the process until they are reassured of 'the irreversibility of reform' (необратимость перестройки). This expression is a further example of euphemism; expressed in full it would mean something like 'no-one will be able to get you if the conservatives regain power and start settling old scores, because we will make it constitutionally impossible for them to do so'. This allays only one part of the worry; the other, unspoken thought continues '... or if the new regime reverts to the tried and trusted methods of the past'.

The fear that 'something might happen' is common to all peoples. It could be argued that because of their history, it has taken deeper root in the Russian psyche than in that of most European nations. The phenomenon is brilliantly described in Anton Chekhov's short story *Man in a Case* where the hero, a provincial school master, consistently shies away from the experiences life has to offer and from his fellow men как бы чего не вышло, 'in case something hapens'. He lives an isolated and paranoid existence which is joyless and sterile, in which he protects himself from the world in a cocoon of nervous dread.

Evgenii Evtushenko revived and reified this notion in a poem published in *Pravda* in 1985, soon after Mr. Gorbachev's accession to power. In it, Evtushenko turns the expression как бы чего не вышло ('in case something happens') into a noun, кабычегоневышлисты, denoting cautious people, all those who throughout history have been afraid to act or take risks. Listing their sins of omission and commission, he castigates them as кабычегоне-вышлистики, 'the nasty little what-if-something-happens-people'. It was they who refused to believe Archimedes and opposed any new development, whether of steam trains, heart operations, aeroplanes or electricity; they banned the publication of Bulgakov's novel *The Master and Margarita*. They were the ones who held back Soviet genetics and cybernetics by decades. In this context, Evtushenko incorporates the name Lysenko into yet another derivation, кабычегоневышлистенко, and refers to the whole atmosphere of fear and excessive caution as кабычегоневышлизм.

Most of the items from the political lexis that have been considered so far are long-established Russian words. There are two other classes of words which should be examined, even in a review as brief as this one. The first group comprises foreign borrowings. One interesting group of words which had existed in Russian before the Revolution had a dual identity: when they were applied to Russia under the old regime or to aspects of life abroad which were being criticised, they were pejorative. When they were used in a post-Revolutionary context, however, they took on a uniquely Soviet meaning. Миллионер ('millionaire') is an example of a word which changed from meaning a wealthy individual to one which referred to a collective farm whose income exceeded a million roubles, or a pilot who had flown over a million kilometres, and so on. Likewise, династия ('dynasty') was no longer applied to a succession of monarchs or aristocrats, but to families where a number of generations were employed in the same trade, e.g. a dynasty of miners, or shipbuilders.

Many of the foreign terms which had been incorporated into the pre-Revolutionary vocabulary were regarded as 'neutral' and retained their previous meaning: лорд ('lord'), ранчо ('ranch'), колледж ('college'), мэр ('mayor'), апартеид ('apartheid'), меджлис ('majlis'). A number of them, however, took on pejorative associations and were applied either to the old regime or to aspects of life abroad which were being criticised. Since 1985 a number of such words have been applied to features of life within the Soviet

Union. One example is the word лидер ('leader') which was often used instead of the more respectful term руководитель. Only Western politicians and trade unionists were dubbed лидеры ('leaders'); while the word could be neutral in certain contexts, it was sometimes used to convey overtones of distaste. In autumn 1988 *Ogonek* printed an article about the new First Secretary of the Astrakhan region, one of the most run-down areas of the Soviet Union, in which he said: Не на почве ли нашей рабской бездумности вырастали дутые лидеры с липовыми заслугами и достижениями ('Was it not on the soil of our servile thoughtlessness that self-important leaders with their fraudulent merits and achievements flourished?') Later in the article he is quoted as saying: ... Не первый день на светеживу и вижу, как иной партийный функционер уже не идет, а что называется, несет себя, сгибаясь под грузом собственной значимости ('I've been around for a while, and I've seen Party functionaries who no longer walk, but, as they say, "carry themselves", bending under the weight of their own importance').[18]

The same arguments pertain to политик ('politician'), a pejorative word applied exclusively to capitalist politicians, with the term политический деятель being employed to indicate a respectful attitude. Политик, however, is now regularly applied to Soviet politicians. Similarly, the word банкир ('banker') was previously only applied to Western bankers, almost always in a pejorative context. Now, however, when the policy of 'plugging into the world market' is being vigorously pursued, foreign financiers are no longer depicted in a deprecatory light. Moreover, the upgrading of the importance of the internal banking and credit system means that the term is regularly used of Soviet banking officials, which would previously have been regarded as extremely distasteful. With the prospect of the fully convertible rouble in sight, one wonders how long it will be before биржа ('stock exchange') will make a come-back in a Russian context.

Another group within the category of foreign borrowings comprises descriptions used by Western scholars and commentators when analysing the political structures of the USSR. Within the Soviet Union, these terms were considered to be not only unacceptable but openly anti-Soviet. Now, terms such as командно-управленческая система (which is a synonym for 'the centralised command economy') are widely used in Soviet publications. Some Russian words which were part of the terminology of foreign Sovietologists have now been given wider circulation within their homeland. For example, the word номенклатура (the *nomenklatura*, a list of top Party posts but also, by extension, an elite group of Party workers) was widely used in the Western literature but within the USSR was confined to an inner circle of the Party. Recently, however, in an attack on the USSR's 'jeunesse doree', a youth paper wrote: Кошмар коррупции, врастание преступности в государственный и партийнный аппарат ... [требует] ... изъятия награбленного у 'потомков' ('номенклатурных детей', так точно назвала эти кастовые ветки 'Комсомолка') ('The nightmare of corruption and the way in which crime has become entrenched in the Party and government apparatus ... [requires] ... that the things they have stolen [i.e. from the people] should be taken away from the 'descendants' ('the *nomenklatura* kids, as *Komsomol'skaya Pravda* aptly named the offspring of this caste').[19] The home-grown descriptions are in any case sometimes stronger than those emanating from abroad: Хрущев, вспомним, был из команды, которую Сталин набирал для уничтожения НЭПа и строительства лагерно-казарменного социализма ('Let us recall that Khrushchev was one of the team which Stalin picked to destroy the New Economic Policy and to construct the socialism of the prison camp and the barracks').[20]

The second class of terms comprises pre-Revolutionary Russian words that have come back into circulation. Many words in common currency before 1917 inevitably strike the contemporary Russian as archaisms. Like the foreign borrowings, they too have a range of stylistic associations. Some, like дума ('Duma') or земство ('zemstvo'—both government institutions) and гимназия ('high school') could be said to be neutral. Others, like помещик ('land-owner') and губернатор ('governor' [of a province]) are pejorative, perhaps even sinister—полиция ('police'), or quaint—престолонаследник ('heir to the throne').

Some nineteenth-century terms have never been absent from the popular speech, even if for many years they rarely appeared in print, for example чиновник ('bureaucrat, clerk'). Now, however, this word is not only on the lips of everyone, but features prominently in press articles which lay bare the obtuseness and corruption of the Party and government apparatus. Other expressions which have reappeared after decades of obscurity have recovered their previous positive associations. Милосердие ('mercy') and бла-готворительность ('charity') were concepts which were virtually outlawed from the Soviet Union during the Stalin years, condemned as part of 'abstract humanism' rather than the 'socialist humanism' promoted at the time and which placed the collective above the individual. At present, an awareness of the extent of the collapse of the social infracture coupled with a new emphasis on moral values and a reinterpretation of socialism as including 'love for thy neighbour' have revived these two notions. The press is full of articles about groups of workers who care for the elderly or the handicapped in their free time. That even the Orthodox church has a role to play in this is openly acknowleged, and photographs of believers, or even nuns, tending the sick in state hospitals are frequently reproduced.

The attempt to revive the country's stultified agriculture by 'giving back the land to the peasants' has brought with it the re-introduction of the old word аренда ('lease, lease-hold'), once again in a positive sense after many years when it served mainly as a deprecatory word. Associated with it is the word подряд ('contract'). The country people can henceforth operate as a семейный подряд ('family work-team') to cultivate land rented from the state or their collective farm on a fifty-year lease. This has been interpreted by some scholars, both Soviet and Western, as prefiguring the eventual collapse of the collective farm system. Such an outcome seems unlikely, however, given the innate hostility of the Russian peasantry to anyone who 'gets above himself'. Moreover, the experience of the кооперативы ('co-operatives', another word which has never fallen into disuse but which is having a new lease of life) and the частники ('self-employed', people working for themselves under the new Law on Individual Labour) suggests that the difficulties facing арендаторы (peasants who lease land) are likely to be so severe that they will present a threat only to the very weakest collective farms for some considerable time to come.

Рента ('rent'), often found in close association with аренда ('lease'), is another word which has come back into use in a non-pejorative context. Although it did sometimes figure in neutral contexts, it tended to be used in Soviet writings to describe aspects of capitalist economic practices in a negative manner and was not normally applied to Soviet conditions. Now that the great trinity of хозрасчет, самоокупаемость, самофинансирование ('full-cost accounting', 'self-repayment' and 'self-financing') are destined to replace central intervention and government subsidisation of the economy, 'rent' is taking on a renewed significance. These three terms all have a substantial pedigree, with 'full-cost accounting' dating back to the days of the New Economic Policy, introduced in the spring of 1921.

There is one other feature of the language of *perestroika* which we should like to bring in. It is not a lexical feature as such, but since it belongs to the realm of metaphor and we started off looking at euphemisms in the political lexis, it deserves a mention. What we have in mind is a penchant for maritime imagery. This is frequently encountered in the speeches of Mr. Gorbachev, who likes to refer to the new course that is being steered, the storm-tossed waters of life's ocean, the wind of change, the reefs and sandbanks that lie in wait for the unwary, and so on. Indeed, it was the notion of *perestroika* as the cleansing wind of change that inspired *Ogonek* magazine to take a photograph of the billowing canvas of a sailing ship as the device for its 1987 calendar.

The record for the most extended use of the marine metaphor, however, belongs to the journalist who wrote up the profile of the First Secretary of the Astrakhan' region already mentioned. This official faces an almost superhuman task in reviving the fortunes of an area long renowned as one of the most dilapidated in Russia. As the quotation in which his plight is described is a long one, only the English version will be given:

> 'Of course, it would be interesting to know what first steps the First Secretary intends to take, and what are his thoughts as he takes the wheel of a ship which has been listing badly for a long time now, and which is shaping a course which will not only overcome the open threat of the storms which have instantly crashed down upon it, but also the invisible reefs and sandbanks of covert resistance, for it would be naive to suppose that those who have become completely accustomed to doing what they like will give up their positions without a struggle and will not want to put the captain himself to the test'.[21]

Perhaps this sentence qualifies for a prize on the grounds of length as well.

A thorough review of the numerous changes taking place in the Soviet political lexis is beyond the scope of a brief article. Even in outline, though, the major processes which are occurring in the endless entropy and renewal of language formations can be discerned (ideally, the 'Brezhnevite' items that are being dropped from the lexis, like 'mature/developed socialism' should be examined as well). The new lexis is largely made up of existing words given new meanings, with neologisms noteable by their absence. This should not be surprisng, however, since it is in keeping with the predominant trends in Soviet lexical history. Mr. Gorbachev has repeatedly described his reform programme as a quiet revolution, and indeed it is by no means a cataclysmic event like the revolutions of 1905 and 1917. It is, all the same, a dramatic re-statement of the classic Russian dilemma of development, and this is reflected in changes in lexis. If the attempt to achieve a better society succeeds, perhaps after all the word свобода—freedom—will also take on a new role in the language and practice of politics.

Notes

1   White, Stephen, *Political Culture and Soviet Politics*. London: Macmillan, 1979; Hill, Ronald J, *Soviet Politics, Political Science and Reform*. London: Martin Robertson, 1980. Chapter 8.
2   Comrie, Bernard and Stone, Geoffrey, *The Russian Language since the Revolution*. Oxford: Clarendon Press, 1978. pp. 135-140.
3   Barnett, Anthony and Bielski, Nella, *Soviet Freedom*. London: Picador Books, 1988. p. xi.
4   Todorov, Tzvetan, *Symbolism and Interpretation*. London: Routledge and Kegan Paul, 1983. p. 69.
5   Bulgakov, Mikhail Afanasievich, *Sobach'ye serdtse*. Paris: YMCA-Press, 1969. p. 143.
6   Glenny, Michael, *The Heart of a Dog*. London: Collins and Harvill Press, 1969 p. 116.
7   Todorov, op. cit. p. 149.
8   Barnett & Bielski, op. cit. p. 34.
9   Toshovich, B, *Izucheniye i funktsionirovaniye russkogo yazyka v mire*. 'Russkii yazyk za rubezhom' No. 4, 1988. p. 51.
10 Gorbachev, M S, *Perestroika i novoye myshleniye dlya nashei* strany i dlya vsego mira. Moscow: Izdatel'stvo politicheskoi literatury, 1987. p. 30.
11 Professor Dennis Ward. Oral comunication at the 18th Scottish Slavonic Seminar, University of St. Andrews, 12 November 1988.
12 Cornwell, Rubert. *Language purists spik out on Russian's degradatsiya*. The Independent, 11 November 1988.
13 Lincoln, W B, *The Problem of Glasnost in Mid-Nineteenth Century Russian Politics*. European Studies Review, XI/2, 1981. p. 176.
14 See, for example the polemic between A Popkova (*Gde pyshnee pirogi?*) and O Latsis (*Zachem zhe pod ruku tolkat'*) in Novy Mir, Nos. 5 and 8 of 1987.
15 Lincoln, W B, op. cit., p. 180.
16 Ibid., p. 185.
17 Cornwell, R, op. cit.
18 *Ogonek* No. 40, October 1988, p. 24.
19 Sobesednik No. 27, June 1988. '*Golosuyem za glasnost'*.
20 *Moskovskiye novosti* No. 42, 16 October 1988, p. 16.
21 *Ogonek* No. 40, October 1988, p. 3.

Communicative Skills Acquisition: a Recommended Resource

Margaret Lang

The communication process may be enhanced by the use of certain linguistic resources which are independent of grammatical structures and which are capable of involving any length of text. These resources may have a vital role in the conveying or understanding of an argument. This paper will examine certain of the resources, their function/s, and various common features. It will consider one resource in detail, namely, the expression of enumeration. Since the initial reason for the study was to determine the pedagogical usefulness and scope of this particular area in communicative skills, the paper concludes with some suggestions of ways of sensitising students to their recognition and use.

It is frequently the case that despite attainment of a certain standard or level in school leaving certificate examinations, English-speaking students of languages remain unable, or are ill-equipped, either to create a structured text or to discern the structure of a text, and this in both mother tongue and foreign languages. It may be considered that a text can rely for its structure on thematic resources, that is on the presence of a lexical field, or fields, alone, provided the theme or themes are not randomly addressed. However, for compelling practical reasons such as advanced academic standards or professional requirements, it is advisable to be able to call on other resources, either in recognition or in production. There is no reason why English-speaking students should not have such resources at their command, and be able increasingly not merely to use them in their normal acceptation, but also to recognise deviant uses. Creating and discerning the structure of a text, by which is meant oral or written discourse exhibiting a logical progression of ideas as, for instance, in a formal speech, interpreting, a report, a summary, or an essay, can be achieved by the use of certain alternative resources, which are known by various names in English and in French.[1]

For present purposes, I shall refer to them simply as cohesive devices. These devices are to be distinguised from structural textual resources, that is resources which are incorporated within sentences and are the expression of semantic relations between clauses. Such resources are more correctly described as constituting elements of syntax and grammar, rather than as being independent of grammatical structures and not bound by a single sentence.

Since cohesive devices are independent of grammatical structures, and since they may involve a length of text beyond the sentence, it might be inferred that they are non-essential textual elements. To a certain extent, this is true: communication is possible without them. Indeed, communication is possible without words. Yet, in the context of advanced, effective communication, oral and written, academic, professional and social, in mother tongue and in foreign languages, there is a substantial case for including them as an efficient method of expressing and of discerning the logic of argument. This does not of course imply that a text is necessarily without logic if the devices are not explicit.

The devices in question are words and phrases such as *yet, indeed, for instance* ... which have a precise function in the argument. They may be polyvalent and consequently context-dependent for meaning, or idiolectal, or have a short-lived, synchronic semantic value. In other words, rigid taxonomies would be particularly inappropriate for these language resources.

It is when one attempts to create a taxonomy of such devices, for pedagogical purposes for example, that the richness of their reference becomes apparent. If, for instance, one wanted to create categories according to their function or functions, one could use labels such as concession, reservation, contrast, refutation, agreement and so on. It might well be modelled on functional classifications such as those of Vigner, or Bloch and Tomasz-kiewicz.[2] However, it would be advisable to work with a list of functions which is fairly flexible for the following reasons. It would quickly become apparent that there are various devices which are classifiable under more than one functional label. Distinctions between functions are not always clear, nor are they always sufficiently justified. Considerable overlap of meaning may occur of seemingly disparate or even contradictory devices. For example, concession may include an element of refutation, or agreement introduce a reservation:

> Obtenir aussi du Conseil le financement de la Communauté pendant la période transitoire. *Certes*, l'arrangement financier qui nous est proposé en guise de budget rectificatif et les conditions de sa présentation provoquent une légitime émotion. Mérite-t-elle de livrer aujourd'hui la bataille de demain? Je ne le pense pas. La responsabilité des gouvernements quant à l'exécution du budget 1987 est engagée.[3]

> Ces établissements ont été créés en 1960 pour répondre à une volonté de formation professionnelle pratique et pas seulement académique, et se sont multipliés. On en compte aujourd'hui environ 70. *Certes*, les étudiants effectuent des stages dans l'industrie, *mais* les resultats sont moins convaincants sur le marché du travail.[4]

In the first example, *certes* expresses agreement or affirmation, but it also anticipates the refutation which comes in *Je ne le pense pas*. In the second, *certes* is concessive, and the following *mais* introduces a reservation. Such polyvalent devices require a measure of context to determine their precise meaning. Generally, when two or more meanings are carried by the device, or set of devices, one is predominant, the other/s implicit.

On the other hand, there are certain functions which can be expressed by means of a variety of cohesive devices. Enumeration, or listing, for example, may be made explicit through the use of *d'abord, puis, ensuite, enfin* or by a selection from these, or by a combination of one or two of these and a selection from other enumerative groups such as *d'une part, d'autre part.* Such combinations serve to illustrate the flexibility of use that is both possible and acceptable with the devices. They serve, in addition, as a reminder that notions of predictability in language, while reassuring for the professional linguist, are not entirely dependable.

Means of expressing enumeration:[5] avant ... puis ... / certains ... les autres ... / d'une part ... d'autre part ... / d'une part ... par ailleurs ... / enfin ... / ensuite ... / ensuite ... enfin ... / il s'agit de ... par contre ... / le premier ... le second ... enfin, le troisième ... / par la suite ... / pour ce qui est du ... tandis que ... / pour certains que ... pour d'autres que ... / précisons d'abord que ... ajoutons à cela que ... / puis ... / quant à ... / tant ... que ... / tout d'abord ... / tout d'abord ... ensuite ... enfin ... / tout d'abord ... puis ... enfin ... / tout d'abord ... quant au ... cependant ... / votre premier point ... d'autre part ... enfin ...

Turning briefly to idiolectal uses, a recent oral example encountered has been the use of *sinon*, which occurred in a liaison interpreting class at the beginning of the present academic year. It seemed slightly odd because it did not have any of the familiar functions which are attributed to it in standard dictionaries that is, the expression of exception, concession, restriction.[6]

> Si l'un des candidats réunit plus de la moitié des suffrages exprimés au premier tour, il est élu. *Sinon*, on procède à un second tour. Il en est de même pour l'élection des députés à l'Assemblée Nationale et pour les Conseils généraux, c'est-à-dire les élections cantonales.

> Il donne son avis sur la nomination des magistrats et statue comme conseil de discipline pour ces mêmes magistrats; *sinon* bien sûr la Haute Cour de Justice et ses 24 juges qui peuvent être appelés à juger le Président de la République ou les membres du gouvernement ...

Clearly, the function of *sinon* in the second example is that of an enumerating, or listing, device. It has occurred frequently, usually preceding the final item in a list. Commenting on it, the lecteur cautioned against this particular use. However, views of several other native speakers support it. Thus one really must adopt a flexible approach not only concerning any classification in terms of functions, but also concerning the devices themselves, which are quite frequently polyvalent.

Before returning in detail to the most common of the devices, that is the set, or sets, which express enumeration, their polyvalence, and their ability to be combined with other devices, it is worth pausing to note the type of text and context in which cohesive devices have a high frequency of occurrence and of which the main purpose is argumentation or exposition, rather than description. Such contexts are likely to be editorials, speeches, summaries ... with a controversial theme and in which the author is seeking to convince, persuade, dissuade ... or where, in the case of a summary, cohesive devices are required to express the underlying coherence of a statement with maximum clarity in a limited time or space.

The six examples which follow illustrate enumerative devices and other incidental devices, in context. In the first example *également* announces a second or third point in the argument and *quant à* a subsequent point. *Ainsi* indicates that an example is provided.

> Ce sont les catégories commerçants et artisans, professions libérales et agriculteurs qui sont surtout représentées. Il convient *également* de noter une différence en fonction des régions. *Ainsi*, l'ouest de la France, traditionnellement religieux, a beaucoup d'écoles privées. *Quant à* votre deuxième question, je crois pouvoir répondre par l'affirmative dans la mesure où ...

In the next example, triple enumeration is expressed by *premier point, d'autre part* and *enfin*. Within the enumerative framework, the speaker provides a contrastive argument following *en revanche*, and a concession introduced by *certes*.

> Votre *premier point* concernant la résistance des enseignants à la volonté gouvernementale de fabriquer davantage d'ingénieurs, d'entrepreneurs et de travailleurs spécialisés par exemple est aussi vrai en France. *En revanche*, les problèmes diffèrent dans le contexte de la classe proprement dite. *Certes*, la revendication salariale existe également mais surtout pour les instituteurs. *D'autre part*, vous savez sans doute que les enseignants n'assurent pas les tâches hors emploi-du-temps de surveillance, d'étude, etc ... qui sont prises en charge par des surveillants nommés par l'Education Nationale. *Enfin*, à la différence des Britanniques, je crois, les enseignants français doivent faire face au problème des effectifs trop nombreux ...

Thirdly, enumeration is denoted by *précisons d'abord que* and *ajoutons à cela que*. This particular example contains in addition the familiar contradistinctive pair *en principe / en réalité*—dear to a French mind—denoting the speaker's veiled rejection as fictional of a generally held conviction, followed by an affirmation of what he believes to be reality. Enumeration and contradistinction are linked by *par conséquent* which (a) is resultative following the second point *ajoutons à cela que* and (b), contiguous with *en réalité*, forges a link between fiction and fact.

> Pour ce qui est du choix de l'université, *en principe*, je dis bien en principe, la seule condition est d'être titulaire du bac. Ceci dit, *précisons d'abord que* très peu d'étudiants reçoivent des bourses, car celles-ci sont attribuées en fonction d'un barème qui tient compte du revenu des parents et du nombre de personnes à charge. *Ajoutons à cela qu*'il n'y a qu'un nombre limité de chambres universitaires qui vont en priorité aux étudiants boursiers. *Par conséquent, en réalité*, de nombreux étudiants français habitent chez leurs parents ...

In the fourth example, temporal devices impose an enumerative structure on the discourse, *autrefois, aujourd'hui*, as do the contrastive pair *pour certains, pour d'autres*.

> Depuis la loi Debré de 1959, l'enseignement privé (religieux ou non) cohabite avec l'enseignement public. *Autrefois*, les parents plaçaient leurs enfants dans

des établissements privés par conviction religieuse. *Aujourd'hui*, les raisons invoquées varient selon les gens: *pour certains*, les écoles privées sont plus petites et donc entretiennent davantage le contact avec les parents, *pour d'autres*, la discipline y est plus respectée, les professeurs plus stimulés et moins enclins à se mettre en grève ...

In the penultimate example, *tout d'abord, quant au* and, to a certain extent, *cependant* perform a listing function. In the case of *cependant*, the predominant function is that of introducing a concession, but it also introduces a third point of information.

Je répondrai *tout d'abord* à cette dernière question: on a évolué naturellement vers la mixité, et le phénomène de séparation 'Ecole de Filles' / 'Ecole de Garçons' que j'ai moi-même connu dans le primaire est maintenant tout à fait exceptionnel. *Quant au* pensionnat, il a tendance aussi à se raréfier. *Cependant*, un bon nombre d'écoles privées sont encore des pensionnats ...

Finally, the use of *pour ce qui est du* suggests a separation of information into discrete units. This is confirmed in the *tandis que* which introduces a contrastive comparison and, in this case, the second point.

Le gouvernement a consacré en 1986 environ 15,7% de son budget à l'éducation. *Pour ce qui est du* corps enseignant, les écoles primaires et secondaires regroupent près de 600 000 enseignants, *tandis que* les universitaires sont au nombre de 42 000 ...

These several examples have touched primarily on enumeration—a fundamental and frequent resource in the structuring of argument. The expression of enumeration has been achieved through chronological devices, it has been supplemented by inclusion of devices denoting concession, refutation and so on. Some devices have been shown to be polyvalent, and there is a striking example of a very French refutation followed by the presentation of the truth—as the speaker sees it. Analysis of these devices can be an informative and rewarding exercise, revealing as it does the measure of coherence—or lack of coherence—in a text.

Exercises which may be introduced to sensitise students to the occurrence and usefulness of cohesive devices in oral and written texts, in mother tongue and foreign language:

identify the device/s and indicate the function/s with reference to the text in question.
classify the device/s, recording context, source and date.
practise summaries, indicating by use of devices the argumentation of the original texts.
develop a plan or structure for a given essay title, debate etc, using controversial, and, wherever possible, topics familiar to students.
identify and develop situations in which students are required to argue a point, provide details, clarify, persuade, summarise, conclude ... .
complete texts from which devices have been removed.

remove devices from a text, arrange sentences in an order different from the original, then ask students to reconstruct the text and provide cohesive devices.
practise note-taking, gist-extraction ... i.e. exercises which require devices for adequate text reconstruction.
in cases where devices are ambivalent, explain the ambivalence and suggest unambiguous substitutes.
identify devices which are non-structural and those which are structural, then match them where possible.

References

Astington, E, *French Structures*. London and Glasgow: Collins 1980.
de Beaugrande R, and W Dressler, *Introduction to Text Linguistics*. London and New York: Longman 1981.
Halliday, M A K and R Hasan, *Cohesion in English*. London and New York: Longman 1984.
—— *An Introduction to Functional Grammar*. London: Edward Arnold 1985.
Nash, W, *Designs in Prose*. London and New York: Longman 1980.
Vigner, G, *Parler et convaincre*. Paris: Hachette 1979.
Bloch, A and A-M Tomaszkiewicz, 'Stratégies pour une pedágogie de l'argumentation en f.l.e.' *Le français dans le monde*. Janvier, 1984.

Notes

1 The following are some of the labels used for the resources: *articulateurs logiques, articulations linguistiques, connecteurs interphrastiques/phrastiques, connecteurs de l'argumentation; cohesive devices, discourse markers, pragmatic connectives.*
2 *Communicative functional classifications.* The following are a selection of useful classifications: G Vigner. *Parler et convaincre* pp. 2-3. approbation, concession, désapprobation, dissuasion, exemplification, explication, illustration, persuasion, protestation; A Bloch and A-M Tomaszkiewicz. *Stratégies pour une pédagogie de l'argumentation en f.l.e.* p.34. chronologie, concession, déduction, démonstration, illustration, mise au point, opposition, persuasion, référence, résumé, temporalité; See also G-D de Salins. *De l'Exercice de lecture à la pratique de l'argumentation*. Same journal as above, p.81; B T Atkins and H A Lewis. *The Mechanics of the Argument/Les Mécanismes de la discussion* in *Collins-Robert French-English, English-French Dictionary*. London, Glasgow and Toronto: Collins 1987.
3 From a speech by M. D'Ormesson in the European Parliament 8.7.87.
4 Unless otherwise indicated, examples are taken from liaison interpreting materials devised by M Lang and I Harris.
5 From the chapter on *Education* in the liaison interpreting materials, Lang and Harris.
6 *The Collins-Robert French Dictionary*, 1987 and *Le Petit Robert*, 1986 offer three acceptations: *sauf, si ce n'est, autrement.*

Some Thoughts on Universities and the Translating Profession

Hugh Keith

There is little danger that the Europe of 1992 will face the same chaos that was visited upon Babel. The problems of communication within the Community have long since been recognised and priority given to their solution. Seventy per cent of the Community administrative budget is now spent on interpreting and translating services alone. Most member countries have training schemes for producing professional linguists, although Britain has been rather slower than some of the other states in developing a proper professional structure for translators and interpreters. There are, however, signs that progress is now being made. In 1986 the *Institute of Translation and Interpreting* was founded in London as a body intended to bring together professional linguists of all kinds. As such it was intended to transcend existing associations such as the *Translator's Guild*, the *Institute of Linguists, International Association of Conference Interpreters* etc. and also to draw together interpreters and translators who had not been members of any such association hitherto. It has developed into a highly active association, with a membership which reached 1,000 in 1989, an annual conference and a number of regional and specialist networks. Under its influence discussions are now taking place on such diverse topics as professional standards, pricing policy, in-service courses for translators etc. Furthermore, professional examinations have been devised for those wishing to become members of the Institute in the future, and it is planned to draw up a register of 'approved' courses whose qualifications will be recognised for admission to membership of the Institute. All in all the trend is clearly in the direction of the establishment of a properly structured profession for translators (and interpreters).

Against this background of increased professionalism amongst translators I intend here to examine the role which can be played in translator training by a university course like the Heriot-Watt Languages (*Interpreting and Translating*) B.A. course created by Henry Prais. When he and his colleagues established the course in 1971 they were already anticipating the increased demand for professional linguists that was to result from the inclusion of Great Britain in the EC. But they were also responding to growing frustration among school leavers with the largely literary orientation of most modern languages degree courses. The course which they created stopped short of providing an exclusively vocational training like the diploma courses offered at continental universities—it remained an Honours B.A. course—but went a long way towards incorporating elements which provided a good foundation for a career as a professional linguist.

The rationale underlying the content of the B.A. course may be summed up as follows: Practical language exercises were to play a much greater role than on 'traditional' courses and particular emphasis was to be given to oral use of the foreign language. The interpreting exercises (simultaneous, consecutive and liaison) were selected not just because of their vocational orientation (need for simultaneous interpreters in the EC, *ad-hoc* interpreters in British industry) but also because they were regarded as offering effective methods of learning the foreign language.[1] Parallel to language classes there was to be a 'background studies' element which, while not eschewing the teaching of literature, placed more emphasis on international, European and national institutions and economic and political affairs in general. A further important aspect of the course was the close linking of the background studies with the language exercises. A class in interpreting thus became not just a language exercise but also a vehicle for the discussion of ideas (with a further structuring being achieved by the use of a topic system which coordinated the subject matter of such classes across language sections). Those students who attended Henry Prais's consecutive interpreting classes or the discussions he led in liaison interpreting classes were able to experience just how engrossing such exercises could become in the hands of an inspired teacher.

The course structure thus combined vocational elements (interpreting and translating) with a general liberal education. The success of this formula could be measured both in terms of the high rate of applications received for the course (and the consequently high standard of student intake) and the large proportion (on average 70%) of students finding language-related employment on graduating. But the success of graduates in also gaining *non-language-related* employment, for example in the Civil Service, also demonstrated another virtue of the course—that the analytical and expressive skills required for interpreting and translating produced graduates who were above average in their ability to process and present information in oral and written form.

In establishing such a course Henry Prais was anticipating the shift in emphasis which has taken place in higher education in Britain in the 1980s. Students now increasingly look to *all* university courses to offer them a strong 'applied' bias. The pressure on undergraduate courses to supply vocational training is increased by the declining interest in supplementing undergraduate studies of a general nature with specialist postgraduate training—a decline explicable partly in terms of the problems students have with funding such studies.

The increased emphasis now being put on training by the translation profession means that courses such as the Heriot-Watt one coming under closer scrutiny from professional bodies such as the ITI as to their suitability not just as 'applied' courses in a general sense, but specifically as training courses for translators. It is therefore appropriate to consider here what demands may legitimately be made on universities by the translation profession.

There has always been a certain disagreement about whether translators a) are born rather than made, and b) should be trained in educational institutions or on-the-job. The number of people subscribing to the belief that translators should be 'trained in the school of life' is probably still quite large.

In Great Britain it is only the more recent generation of translators which has had the benefit of a specific vocational training. Previous generations— many of whom became highly skilled translators—had to rely on acquiring the necessary skills gradually, and many only entered the profession after gaining experience in other walks of life:

> '... grandparents of different nationalities, a good school education in which you learn to read, write, spell, construe and love your own language. Then roam the world, make friends, see life. Go back to education, but to take a technical or commercial degree, not a language degree. Spend the rest of your twenties and your early thirties in the countries whose languages you speak, working in industry or commerce but not directly in languages. Never marry into your own nationality. Have your children. Then go back to a postgraduate translation course. A staff job as a translator, and then go freelance. By which time you are forty and ready to begin.' (Castellano 1988).

Despite having her tongue in her cheek when she made these remarks, the author—herself an experienced translator—is also making a serious point: professional translation requires a breadth of knowledge and an experience of language which increase with age and intellectual maturity. However her suggestion that such knowledge and experience should be gathered prior to undergoing training is only likely to be practicable in a minority of cases.

Even if some practising translators still harbour some scepticism about the usefulness of translator training programmes, very few of them actually express their views formally. Pilley (1962) was one of the last to do so, and as Chau (1984) points out, since then most discussion has centered on the question of *how* to train translators rather than whether to do so.

In 1986 the *Bundesverband der Dolmetscher und Übersetzer* in the Federal Republic of Germany published its recommendations for the training of interpreters and translators at West German universities. This exhaustive document, produced by a committee consisting of representatives from universities, industry and the profession, lists the elements regarded as necessary for inclusion in institutional training programmes for translators and interpreters. I have myself discussed elsewhere (Keith 1989 A & B) the skills which an individual requires to work effectively as a translator:

> foreign language competence
> mother-tongue competence
> translation competence
> practical skills
> procedural skills
> specialist knowledge

This list (in which *practical skills* refers to skills such as typing and word-processing and *procedural skills* refers to terminology work, glossary building etc) largely matches the requirements laid down by the *BDÜ*. What is debatable, however, is the extent to which these skills can be acquired *during (institutional) training*. The assumption of the *BDÜ* memorandum appears to be that one can demand of the universities that they train students exhaustively in all the areas described above. One should remember, of course, that the university institutes of translation and interpreting in the Federal Republic offer vocational courses leading to a professional diploma qualification and are not as such, therefore, strictly comparable to the more general British B.A. qualification, which can allow an individual to enter a variety of professions, including teaching, which would not be open to German diploma holders. Nevertheless one has to ask how realistic the *BDÜ* are being in including as desiderata for a university course *all* the elements listed above. The only concession they make to the limitations of institutionalised training are in the area of specialist knowledge, where they merely recommend that every student studying two foreign languages should be examined in a special subject, which is studied: '...to show students of translation ... the approaches and methodologies used in other disciplines. Thereby stimulating system and problem-oriented thinking in addition to the primarily text-related, analytical approach.'

However, under a separate heading of 'general background knowledge', in addition to those areas normally included under such a heading, they include: Economics (e.g. systems, trade, taxation systems), Law (e.g. systems, law of contract), Technology (e.g. standardisation. measurement systems) and Art (e.g. literature, pictorial arts)! The *BDÜ* would appear to expect of the universities that they pass on to their students in four years the sort of comprehensive knowledge and experience which Castellano suggested would require forty years to acquire!

Any discussion of what elements can be included in institutional training needs to take into consideration the particular circumstances of the country concerned. It is not my intention to discuss the feasibility of the *BDÜ* proposals in the German context, but rather to look at what can be achieved in the British context. Here the background to any discussion has to be the precarious position of languages in the secondary school system. At present a very high proportion of secondary school children in Britain give up studying a modern language after the age of 14. The introduction of the common core curriculum may now ensure that one language—usually French—will be taught to age 16 in future, but the corollary of this development is that other languages will decline. There is, moreover, an acute shortage of language teachers at secondary level. This is already having a knock-on effect on universities, which are increasingly forced to offer undergraduate courses *ab initio*. It seems, therefore, that the first priority for any undergraduate training course for translators in Britain has to be achievement of the necessary level of foreign language skills. Even in the German context there is awareness of this necessity: the *BDÜ* recommendations include testing of foreign language competence prior to entry to translator training and the setting up of preparatory courses in those languages not studied at secondary school.

Apart from raising foreign language competence to the threshhold level at which acquisition of *translation* competence can occur, the more problematic question is what other skills can and should be taught on a university course. One method of deciding which elements need to be included is to consult the employers of in-house translators. In March 1989 I conducted a small survey among British firms and institutions known to employ full-time translators. A questionnaire was sent to eight major firms and institutions employing a total of 47 translators, of which 43 had been employed within the last five years. Thirty of these had received institutionalised training as translators either at undergraduate or postgraduate level. Questions were asked concerning the degree of satisfaction among the employers with the level of competence their recruits displayed in various areas: mother tongue (English), foreign language, typing/word-processing skills, specialist knowledge. The results may be summarised as follows:

Generally speaking the employers seemed satisfied with the level of knowledge of the foreign language which had been achieved. Language skills were judged to be most inadequate where the mother tongue was concerned. Only one employer expressed dissatisfaction with the degree of foreign language competence of some of the recruits, whereas five criticised recruits' command of English (all concerned were native-speakers of English). Recommendations that more attention be devoted to improving English skills are frequently made when translator-training is discussed (cf. McCluskey 1987), though ideas are rarely put forward as to how this can be done.

Of significance was the employers' attitude towards the acquisition of specialist knowledge while at university. All eight employers stated that the level of specialist knowledge of their recruits was inadequate for the tasks they were to undertake, but six of them stated clearly that they saw training in their specialist areas as something which should take place within the firm/ institution and many of them detailed the in-house courses which were offered to this end. Four of them emphasised, however, that students should be given some experience of tackling a highly specialised area, of how to approach terminology problems, research an unknown subject, prepare glossaries etc, but they made it clear that the precise area selected was unimportant. In other words they recommended the acquisition of general, transferrable skills, rather than specific specialisations. Only two employers suggested anything more specific: one recommended the familiarising of the students with computer terminology, the other suggested that a basic grounding in physics and chemistry would be desirable. Both stated that their companies offered in-house training in specialist areas as well. It would appear that in the British context extensive training in specialist areas by the universities is not regarded as an urgent need by the employers, provided students are offered *some* opportunity to become familiar with the problems associated with translating texts from a specialised subject area.

Finally, the employers surveyed seemed to play down the necessity of students being taught extensive word-processing skills before they took up their posts. Five of them did state that recruits lacked word-processing skills, but added that these could be acquired in-house.

Inasmuch as it is possible to draw any conclusions from a survey of such limited scope it would seem that employers of translators seem to regard the primary function of university courses as being the development of general language skills (foreign language *and* mother tongue), the skill of transferring between those languages (translation competence), and an ability to tackle unfamiliar areas of specialist knowledge. Many of the replies received revealed an awareness among the employers that it was unrealistic to expect the training institutions to produce 'complete' translators with a comprehensive knowledge, who required no further training. Most seemed to accept that there was a role to be played by their companies in complementing the university courses and supplying training in special subject areas, terminology and word-processing skills. The eight firms and institutions surveyed were relatively large and appeared to have the resources to offer training schemes beyond mere checking of young translators' work by a senior colleague. Five of them claimed to offer induction courses, briefings or even language training courses. Whether or not smaller firms would be in a position to offer similar facilities would require investigation.

In many respects a course such as the Heriot-Watt B.A. course would seem to meet the criteria for a university training for translators as outlined in the previous paragraph. The high level of foreign language competence attained by students on the course prepares them well for the profession (though, given the situation of language-teaching in secondary schools, it is uncertain how long the high standard of students' language skills on entry can be maintained). In addition the course probably places more emphasis on mother-tongue (English) skills than most other modern language degree courses, on which the teaching concentrates almost exclusively on foreign language skills. The criteria for selection of students include an assessment of their ability to express themselves in English and there is, throughout the course, a high preponderance of exercises involving translating or interpreting *into* English, and consequently much discussion of aspects of that language. Furthermore there is now a course in text analysis during first year which involves the close study and discussion of English texts. It is interesting to note the three recommendations made in the *BDÜ* document regarding mother-tongue skills:

> the testing of mother-tongue competence prior to admittance to translator training courses
> the application of rigorous standards of assessment of the mother-tongue in all examinations,
> the offering of courses on topics such as:
>
>> text analysis
>> résumé/summary writing
>> text production
>> correction of defective texts
>> oral work (including public speaking)

All of these recommendations are met at least to some extent by the Heriot-Watt course in its present form.

The only recommended element in translator training which the Heriot-Watt course does not formally cater for is the exemplary study of specialist areas. Yet the potential exists for this to be established at a satisfactory level.

The system of elective subjects offers the possibility of in-depth study of a special subject, while the topic system operated for language classes offers the possibility of translation problems associated with particular fields to be discussed. All that would be required would be for topics of a technical nature to be substituted for the more general background topics at present used.

One of the questions posed in this paper was: what demands can be made on the universities by the translation profession in Britain? The evidence of the employers' survey carried out suggests that the priorities listed in the *BDÜ* memorandum are probably unnecessarily ambitious in the British context. The larger firms, at least, appear to be prepared to recruit linguists who have excellent foreign language and mother-tongue skills and who are familiar with the problems of translation and the methodology of tackling unknown specialist areas, but who do not necessarily have extensive or in-depth knowledge of particular areas. There is evidence of a willingness to supply such specific subject-training *in-house*, though in future years, when the translation profession has expanded further, it may well be possible for elements of this training to be provided in the more cost-effective form of short courses by tertiary institutions such as universities or polytechnics.

Where does the Heriot-Watt course fit into this picture? I stated at the outset that Henry Prais's original formula was intended to produce highly competent linguists for a variety of forms of employment, but also to offer elements of a general liberal education. I also stated that university courses were now under increasing pressure from all sides to provide a specialised vocational training. If one considers the Heriot-Watt course specifically from the point of view of translator training in the 1980s, then the evidence suggests that, with minor adjustments, the course can offer an excellent basic training for the professional translator in the British context, but without assuming an *exclusively* vocational nature and losing those aspects of a general education which Henry Prais regarded as so important.

Note

1   A controversial point: while consecutive intepreting, involving a form of aural comprehension, may be regarded as a useful language-learning exercise, and liaison interpreting *can* also form the focus of a number of different language-learning activities (see Keith 1985), it is difficult to see simultaneous interpreting as more than a high-level *test* of certain language skills. Certainly for simultaneous—and, to a certain extent also for liaison interpreting—there is a threshold level of student language competence below which they lose usefulness as exercises.

References

Castellano, L, 'Get rich—but slow', in *Translators and Interpreters mean Business*, Proceedings of the Second ITI Conference, London 1988

BDÜ Memorandum 'Praxis und Lehre' in *Mitteilungsblatt des Bundesverbandes der Dolmetscher und Übersetzer*, 5/32, 1986

Chau, S, Doctoral thesis (unpublished) presented to the University of Edinburgh, 1984

Keith, H A, 'Liaison interpreting as a communicative language-learning exercise', in *Interpreting as a language-teaching technique,* ed. Thomas and Towell, London 1985
—— 'University versus in-service training', in *Proceedings of the Fourth ITI Conference,* London 1989A
—— 'Training of translators', in *The Translator's Handbook,* ed. Picken, London 1989B
McCluskey, B, 'The chinks in the armour: problems encountered by language graduates entering a large translation department', in *Translation in the Modern Languages degree,* ed. Keith and Mason, London 1987
Pilley, A T, 'The Training, Qualifications and Professional Status of Translators', in *The Incorporated Linguist,* 1,3, 1962

Overcoming Babel: the Role of the Conference Interpreter in the Communication Process

Janet Altman

Conference interpreting has become an essential feature of the modern world: it is by now taken for granted that no superpower summit or other international meeting could function without the presence of interpreters. Organisations like the United Nations and the European Community rely very heavily on them: indeed, in 1987 alone the European Commission's expenditure on its interpretation service totalled £26 million, which clearly illustrates the considerable use made of interpreters.[1]

The purpose of this article is to investigate the role of the conference interpreter in the process of communication across linguistic and cultural barriers. This will be done by examining interpreters' own perception of the factors governing their success in fulfilling this role. The article is based on the findings of a survey conducted among conference interpreters in Brussels.

The survey

During a one-week period in April 1989, 48 interpreters working for the Commission of the European Communities in Brussels were requested to complete a questionnaire (see annex for a copy of the questionnaire and details of responses). The rate of response was excellent: 40 (83%) of those approached agreed to fill in the form. Predictably, perhaps, 95% of the respondents consider their effect on the communication process to be positive, if not very positive (see Question 1). The findings are complemented by events observed in Brussels during that same week.

Copies of the questionnaire were handed out at the start of the day to the interpreters in their booths, who completed them anonymously and returned them after the meeting. Although participants were invited to base their comments on simultaneous interpreting and to refer separately to consecutive where appropriate, very few distinguished between the two modes. In addition to replying to the questions according to a differential scale, respondents were also asked to provide extra comments wherever possible: 27 did so. When quoted they will be referred to as R (Respondent) 1-27. Their input ranged from minor annotations to (in one case) six additional pages, and was helpful both in terms of extending the range of issues covered and adding nuance to what were inevitably rather crude categories. Many points of interest emerged.

With respect to the respondents themselves, over a quarter had English as their main target language; the remainder were fairly evenly divided between

French, German, Spanish, Italian and Dutch (there were no interpreters of the
other three Community languages—Danish, Greek, Portuguese—available).
Their length of service varied from one to 32 years.

years' experience	1-4	5-9	10-19	20-29	30+	n.a.	total
number	9	4	15	7	2	3	40
%	22.5	10	37.5	17.5	5	7.5	100

The following sections contain an analysis of the most striking features of
the information obtained. The survey results will be evaluated according to
certain themes: the relative importance of cultural and linguistic obstacles to
communication (Question 2); the extent of and reasons for breakdowns in
communication (Qs 4, 5, 6 and 7); the effect of relay interpreting on the
interpreting process (Qs 10, 11 and 12); the effect of other factors on the
bridging of the communication gap by interpreters (Q9); when and for what
reason the interpreter sees fit to intervene actively in the communication
process (Qs 3, 8 and 13). Before drawing conclusions we shall consider
interpreters' opinions about the likely effects of future developments on their
role in the communication process.

Cultural versus linguistic obstacles

'Cultural differences are a greater obstacle to communication than linguistic
ones' (Q2). Over two-thirds of those who answered Q2 agreed entirely or
partially with the above statement. But R9, in rejecting the statement,
claimed: 'There *can* be superb communication across both cultural and language barriers or they can be used as an excuse for non-communication.'
R19 added: 'perhaps with very different cultures (Chinese, Arab) but not in
the European context'. This is a point worth making: whereas there is a
certain amount of cultural similarity in the EEC, interpreters working in
another forum might have replied quite differently to Q2.

An incident which served to indicate the significance of cultural differences
even within Europe occurred when a United Kingdom delegate needed to
distinguish between motor vehicle types N1 and M1. Unlike the French-
speakers, who used the universally recognisable gloss 'Napoléon 1', he
described the former as 'Noddy 1'. This culture-bound reference was incomprehensible even to my American colleague in the booth, and certainly
unlikely to facilitate communication for Greek and Danish listeners. And as
to the interpreters working from English into other languages, surely no-one
who had neither grown up in Britain nor raised a child here could be expected
to grasp such a reference.

Clearly, therefore, there is a need for not only interpreters but also delegates
at meetings constantly to remain alert to cultural differences. Even where
linguistic obstacles are minimal (the Greek and Danish delegates had a good
grasp of the English language), cultural ones can hamper communication.

Communication breakdown

None of the respondents ventured to define their understanding of the term 'communication breakdown'. It applies to a situation where a listener has failed to grasp the speaker's message. This may become apparent in one of two ways: either the listener, unaware that s/he has misunderstood, will respond in such a way that reveals a lack of comprehension; or proceedings will be halted by a request for repetition/clarification. In other words, the normal flow of communication is disrupted in some way.

One could not, of course, allege that communication breakdowns occur solely in situations where interpreters are mediating. The reaction of an American serviceman stationed in Italy, recently asked when conscription ended in the United States, was a blank expression and the words 'Excuse me?' Communication had broken down because of one of the many differences between British and American English, but was restored as soon as the question was repeated substituting the word 'draft' for 'conscription'. In terms of international meetings and the role of the interpreter, R9 commented:

> I attend as many monolingual as multi-lingual meetings and have the impression that *real* breakdowns in communication (as opposed to deliberately engineered ones where interpreters are scapegoated) happen slightly less, possibly because interpreters 'filter' out some of the more confrontational aspects of speeches.

As to the frequency with which communication breakdowns happen at international meetings, almost three-quarters of respondents said 'often' or 'occasionally' (Q5). Perhaps more significant are the causes. When asked whether delegates make allowances for the presence of interpreters (Q4), a small majority replied in the negative. Two people distinguished between delegates to meetings at organisations like the EEC and those to private meetings who make fewer (or no) allowances. It may be that the latter have less experience of working with interpreters and are ignorant of the ways in which they can help (supplying documents to the interpreters, speaking clearly and concisely, pacing their delivery appropriately and avoiding highly idiomatic language).

Two-thirds of respondents admitted that interpreters are themselves responsible, occasionally, for communication breakdowns (Q7). R15 emphasised the need to take 'pre-emptive measures (reading all conference documents before the meeting, boning up on 'new' subjects, drawing up vocabularies...).'[2] One could add that the amount of attention paid by interpreters during meetings is relevant, as evidenced by one incident. After the chairman's summary—'the Greek and Irish delegations enter a reservation'—an agitated Dutch delegate protested 'No, Mr. Chairman, we have no reservation on this point'. The Dutch interpreter, having misheard 'irlandais' as 'néerlandais', had mistranslated the delegation's nationality. Such acoustic problems (which frequently occur even in monolingual discussion) can be compensated for by constant attention to the communicative context: the interpreter in this case should have remembered which delegations had raised objections during the preceding discussions.

   Three-quarters of respondents felt that interpreters are at least occasionally blamed unjustifiably for breakdowns in communication (Q6). At one stage in a meeting the Spanish chairman accused his interpreter of rustling papers in the booth and therefore rendering her interpretation incomprehensible (an accusation for which he later apologised publicly and profusely). The chances are that a moment of inattention had caused him to miss a point, and that he had chosen this method of concealing his embarrassment. To use R9's term, the interpreter had been 'scapegoated'. But, as R13 put it, 'blaming the interpreter is a form of courtesy among delegates'. Others agreed. It seems that to bear the brunt of such criticism is one aspect of the interpreter's role which s/he must, unwillingly, accept.[3]

Relay interpreting[4]

If, as has been shown, the involvement of interpreters can in some cases hamper the communication process, the risk of breakdowns must double when the message passes through two intermediaries. An internal working document recently issued by AIIC (International Association of Conference Interpreters) illustrated the Babel which can ensue when relay interpreting is taken to extremes:

> Should the English booth interpreter seek relief, a situation can arise whereby an interpreter with an English B (who has probably just completed 30 mins. work in his/her A language) stands in and, when Spanish or Russian is spoken, takes relay from a C language (French), interprets into a B language (English), and is in turn taken on relay by the Chinese and also the Russian or Spanish booths.

The interpreters canvassed were practically unanimous in their distaste for relay interpreting. Almost three-quarters of the those who replied do not prefer working on relay under any circumstances (Q12):

Q12. I prefer working on relay to interpreting 'direct':

	often	occasionally	hardly ever	never	total
no.	0	3	7	28	38
%	0	7.9	18.4	73.7	100

   When asked for their opinion of the effect of relay interpreting on the communication process (Q10), not a single respondent described it as either very positive or positive. R15 likened it to 'Chinese whispers on a tight-rope'. Seven others stated that its effect depends entirely upon the quality of the relay interpreter. This reference to quality raises a separate, and very important, issue which has been dealt with elsewhere to a certain extent.[5]

   Although the questionnaire was not specifically designed to elicit opinions about quality of performance, it can be inferred from the reaction to Q11 that interpreters strive to improve the service they provide when they know that other interpreters are relying on them as a relay. Furthermore, the nature of their work alters, as is shown by several comments: 'I try to structure my delivery better' / 'J'essaye d'être plus claire, de faire des phrases plus simples' / 'I avoid idiomatic expressions or qualify them' / 'Maybe I "edit" more'.

It is interesting to note that some interpreters take greater pains to simplify and clarify the message when working for colleagues than they do normally. Could it be that they lack faith in their colleagues' language competence? Possibly, but this phenomenon could likewise be attributable to a variety of other causes, for example: an attempt to avoid the 'Chinese whispers' syndrome; the knowledge that a wider audience than usual is reliant upon them; the fact that interpreters are notoriously more critical of one another than delegates are of interpreters, and hence the desire to make a good impression; or else the awareness that the demands made of the interpreter-listener (hearing, understanding, processing and reproducing a message) are much greater than those made of the delegate-listener (hearing and understanding only).

Bridging the communication gap

Turning now to specific influences on interpreters' ability to bridge the communication gap (Q9), the quality of sound transmission is found without any doubt to be the factor which has the greatest impact on their ability to perform effectively:

Q9d. quality of sound transmission	5	4	3	2	1	total
no.	24	14	1	1	0	40
%	60	35	0.25	0.25	0	100

The fact that 60% of participants replied 'enormously' here (a rating of 5) is unsurprising. Unless the original speech is clearly audible, it is impossible for the interpreter to understand or analyse, let alone re-express, it: there can therefore be no communication at all. This finding contrasted starkly with the results of Q9c: even though AIIC regards a clear view of the speaker from all booths as essential,[6] only 8% of the interpreters consulted selected a rating of 5 on the differential scale, whereas 15% rated its importance as 1.

Four of the other factors listed under Q9 relate to the nature of the raw material with which the interpreter works. Almost half of the respondents felt that for delegates to speak languages not their own (Q9h) was only 'somewhat' significant, yet almost all the remainder rated this factor at 5 or 4 on the scale ('enormous' or 'considerable' effect): we can therefore deduce that it is preferable for delegates to speak their own language whenever possible (but not, presumably, if this necessitates relay interpreting—see previous section).

The speaker's speed of delivery (Q9e) is slightly more relevant than the above, with over 50% rating it at 5 or 4. The quality of his/her speech (Q9g) is more relevant still: according to 73% of respondents it affects their ability to bridge the communication gap either enormously or considerably. It might have been interesting to discover what the interpreters in the survey read into the word 'quality' in Q9g, where it clearly has a more subjective and far-reaching meaning than it does in Q9d, referring to the technical installations.

Q9f, which also relates to input, provides some insight into respondents' assessment of their own language knowledge. An admission that the ability to perform effectively is affected by whether or not the language spoken is one's strongest can be taken to imply that an interpreter has weaknesses in one or more working languages. In fact, opinion was spread more evenly across the differential scale on this issue than on any other:

Q9f. whether s/he uses your strongest foreign language

	5	4	3	2	1	total
no.	9	10	5	7	7	38
%	23.7	26.3	13.2	18.4	18.4	100

Familiarity with the subject matter is considered crucial (Q9a), second in importance only to sound quality.

Q9a. your familiarity with subject matter

	5	4	3	2	1	total
no.	21	12	3	3	1	40
%	52.5	30	7.5	7.5	2.5	100

One of the few interpreters who diverged from the majority view in fact corroborated it by writing: 'if you always work at the Commission you know the subject matter'.

The survey also bore out interpreters' well-known dislike of being involved in discussions of an unavailable document, since two-thirds of respondents gave Q9b a rating of either 5 or 4. Even worse, according to R14, is a speaker reading aloud a document, particularly when s/he does so at speed and/or the interpreter is not in possession of the text. If the interpreter's role is to convey a message, and if that message is contained in a document, it is vital for the interpreter to have access to it during—and, more especially, before—its presentation, in order to be able to digest its ideas, logical progression and specialised terminology.[2] And even if the text has been studied in advance by the interpreter, its effect will be lost on the listener unless the presentation is given at a measured pace. This point highlights the need for both conference organisers and delegates to be enlightened as to the steps they could take to facilitate the interpreter's task and thereby to improve the communication process.

The two enquiries relating to the practitioner's physical condition met with a less clear-cut response than other factors. Their state of fatigue (Q9i) emerged as being slightly more significant than their state of health (Q9j): over a quarter said that the latter affected their performance either 'hardly' or 'very little'. One reason for such a discrepancy could be the one advanced by R23: 'If I'm in such a poor state I stay at home'.

And finally, the factor which emerged as least relevant of all (Q9k) was the recording/broadcasting of an interpreter's performance. It affects only two respondents 'enormously', but eleven 'very little' (one of whom pencilled in 'or zero'). This result was perhaps somewhat unexpected, in view of the additional stress occasioned by such work, a fact recognised by AIIC.[7] The explanation could perhaps lie in the fact that the interpreters consulted preferred to answer on the basis of experience rather than conjecture but had never themselves been recorded/broadcast.

Other factors

At the end of Q9 respondents were invited to add any additional factors which affect their ability to bridge the communication gap. Most of the comments made relate to the atmosphere either within the booth or in the meeting room itself.

The atmosphere in the booth includes physical comfort: R27 mentioned 'quality of air/lack of oxygen'; R15 inveighed against smokers. Only one respondent referred specifically to 'nice and co-operative colleagues', which one might have expected to feature more prominently in that the level of stress is inevitably reduced if one feels relaxed with one's booth colleagues. R15 made this point very strongly elsewhere:

> Individualistic and opinionated interpreters are part of a team (delegates, organisers, technicians, other staff, colleagues in other booths and LAST BUT MOST IMPORTANT colleague(s) in the same booth). Being in bed together is barely more intimate.

'Speaker commitment/enthusiasm helps', wrote R8. R16 appreciates 'signs of direct interest/attention/involvement from the listener', and R22 refers more generally to the 'Gruppendynamik im Saal'. Once again, surprisingly few respondents made comments along these lines, although most interpreters would probably readily agree that the mood of a meeting and responsiveness on the part of their customers do affect their performance.

One factor of a different type, finally, was mentioned by only one respondent although it could be assumed to be highly relevant: 'Interesse am Thema'. Perhaps others considered this area to be subsumed under Q9a; yet the distinction between familiarity with and interest in a topic is a valid one.

Active intervention by the interpreter

Conference interpreters convey messages from one person to another/others. Their job is to transmit, not to generate, ideas and information. But do they ever cast aside this low profile? Three questions (3, 8 and 13) sought to discover when and to what extent interpreters consider it appropriate to intervene more actively than usual in the communication process.

Q3 asks whether interpreters 'amplify' their interpretation to explain either cultural or linguistic differences. An 'amplification' could be a gloss along the lines of 'poll tax: the new form of local taxation'. Opportunities to provide such explanations are obviously severely limited in simultaneous interpreting, but according to R15: 'Consecutive meetings lend themselves more to explanations and amplifications as part of the interpretation.' As to the respective frequency of provision of linguistic and cultural amplifications, the table below shows that the former are given more readily.

Q3.	often	occasionally	hardly ever	never	total
a) linguistic amplifications	20.5	64.1	15.4	0	100%
b) cultural amplifications	2.7	70.3	27	0	100%

These data seem to conflict somewhat with the findings of Q2, where 69% agreed that cultural differences are a greater obstacle to communication than linguistic ones, but the discrepancy may derive from the wording of the questions. The fact that both of the 'never' columns in the above table contain zero entries indicates that all the interpreters consulted consider it to be part of their role to explain both linguistic and cultural phenomena at times. One reason for the apparently greater readiness to provide linguistic explanations than cultural ones could be, as asserted by R13, 'I mainly work at technical meetings'. The response to this question may have been quite different if the questionnaire had been distributed to interpreters working in a forum where the issues discussed were less technical and the cultural backgrounds of the participants more varied.

Positive action to correct or compensate for mistakes made by colleagues is something that interpreters are extremely reluctant to engage in: 82% would never or hardly ever do so (Q8). R6 wrote: 'Even if necessary I would never do it! I would use my terminology but unobtrusively.' R15's comment was:

> I write things down, in case (colleagues) can use them in the best way for them. Booth manners are vital. Far better to provide colleagues with the means to correct themselves than compensate obtrusively.

It would seem from the above comments—and also from that of R23: 'I leave them (the mistakes)!'—that although interpreters hesitate to correct mistakes made by colleagues, they are not infrequently aware of such occurrences (see also the responses to Q7). So the question arises as to why they decline to do so. The reason would seem to be that interpreters consider 'booth manners' (to quote R15, above) to be even more important than accuracy of information: they wish to preserve a harmonious working relationship with their immediate colleagues, even at the cost of allowing misunderstandings to persist. This casts an interesting light on the role of the interpreter (faithful representation of a speaker's message): it is a role which cannot be evaluated in isolation from its situational and human relations aspects.

Another reason for the interpreter to intervene actively in the communication process might be to improve upon the quality of a speech (Q13). Respondents were confident of their ability to do this: 93% of them said that it could be done either often or occasionally. However, some queried the rectitude of taking such action: R2 circled the word 'occasionally' and added 'but I'm not sure if one should, except to make things clear'. Others concurred. R9 supplied the most revealing (and amusing) remarks:

> Why should the interpreter improve the speech? Surely if the speakers can't put their ideas together coherently the interpreter should be passing that message on to the listeners to the other languages. On the other hand, if a speaker has a GENUINE speech (as opposed to brain) defect, I feel the interpreter should make an effort to improve the speech to get the message across as effectively as possible.

Perhaps a tentative conclusion here is that interpreters do not necessarily live up to their popular image in some quarters, namely that they are aggressive, extrovert, 'prima donna' figures. In fact, they show sensitivity towards colleagues' feelings and hesitate to adopt a high profile in the communication process.

Future developments

Although Q14 ('How are future developments in the profession likely to affect the interpreter's role in the communication process?') was deliberately left open-ended, three respondents criticised its lack of focus. What was remarkable about the twelve who did advance ideas was the almost universal pessimism. Its causes fall into two groups: developments brought about by technological progress, and those attributable to the spread of English as an international language.

The technological innovation which interpreters dread the most is the tele-conference, or video-conference.[8] They fear a deterioration in working conditions both from the technical point of view (including a loss of sound quality, the paramountcy of which has been shown above) and from that of their isolation from the meeting as such. To quote R7:

> Teleconferencing—more stressful for the interpreter—conditions need to be considered carefully. TV link-up—again, the conditions are often difficult (e.g. inability to hear the other half of the link, difficult audio systems).

R20 sincerely hopes that such trends 'won't amount to hiding the interpreter away in a closet altogether to act as an "interpreting machine"'. Computers were mentioned only by R15, who does not (yet?) consider them to be a serious threat to her/his job: 'I might worry about computers when they can do quality newspaper crosswords better and faster than I can—but not before.' R13, agreeing with others that 'video-conferencing will tend to divorce interpreter from client even more', states that the profession must be prepared to adapt to future needs with 'an openness to new tasks i.e. broadcasting/journalistic knowledge'. It would be interesting to know how many practitioners would show such flexibility.[9]

The other main cause of concern is the increasing tendency for meetings to 'make do with' English or to employ the minimum number of interpreters possible. The bleakest prediction came from R25: 'I imagine we'll be obsolete in 20 years' time'. R19 gave a somewhat more reasoned response:

> I fear that more and more speakers speak languages other than their mother tongue which makes the interpreter concentrate on what they might have meant rather than transmitting what they actually said.

Such a trend can, undoubtedly, be detected at the European Commission: no interpreters of the Community's three 'smallest' languages (Danish, Greek and Portuguese) were employed in meetings at which the questionnaire was distributed; and delegates of these three nationalities, but also others, frequently spoke foreign languages—and exhibited varying degrees of competence in them.

However, precisely the opposite trend is predicted by R13: 'The interpreter's role can only increase in importance with increasing international contacts for which basic English is inadequate, e.g. economics and law.' It should, perhaps, be pointed out that R13 was one of the most junior respondents in terms of experience if not age. One hopes that increasing years in the profession will not dampen her/his optimism.

Conclusion

Although the rate of response to the questionnaire was remarkably high and a good deal of interesting data came to light, certain issues were inevitably over-simplified owing to the need to restrict the answer form to a length which would not discourage respondents. Future investigations might usefully make a greater distinction between the interpreter's role in consecutive and in simultaneous interpreting and differentiate between the views of free-lance interpreters and those in permanent posts. The distribution of an identical questionnaire at non-European Community meetings would provide material for a comparative study, and an equivalent survey could be conducted among delegates and conference organisers, two groups whose opinions on the role of the interpreter would be worth canvassing.

The average length of experience of those who replied 'very positive' to Q1 ('What effect do you think the interpreter has on the communication process?') was 9.4 years, which is somewhat lower than the overall average of 13.1 years,but perhaps not sufficiently so for us to conclude without further evidence that disillusionment increases with length of service. Another potential area of research was helpfully proposed by R19: 'It might be an idea to identify what exactly makes a speaker an 'interpreter's dream' or 'interpreter's nightmare' and find out how many fall into each category.'

Let us now summarise the main findings of the survey conducted. Cultural and linguistic obstacles to communication could perhaps be minimised, given appropriate changes in delegate (and, to a lesser extent, interpreter) behaviour. Where communication temporarily breaks down altogether, it seems that interpreters must be prepared to shoulder the blame whether or not they are at fault.

The distinct aversion of interpreters for relay interpreting emerged very starkly, even though a large majority stated that their work is affected positively when they are working as a relay. It would be over-simplistic merely to recommend the abandonment of relay intepreting, given the relevance of issues such as national pride, Community language policy and interpreter training. But a reduction in its use at EEC meetings would undoubtedly be welcomed and beneficial to the communication process.

Various factors were identified as having a particular effect on the interpreter's ability to bridge the communication gap: first and foremost the quality of sound transmission. Second in importance came familiarity with the subject matter under discussion, but least significant was the recording/broadcasting of their performance.

As far as the active intervention of interpreters in the communication process is concerned, some might be surprised at respondents' reluctance to correct their colleagues' mistakes and to improve upon the quality of a speech.'Quality' is a wide-ranging term which is used in different ways in this article. The whole issue of quality in intepreting, which has thus far received little attention in the literature, would merit a good deal more research.

Looking to future developments likely to affect the interpreter's role in the communication process, the two areas of change identified by respondents were technological (tele-conferencing) and linguistic (the ever-increasing use of English). But what was most striking about the thoughts proffered in this section was their gloominess: even though in response to Q1, 96% of subjects saw their role as positive or very positive, their verdict on the future of the profession was overwhelmingly negative.

Whether or not the respondents were being over-pessimistic in their assessment of what lies ahead there is no doubt that, as times change, so must the interpreting profession. Conference interpreters will need to show flexibility and adaptability as they enter the twenty-first century, but their international importance is scarcely likely to diminish. They will undoubtedly continue to perform the crucial role of helping mankind to overcome Babel.

Annex—the Questionnaire

Role of the Conference Interpreter in the Communication Process: Overcoming Cultural and Linguistic Barriers between Nations

Into which language do you normally work?
For how many years have you been an interpreter?

1. *What effect do you think the interpreter has on the communication process?*

very positive	positive	neutral	negative	very negative	
7	28	0	2	0	(total 37)

2. *Cultural differences are a greater obstacle to communication than linguistic ones.*

true	partly true	partly false	false	
8	17	7	4	(36)

3. *I amplify my interpretation to explain:*
    a) *linguistic differences*

often	occasionally	hardly ever	never	
8	25	6	0	(39)

    b) *cultural differences*

often	occasionally	hardly ever	never	
1	26	10	0	(37)

4. *Delegates to meetings make allowances for the presence of interpreters:*

often	occasionally	hardly ever	never	
7	10	19	2	(38)

5. *I am aware of breakdowns in communication during meetings:*

often	occasionally	hardly ever	never	
9	20	11	0	(40)

6. *Interpreters are blamed unjustifiably for breakdowns in communication:*

often	occasionally	hardly ever	never	
8	21	10	0	(39)

7. *Breakdowns in communication are attributable to interpreters' mistakes:*

often	occasionally	hardly ever	never	
2	24	13	0	(39)

8. *I need to correct/compensate for mistakes made by colleagues:*

often	occasionally	hardly ever	never	
0	7	25	7	(39)

9. *To what extent do the following factors affect your ability to bridge the communication gap?*
    (5 = enormously, 4 = considerably, 3 = somewhat, 2 = hardly, 1 = very little)

	5	4	3	2	1	
a) *your familiarity with subject matter*	21	12	3	3	1	(40)
b) *discussion of a document not available to you*	10	18	7	1	4	(39)
c) *clear view of speaker*	3	12	14	5	6	(40)
d) *quality of sound transmission*	24	14	1	1	0	(40)
e) *speaker's speed of delivery*	7	15	12	4	1	(39)

f) *whether s/he uses your strongest for. language*	9	10	5	7	7	(38)
g) *quality of speech*	11	18	7	4	0	(40)
h) *delegates speaking a language not their own*	7	11	19	3	0	(40)
i) *your state of fatigue*	10	10	12	6	1	(39)
j) *your state of health*	6	12	11	9	2	(40)
k) *whether you are being recorded/broadcast*	2	10	10	6	11	(39)
l) *other factors (please specify)*						

10. *What is the effect of relay interpreting on the communication process*

very positive	positive	neutral	negative	very negative	
0	0	12	20	2	(34)

11. *What is the effect on your work when you know you are being used as a relay?*

very positive	positive	neutral	negative	very negative	
4	20	9	1	0	(34)

12. *I prefer working on relay to interpreting 'direct':*

often	occasionally	hardly ever	never	
0	3	7	28	(38)

13. *The interpreter can improve on the quality of an original speech:*

often	occasionally	hardly ever	never	
16	21	3	0	(40)

14. *How are future developments in the profession likely to affect the interpreter's role in the communication process?* (16)

Notes

1   Figure given by Renée van Hoof, Director of Conference Services at the European Commission, in the course of a lecture at the University of Edinburgh, 1988.
2   This topic is explored in more depth in H Janet Altman, 'Documentation and the free-lance interpreter', in *The Incorporated Linguist* 23/3 1984, pp. 82-85.
3   The phenomenon of the interpreter as scapegoat is not new. In his 1952 classic, *The Interpreter's Handbook*, Jean Herbert suggests an appropriate reaction: the interpreter 'should relentlessly shelve all amour-propre' and in some cases even apologise (Geneva: Georg, 2nd edn, 1968, p. 81).
4   Relay interpreting—the process in the simultaneous mode whereby (for example) a Spanish interpreter who does not understand Dutch will listen to the French booth's version of the Dutch speech and interpret from French into Spanish.
5   See in particular Daniel Gile, 'Aspects méthodologiques de l'évaluation de la qualité du travail en interprétation simultanée', in *Meta* 28/3 1983 pp. 236-243, and Hildegund Bühler, 'Linguistic (semantic) and extra-linguistic (pragmatic) criteria for the evaluation of conference interpretation and interpreters', in *Multilingua* 5/4 1986, pp. 231-235.
6   See Article 7e of the Code of Professional Conduct and Practice (AIIC 1983).
7   AIIC stipulates that no interpreter may be recorded without prior consent. It also recommends that, where recordings are made, remuneration should be increased by at least 50%, and by 100% where copyright applies. (*AIIC Bulletin* XVI/3 1988, p. 25).

8   Both designations refer to the system whereby participants—and interpreters—
    do not travel to meet each other, but communicate by means of video systems.
9   Annex IV to the AIIC Code of Professional Conduct and Practice, dating from
    1983, is entitled 'Guidelines for remote conferencing'. However, four years later
    an AIIC report stated that 'le développement de la visioconférence est beaucoup
    plus lent que prévu, e.a. parce que les coûts ne baissent pas contre toute attente'.
    (*AIIC Bulletin* XV/4 1987, p. 77).

Foreign Languages for British Engineers:
A Vision of a Better Europe

Mireille Poots

The purpose of this short essay is to discuss the significance of the introduction of foreign languages to the engineering curriculum, both in terms of the obstacles which this development has already encountered and of the advantages which the students can be expected to gain. It is hoped that the introduction of foreign languages should help them to overcome social, cultural and linguistic differences and should add to their highly specialised training a new dimension, the lack of which has only been tolerated and condoned because of tradition and short-term economic advantages.

The fact that some academics and industrialists are genuinely convinced of the validity of such developments is of great significance. The fact that some students are also starting to be convinced is even more promising.

Although this paper is addressed to engineers, it could equally be addressed to scientists.

Preliminaries

> 'If we are to form a United States of Europe ... we must begin now'. Churchill, 19.9.1946.[1]

Forty-three years later the task is incomplete for a variety of reasons, in particular the insularity of the majority of British citizens, the feelings of the political establishment, the present-day values essentially based on 'financially-viable' criteria, the general mood of the press which, with a few exceptions, still offers to readers an essentially English-coated world. There are, however, some very encouraging signs. Since 1981, the concept of Europe and the European citizen has gained momentum and lately acquired a shape which is worth fighting for. A Europe prepared at last to adhere to ambivalent values: recognising (while controlling) the inevitability of a certain uniformity and the convenience of an international language, while maintaining the plurality of European cultures and languages and preventing the resurgence of nationalism. Two necessary forces pulling in opposite directions. With this movement as a background, an increasing minority has become aware of the need to 'accelerate and dynamise intellectual communication in Europe ... to overcome our cultural tribalism', to quote the concluding words of Robert Picht, political scientist from the German Federal Republic, at the International Symposium on 'L'Identité Culturelle Européenne' held in Paris on 13 and 14 January 1988.[2] This view was echoed by a group of enlightened British engineers who decided to take the European bull by the horns and discuss 'The Formation (delicious gallicism) of Engineers in an Integrated

87

European Framework' at an international conference organised by the
Institute of Civil Engineering, held on 6-7 September 1988 in Southampton
University. Last and most important, the enthusiasm, during the last few
years, of some young engineering students who have taken the trouble to
learn a European language and to study in Europe.

Against this background, nonetheless, remains the well-known insularity
of the majority of British citizens, nourished by the ruling party's presentation
of their continental neighbours. A recent flagrant example deserves a special
mention.

In 1986-7, the Conservative Party's pre-election poster was to be seen on
walls, hoardings, newspapers and TV screens all over the country. Beneath
the caption 'Now we've the fastest growth of any major economy in Europe'
sat three dogs: to the right a large British bulldog, in the centre a medium-
sized German Shepherd dog and to the left a small French poodle. Without
embarking on a detailed text analysis of this poster, it might be useful to note
that, apart from the horse, no animal speaks so directly to the British heart
as the dog. The bulldog, although not beautiful, is of Churchillian strength,
reliability and ugly charm; the German Shepherd, while smartly turned-out,
is no longer a force to be reckoned with; the poodle, irremediably rustic, with
peasant beret and onion string, appears to be unaware of even the most basic
industrial development. The subliminal effect of such publicity on the young
must not be overlooked by those engaged in their education. This brilliant
poster reflects and encourages long-standing cultural clichés. It is not suggested that witticisms be banned, but since wit can only be successful if it
relates to a measure of reality in the minds of those who enjoy it, the
perpetuation of these amusing clichés has to be counteracted by reliable facts.

In spite of (possibly because of) these forces working in the background,
overcoming social, cultural and linguistic differences appears to be even more
imperative. To overcome is not to ignore or to abolish but to find out, learn
and master. To overcome social, cultural and linguistic differences is therefore
to discover these differences, learn about them and learn to like them. The
mastering of linguistic differences should be a very good way of dealing with
the first two. 'A well-conceived language teaching programme should be a
powerful mind-broadening tool to develop cultural maturity and an indispensable means of "rapprochement" between men of different ethnic origins.'[3]
Learning a foreign language should not only give us the opportunity of
discovering a new vision of the world, it may in some cases trigger-off our
first conscious vision of it. It may bring about the first conscious appraisal of
our own culture and is therefore likely to generate psychological reactions
which can be both positive and negative. Because language acquisition is
based on comparison, because the discovery of the unknown is related to an
existing cultural background, it is normal to make a value judgement. This
explains why those who learn a foreign language (and to a greater extent
those who expatriate themselves) usually end up belonging to one of the
following three groups. There is the individual who, like the recent convert,
becomes more fanatical about his newly-adopted language/culture than the
native and who may eventually renounce his origins in a very self-destructive

way; the individual who rejects every new feature, as a matter of principle, for whom a stay abroad only succeeds in further narrowing his tolerance and field of vision; lastly, the privileged individual who enriches his new vision of the world by approaching his new experiences positively, enabling him to choose and integrate the many good features of the foreign 'landscape'.

Ideally, the educational system should enable the student to fit into the third category.

The realities

There are major obstacles to the introduction of foreign languages to the engineering curriculum, some of which having so far proved insurmountable for the majority of engineering departments.

First, there is the lack of awareness, on the part of most members of academic staff as well as students, of the usefulness of foreign languages in the curriculum as a very good way of a) broadening the student's general culture, b) improving his/her knowledge of his/her mother tongue and his/her ability to structure an argument, c) enhancing his/her employability. This is confirmed by those very few engineering departments which have for many years had a language component in their course. To witness the sudden awakening of interest in the mechanisms of a student's own mother tongue, due to the demands made by the foreign language, is a moving experience for a teacher. Wittgenstein's statement 'The limits of my language are the limits of my world', allows us to suggest that the learning of a foreign language at a mature age (no longer adolescent) should be an enriching experience which many students do not hesitate to qualify as the most exciting in their student career.

Recently, some engineering departments have turned to languages as a means of boosting their ailing economy. This attitude requires caution since it could have negative repercussions on the course structure offered to students. Equally, the boost would probably be of short duration and might lead to students' failure and disappointment. Sir George Porter, President of the Royal Society, has warned that 'In this perceived hour of need, scientists are being drafted into the short-term exploitation of science, even if it means that ultimately we shall have no science to exploit.'[4] Languages must be saved from a similar fate and must be considered as an educational and cultural asset. Their recent commercial value should rank lower.

Secondly, there are difficulties in integrating a language component into an engineering course already so heavily loaded as to stretch students to their limit. Even those who wish to accept the extra 'burden' of learning a foreign language have difficulty in finding space within the timetable. Nevertheless, the need for nationally and internationally competitive 'quality graduates' is real and constantly emphasised by our political leaders. In order to fulfil this need, it will be necessary to lengthen the period of study, increase university staffing levels and end overspecialised secondary education, three conditions stubbornly opposed by the present government.

Thirdly, there is only lukewarm enthusiasm in many languages departments for the investment of time, energy, knowledge and creativity in what is considered as 'service teaching'. The contempt for the apparent lack of intellectual content of 'service teaching' is reminiscent of that found in traditional languages departments when the new languages departments of the late 1960s and 1970s were created and applied language degrees appeared. It remains to be seen whether the relatively new emphasis on the development of communicative skills in schools and universities may not in the long term run the risk of developing Form at the expense of Content. This, however, is not a defect inherent to the objectives of applied language courses but to some of their obsessive teachers. In a university world perverted by the lack of resources and the standardisation of criteria for promotion based essentially on research, who would enthusiastically spend the necessary time on 'service teaching'? In the meantime, in the name of research and publications, forests are laid waste.

Lastly, most engineering students lack language skills on arrival at university. So far, universities are not in a position to compensate for inadequacies generated at secondary school, where the pursuit of general culture is sacrificed to the acquisition of grades. The lack of language acquisition at school should not, however, prevent future generations from having access to languages at university. At the risk of over-simplification, students, whether at school or at university, fall broadly into three categories. The 'high-flyers', who learn a foreign language with the same ease as they do scientific subjects, who could (and often do) add a foreign language at school or later on. This minority's ability to learn does not depend upon the level of pedagogical competence of the teacher. The 'good at science but poor at languages' who struggle with languages at school or drop them at an early stage but who are eminently recuperable. For psychological reasons already given, these students are often likely to develop an interest in languages later on, when maturity and motivation are present. If languages are to be taught in a meaningful way, they must, of necessity, include a corpus of ideas which does not necessarily fascinate every adolescent struggling with his own tormented development. Those in the third category require special help.

The programme offered must therefore ensure that the pick-up points be numerous.

The way ahead

A realistic programme of measures should enable the majority of students to broaden their education, with the introduction of foreign languages to the curriculum, backed up by the study of European culture. During the Paris Symposium of January 1988 the French historian Pierre Nora presented his radical approach to history as 'Les Lieux de Mémoire dans la Culture Européenne'. In this 'Memory Lane of European Culture', students would learn and compare the similarities in and differences between our cultural heritages. They would '... find collective values but within a national context; ... arrive at general principles but from specific cases; ... and seek out what is of universal value from the study of individual instances'.[5] This exploration of the cultural identity of Europe would create bonds and might generate responsibilities towards each other which so far are lacking. Hugh Seton-Watson, the eminent Scottish historian, whose vision included the whole of Europe, encapsulated this spirit in the following words: 'The unity of European culture is simply the end-product of 3000 years of labour by our diverse ancestors. It is an heritage which we spurn at our peril, and of which it would be a crime to deprive younger and future generations. Rather it is our task to preserve and renew it.'[6]

This realistic programme should be comprehensive and should cater for many needs, from those of the student engineer who wants to add a language option, to those generated by a joint engineering/language degree. The potential and ramifications of such developments are enormous. In the context of the making of Europe, it should be possible to generate enthusiasm in academic circles to experiment with this new type of service teaching. A realistic programme should also include sponsored summer holidays abroad, foreign industrial placements and studies abroad as a matter of course. This entails the participation of industry, sponsored by organisations like ESPRIT, RACE, BRITE, EUREKA, to create a wide and accessible network of placements and the easy availability of funds. ERASMUS was a great spur, triggering-off a momentum of activities. It will soon become a brake unless it is more generous and less cumbersome to administer. Language courses should be offered to university engineering staff and provided by languages departments' staff. This would bring about a 'rapprochement' between disciplines which rarely meet and offer a chance to a whole generation of staff to fill the lacunae created by years of over-specialised secondary education. It would explode the myth that language teaching is no different from the rest and stress that the study of foreign languages has financial implications (small groups, repeated exposure) and psychological effects, not shared by many other disciplines.

Conclusions

Such a profound change is difficult to envisage without an increase in the length of engineering degree courses and without considerably enhanced funding. With rare exceptions, the introduction of languages to the engineering curriculum has been done timidly and without a proper budget. The authorities have relied on the goodwill, the conviction and the generosity of the few members of staff involved. Proper financing is essential and is not so far forthcoming, due to the savage 'rationalisation' of the universities' budgets. The absence of tangible economic benefit of such a national programme would undoubtedly deter politicians from supporting it. They might even remind us that when Schuman and his European colleagues created the European Community, they no doubt thought that progress would be more quickly reached in the economic field than in the cultural. However, these same politicians might usefully reflect at this stage that it is unlikely that economic progress will be sustained in the absence of a sense of cultural unity and a respect for cultural differences. The Single European Act repeatedly refers to the European Union and not, as Lord Young would have us believe, to the 'European economic union'. Therefore, when Lord Young tells Jonathan Dimbleby that '... The whole of the Single European Act is about creating a single market in Europe, which is about the removal of non-tariff barriers in Europe',[7] we must refer him to the Single European Act which states quite unequivocally that 'The European Communities and European Political Cooperation shall have as their objective to contribute together to making concrete progress towards European unity'.[8]

Nor is reassurance forthcoming from the Minister of Education at the Scottish Office, Mr Michael Forsyth, who advocated to an audience of 200 teachers, lecturers, headmasters, HMIs and education officers that 'schools would have to shift resources from the subjects which future pupils will drop in favour of languages.'[9] Considering that this conference had been called to rescue languages from the oblivion to which an ignorant education policy had consigned them for the last 25 years, it would have been tempting immediately to book the minister for a conference to be held in 25 years' time to retrieve those subjects he is advising us to drop now.

But it would be improper to finish on a pessimistic note. Too much has happened already, which would have been unthinkable a few years ago, not least the Southampton Conference mentioned earlier. No less the success of a young student from Galashiels, whose qualities of perseverance, audacity, endurance and humility were suddenly awakened by the intellectual challenge presented by an industrial placement for two and a half months in Schlumberger in Paris, by the linguistic challenge of learning French and the social adaptation required while looking after 3 young French children for a month in the South of France. All this without a doubt proved a very enriching experience in more respects than one. For those who might fear for his academic performance, it should be noted that his rating improved from ordinary II 2 during his first 3 years at university, to a very good II 1 at graduation. He is now working for ICI, being 1 of 14 chosen from an initial 232 applicants.

To ask our young engineers thus to overcome social, cultural and linguistic differences would effectively broaden their education and in the process should help them to ask 'why' as well as 'how'. Such an approach may contribute in its own way towards world peace.

'The splitting of the world into antagonistic groups is essentially attributable to a lack of mutual understanding among peoples ... I believe that the most crucial key to world peace is the promotion of understanding among people. When an overflowing stream of common feeling underlies the speech and actions of all people, the hostility of governments will become absurd.'[10]

Why deny them this right?

Notes

1   Churchill, 'Churchill Speaks 1897-1963', Robert R James, Windward, 1981, p. 892.

2 For the collected contributions of this symposium, see 'Europe Sans Rivage: De L'Identité Culturelle Européenne', Albin Michel, 1988, pp. 343-5.
3 Professeur Robert Galisson, Université de la Sorbonne Nouvelle, Paris.
4 Sir George Porter, Richard Dimbleby Lecture, BBC1 TV, 10.4.1988.
5 '... trouver le collectif, mais dans le national; ... trouver le général, mais dans le spécifique; ... rechercher dans le particulier ce qui nous reste d'universel'. Pierre Nora, 'Europe Sans Rivage: De L'Identité Culturelle Européenne', Albin Michel, 1988, p. 42.
6 Hugh Seton-Watson, 'What is Europe, Where is Europe?', in Encounter, July/ August 1985, vol. LXV, number 2, p. 17.
7 'On the Record', BBC1 TV, 9.10.1988.
8 Single European Act, Title 1, Article 1, in 'Treaties Establishing the European Communities' (Abridged Edition), Luxembourg: Office for Official Publications of the European Communities, 1987, p. 533.
9 'Foreign Languages In Scotland: The Way Ahead'. Conference held in Stirling University on 5.11.1988.
10 Arnold Toynbee and Daisaku Ikeda, 'Choose Life: A Dialogue', Oxford University Press, 1976, p. 241.

Nation Shall Speak Unto Nation: the BBC World Service

Alan Thompson

In the aftermath of the Second World War, during which I had served in the infantry, I found myself transferred to a small radio station in Italy (and subsequently Austria) where my job was to broadcast propaganda talks to the troops. I had exchanged my gun for a microphone. Over thirty years later I found myself appointed a Governor of the BBC. I do not believe the two events were in any way connected, but it gave me the opportunity of contrasting the two broadcasting roles which I had performed in my life—propaganda on behalf of a victorious military alliance, and the maintenance of a free broadcasting system which mirrored the values of democracy. I had moved, one might say, from ideology to idealism. The BBC in general (and the World Service in particular) stand, in my view, at the idealistic end of the scale.

The BBC External Service (originally known as the Empire Service) was set up in 1932 to reflect on an international level what the BBC provided domestically under its charter:[1] a public service influenced neither by party politics nor commercial considerations. It was to be politically neutral and provide a wide variety of viewpoints on current issues. There was one difference: whereas the domestic service was financed by license holders, the External Service was financed directly by government grant (on the grounds that British licence holders should not pay for a service which they could not hear). Although the system of direct grant carries a greater risk of government interference, the World Service is remarkably free of any such interference (although this does not mean that it has never been attempted).

The expansion of the Empire Service into a wider External Service (and subsequently what is now called the World Service) was accelerated by rival overseas services by Germany, Italy and Russia, whose messages were unashamedly propagandist, strident and aggressive. Of the three, the German service was the most influential.

Soon after they came to power the Nazis expanded a short-wave station at Zeesen, a village about 20 miles south-east of Berlin. They encouraged their overseas listeners by organising competitions, giving away programme details and free material for rebroadcasting on local stations—practices which are all now commonplace among international broadcasters—and sometimes, as in Latin America, even buying up such stations. They attacked both the Bolsheviks and the 'decadent' Western plutocracies in violent and picturesque terms, and there is no doubt that in the short term their propaganda was brilliantly effective.

In the face of a torrent of abuse the British authorities decided that in sheer self-defence they too would have to go into the business of broadcasting in foreign languages, particularly Arabic. A Cabinet committee was set up to consider the problem. One suggestion was that the Foreign Office should organise broadcasts to the Arab world from a transmitter in Cyprus. Reith, however, argued that only the BBC had the necessary expertise. There was opposition among senior members of the Corporation who were afraid that such broadcasting would be mere propaganda (a hate word) and would detract from the credibility of the Empire Service.

Their fears were eventually overcome but they had not been altogether misplaced. The then head of the Foreign Office news department thought that for the Arab world news items should be selected which were in the interests of Britain, omitting those which in the opinion of the Foreign Office 'it would be inadvisable should be given the emphasis that broadcasting by wireless would give'.[2] This was seeing the problem through the eyes of a diplomat, but it was not the BBC way. Fortunately for posterity Reith insisted that in its language broadcasts the Corporation should have the freedom from government control possessed by its other services. Prestige, he argued, depended on broadcasting that was both truthful and comprehensive; the External Services owe him a great debt.

He also made it clear that if the government wanted foreign language broadcasting it would have to pay; the money was not coming from the licence payers this time. The government somewhat nonchalantly agreed— it could hardly be expected to visualise the enormous expansion that would come—and presented a small supplementary estimate to Parliament without defining the precise responsibilities of each side. The arrangement was, in typical British fashion, blurred at the edges, but essentially the BBC was in the position of a specialist contractor hired to do a particular job in its own way.[3]

The opening of the Arabic Service on 3 January 1938, was accompanied by a demonstration of the Corporation's editorial independence. The news bulletin carried an item (translated from the Empire Service) about the execution of an Arab by the British authorities in Palestine for possessing a rifle and ammunition during anti-British riots. This was precisely the sort of item which under the Foreign Office formula would have been tactfully omitted, and it did in fact lead to complaints. In the words of the historian Asa Briggs: 'Only the BBC would have jeopardised the start of Arabic news bulletins by telling the truth in a bald, factual way.'[4]

Broadcasting to the Arab world alone would have seemed like a direct challenge to the dictators. That, of course, is what it was, but in the age of appeasement the government felt it inexpedient to make this obvious. So in March transmissions began in Spanish and Portuguese to Latin America, where Britain had commercial, if not strategic, interests to defend.

The Munich crisis in the autumn of 1938 led to a further growth in the External Services. Shortly before the war, the Foreign Secretary of the time, Lord Halifax, expressed the view that in broadcasts to Germany the BBC 'could hardly be expected to possess sufficient knowledge of facts to enable it always to be the best judge of what should or should not be included in a bulletin',[5] thus once again showing the confusion in the official mind between news and propaganda. In the end he settled for a system of consultation rather than actual Foreign Office control, but just before the outbreak of war in 1939 the government prevented the German service from carrying a message to the German people from the National Council of Labour. This decision was later reversed, and the message was eventually carried—five days late.

When war broke out the BBC was broadcasting in English and seven foreign languages (Afrikaans was added to the list in the summer of 1939 and Spanish and Portuguese transmissions were directed to Europe as well as Latin America). When it ended six years later it was speaking to the whole world in 45 languages.

With the end of the war the External Services, which had grown in such a rapid and unplanned manner, were put on a formal basis. The BBC Charter and Licence of 1946 specified that the Corporation should broadcast abroad in the languages and for the number of hours laid down by the government. For its part the government would make available the necessary finance as voted by Parliament. It was specifically stated that the BBC would remain independent in preparing programmes but would obtain from the government 'such information about conditions in those countries and the policies of His Majesty's government towards them as will permit it to plan its programmes in the national interest'.[6]

What this meant in practice (and still means) was explained by the Lord President of the Council, Mr Herbert Morrison in the debate on the 1946 charter in the House of Commons:

> The Corporation will accept the guidance on the nature and scope of its foreign language services, and there will be a very close liaison between the two of them... But once the general character and scope of a service has been laid down, the BBC will have complete discretion as to the content of the programmes themselves. This compromise may result in some regrettable incidents, but unless such incidents are to be much more numerous than we have reason to expect, they will, I think, be a small price to pay for letting the responsibility for broadcasting programmes lie with those best quailfied to exercise it.[7]

This was very different from the thoughts of Lord Halifax in 1939 and shows how greatly the prestige of the BBC had grown because of its wartime record. The Director General, in a paper presented to the Board of Governors soon after this, put forward the principles which continue to guide the External Services. Among these were the following: news which might be in the short term inconvenient must on no account be suppressed; news bulletins should not seek to persuade; it is not the function of the BBC to interfere in the domestic affairs of any other country; the European and Overseas Service would be separate (i.e. all the outside world except Europe). The Empire Service itself changed its title and incorporated at various times the General Overseas Service, the Overseas Forces Programme, the General Forces Programme and (after the war) back to being the General Overseas Service and then the World Service. It developed a number of regional services, broadcasting for example to Africa, the Pacific and North America.

Since the end of the war the BBC World Service has preserved its independence of government control, although it came under considerable pressure at the time of the Suez war in 1956. The BBC felt it should broadcast in detail the views of Hugh Gaitskell and the Labour and Liberal Parties opposing the war. The Prime Minister, Mr Eden, attempted to impose censorship, and was considering the possibility of a bill to curtail the powers of the BBC when the war came to an end and the controversy died away. Although subsequently during the Falklands War relations were sometimes strained between the Government and the BBC, there was nothing like the anger and hostility provoked by the Suez War.

On another occasion, during the last days of the Shah of Persia's rule in 1978, there was criticism of the BBC for alleged anti-Shah bias of its overseas broadcasts, and the British Ambassador to Persia expressed his concern. Some people still believe that there was substance in these allegations, but other observers who investigated the matter concluded that there was no evidence of bias.

Compared with Suez and Iran the Falklands war involved the BBC World Service in little criticism for its coverage. The fact that (unlike Suez) the Government and Opposition was united in defending the legitimacy of the war may have helped to defuse any parliamentary criticism which may otherwise have been voiced, but the main reason was the highly responsible and balanced coverage by the BBC.

The growth in the range and influence of the BBC World Service in recent years has been greatly assisted by a technological development. This is the transistor, an innovation which has had tremendous repercussions on radio listening habits. Young people not only listen to their favourite pop groups as they walk down the street or travel on bus, tube and train, but also in towns and all over the Third World they use transistors for serious listening. In these countries it is the most important medium of mass communications. Television and the printed page are in many instances for the urban elite, but radio, comparatively cheap and portable, is for the people. Thanks to the transistor there has been a huge increase in the number of radio sets in the world. In Africa, for example, the number increased in a period of 20 years from less than half a million to over 22 million; in India from one million to 18 million. This means that there is a mass audience for which many broadcasters compete; well over 80 countries now broadcast to people outside their own borders.

Nevertheless, the BBC manages to retain the largest number of listeners. It measures the size of its audience overseas—and those of other international broadcasters—by commissioning sample surveys. These are always carried out by experienced, independent research companies by means of personal interviews. Surveys also provide information about the characteristics of audiences, reception conditions, set ownership and so on. They cannot be carried out in all countries; either they are forbidden, as in much of Central and Eastern Europe, or there may be no suitable company to undertake the work, or the cost may be too high. However, the BBC now has information from some 60 countries, enough for deductions to be made about the size of its worldwide regular audience—about 120 million adults, not including China. Of these no fewer than 35 million listen to the Hindi Service and 25 million to the World Service in English.

What then, are the main achievements of the BBC World Service which are as valid (if not more so) today as they have been in the past.

First, the maintenance of the independence of the service from government control. This means that it can provide a news service that reports fully, accurately and speedily about the world as a whole. There is the celebrated instance of a government-run news conference in Baghdad when the entire meeting broke up while everyone, including the official spokesman, tuned into London to find out what was really happening in the Gulf War. During the Helsinki Review conference in 1986 in Stockholm, when East and West were arguing over the fine points of the size of manoeuvres that had to be notified to the other side, World News carried the story that agreement had in fact been reached on the lower figure. Once it was carried on the World Service diplomats speedily moved to the appropriate agreement. But the BBC can only play that kind of role in world affairs if it is trusted in the first place.

Second, there is the question of the tone of the programmes. There is a tendency for governments to urge the BBC to proclaim British exploits and achievements loudly to the world: the World Service, of course, does this in programmes about industry, arts, sport and politics. In each of these topics it also informs the audience about what the world is doing as well. British writers, artists and industrialists gain by being set and seen in the total global context. They live and work in a fierce international competitive market place in their every day lives; they would not gain, and we would not be listened to, if the BBC provided a protectionist broadcasting environment where the mere fact of being British earned them the right to uncritical broadcasting attention.

Third, the BBC broadcasts to people in their own tongue as well as in English. It talks to masses as well as to elites. It does not believe that as long as a foreign head of state hears the broadcasts that is all that matters (it is the job of our ambassadors to inform heads of government).

Fourthly, the BBC addresses open societies as well as closed ones, to friends as well as to enemies. Government priorities inevitably tend to emphasise the latter; the BBC insists on not overlooking our friends, such as the American audience. Who can argue that the need to communicate with Americans is not of prime importance in matters of foreign policy today and their perception of Europe's readiness to stand and devote resources to its defence, a vital part of the dialogue between allies? On a more Macchiavellian level friends and enemies change backwards and forwards over time, but the BBC should be speaking to both all the time.

In any area of public activity, however, it is not enough from an economic point of view to applaud the objectives: we also have to measure its efficiency. It is true that public sector broadcasting in general and the BBC World Service in particular do not lend themselves to all the normal tests of the market. There are, however, certain guidelines which can be laid down to minimise waste, extravagance and blatant misallocation of resources.

The Managing Director of the service, Mr John Tusa, in 1987 introduced various measures to secure increased efficiency (and, incidentally, equip the BBC to meet the stern and challenging interrogation to which the House of Commons Public Accounts Committee subjects public bodies).[8] Mr Tusa introduced a new budgeting system where every department in the External Services directorate had to relate its programmes to stated purposes and objectives, and then justify their expenditure in relation to those purposes. Further, every department had to identify 5% of their budget as being of lower priority than the rest, and also proposed projects which could cost a further 5%. This enabled management to look across the World Service as a whole and decide to reallocate money from relatively higher priority activities. It was discovered that over 90% of senior managers, as a result of a long and demanding process, carried out under acute pressure of time, believed they knew more about their department than they had before as a result of this process. It was both a management, and in the end, an editorial instrument.

The Service is also the subject of regular 'activity for value of money reviews' undertaken by the BBC's auditors on a rolling basis. The World Services' timetable is for the whole place to have been scrutinised in this way over five years. So far the Eastern Service and the South European Service have been reviewed to see if their organisation and administration are properly run to use resources in the best possible way. These reviews both make suggestions about ways in which departments could be better run but also identify areas where departments have less money than they need—in the case of the Eastern Service, it appeared that certain categories were under-funded.

Economic scrutiny is clearly important, but there is also need for editorial scrutiny. This is important, for instance in the vernacular services to ensure that they are reaching good translation standards, meeting common editorial standards and producing good and effective programme material. The method is to record three days output, back-translate it, compare the two, and then examine the two texts in a six hour session. This editorial scrutiny had to date covered the Hausa, the Poles, the Indonesians and the Turks, the Finns and the Hindi and is proving itself a useful method of keeping standards matching across the Service as a whole, as well as showing people in one service how colleagues in other services meet similar problems and challenges. It means that senior management can get closer to the output and the sections than was formerly possible. So the process of scrutiny is constant, varied, and both internally and externally run.

The World Service's quality of output, in my view, entitles it to a wider audience within the U.K. It should be fully and deliberately audible to domestic listeners. The costs, however, would have to come partly from the licence fee and could not be a charge on the grant-in-aid; and, there would have to be re-negotiation of fees with the unions involved. These arrangements would not be difficult to secure, but if not properly discussed and negotiated could lead to considerable political controversy and procrastination.

The achievements of the World Service spring in no small measure from the calibre of the men who have guided its destiny. The three managing directors within my personal acquaintance, Gerald Mansell, Douglas Muggeridge and John Tusa have all been men of academic and cultural distinction as well as thoroughly-trained professional broadcasters. They have also been helped by the composition of the Board of Governors. Although the Board has sometimes been criticised for its elitist outlook (arising from the number of professors, and vice-chancellors among its membership) this has probably helped in the special interest it has usually shown in maintaining the quality and integrity of international broadcasting.

Whatever changes face the structure of broadcasting in the UK in the aftermath of the Peacock Report and government proposals for the future, the arguments for retaining a strong publicly funded World Service remain as strong as ever. Its fifty years of professional broadcasting is unrivalled by any other nation in the world, and its objectives do not make it a suitable body for privatisation. Together with the British Council, whose activities the BBC regards as complementary, the World Service plays a vital part in what might be loosely called 'cultural diplomacy'. It may not always have pleased the Foreign Office and it may occasionally have caused anger and outrage at Number Ten Downing Street but it supplies a standard against which all news correspondents in the world compare their work.

Notes

1   *BBC Year Book* (1933) p. 263
2   BBC External Services Publicity Unit, *Voice for the World*, 1982, p. 7
3   *Report of Broadcasting Committee* (Ullswater) Cmd. 5091 (1936) paras 12, 16, 21, 23, 115-124
4   Briggs, Asa, *The Golden Age of Wireless* (OUP) 1965 p. 404
5   Notes of a meeting at the Foreign Office, 1 Nov 1938 between the Foreign Secretary and the Chairman of the Board of Governors (Professor F W Ogilvie) (*BBC files*)
6   BBC External Service Publicity Unit, *Voice for the World*, 1982, p. 14
7   Ibid. p. 14
8   Tusa, John, Managing Director, BBC World Service: 'Radio Around the World': address to the Bristol Radio Festival, 17 July 1987.

Devolution: Scottish Solution or British Expedient?

David Harron

Since the 1987 General Election, when the Conservative Party was elected to a third term of office, constitutional reform has moved to the top of the Scottish political agenda, given that the governing party's parliamentary representation was cut to just ten of the country's 72 MPs. This fact, and the subsequent unwillingness of Mrs Thatcher's government to moderate any of the policies which had been so decisively rejected, has led to much radical re-evaluation of Scotland's role both within the United Kingdom and in the wider area of the European Community. The purpose of this essay is to examine the concept of legislative devolution in its two most common guises—i.e., as advocated by the Labour Party and by the Social and Liberal Democrats—and to ask whether a Scottish Assembly within the UK framework, once seen as a panacea, would now be merely a politically motivated attempt to patch over the irreconcilable differences between Scotland and England.

> Much ink is wasted on the question of whether the Scots are a nation. Of course they are. They were both a nation and a state until 1707. The state was wound up by a Treaty which clearly recognised the nation and its right to distinctive government in a fundamental range of home affairs. The fact that institutional forms, however empty, reflecting these distinctions have been preserved to the present day demonstrates that no-one in British government has dared to suggest openly that the nation no longer exists, or that the case for distinctiveness has now disappeared.[1]

With these words, the *Claim of Right For Scotland* document, published by the *Campaign for a Scottish Assembly (CSA)*, begins its presentation of the political case for legislative devolution. There has been considerable debate on Scotland's future since 1707, but this debate reached its two most significant peaks in the devolution proposals of the 1970s and the current supposed consensus on constitutional reform, a consensus based on a perceived subservience of Scottish intrests to the wishes of an English-dominated parliament.

The battle-lines in the constitutional debate are drawn with reasonable clarity: the ruling Conservatives favour no change from the status quo; the Labour Party advocate the devolution of certain powers to a Scottish Assembly; the Social and Liberal Democrats (SLD) believe in the need for a renegotiation of the Treaty of Union, with the subsequent establishment of a federal structure throughout the UK; and the Scottish National Party (SNP) propose the creation of an independent Scottish State within the European Community. An up to date indication of levels of support for these parties is provided in Table 1.[2]

Table 1: Scottish voting intentions, May 1989

	%	1987 General Election %
CONS.	22	24
LAB.	44	42
SLD	5	
SDP	3	19
SNP	25	14

The anomalous position of the Conservatives as, in the words of *The Scotsman*, 'an opposition in government', with minimal support and yet complete freedom to implement their policies, has been a major factor in fuelling constitutional debate in Scotland and has led the *Claim of Right* authors to note that 'the machinery (of Britsh government) is also constitutionally unsound in that it can work only if the governing party in the United Kingdom has a certain minimum of support in Scotland'.[3] However, consensus has been difficult to achieve: considerable hostility has built up between Labour and the SNP, with the result that cross-party co-operation has been restricted thus far to the participation of Labour and the SLD in the *Scottish Constitutional Convention*, organised by the CSA, which met for the first time in Edinburgh on March 30, 1989. This is hardly a surprise, given the unbridgeable gap which exists between the unionist Labour Party and the pro-independence SNP.

In many ways, 'devolution' remains a concept most closely associated with the constitutional debate of the 1970s, a debate which culminated in the then Labour Government's 1978 Scotland Act. Though approved in a referendum on March 1, 1979, the devolutionary proposals were never implemented because less than 40% of the total electorate had voted in favour. In its most basic form, devolution entails the transfer of responsibility for certain areas of Scottish government from London to a Scottish Assembly, or parliament, in Edinburgh. However, Scottish political debate has moved on considerably since 1979, and it is my purpose here to look at the thinking behind devolution in the late 1980s and to examine how it relates to current political realities.

The effect of the Thatcher years is illustrated by the more wide-ranging devolution now proposed by the Labour Party. The Party's 1984 Green Paper envisaged the establishment of an Assembly with responsibilities in a wide number of areas including health, education and local government. The crucial difference, of course, between devolution and full independence remains the UK dimension, and the problem of Scottish MPs being able to vote on purely English legislation, while their English counterparts exercise no such powers over Scottish government, is not satisfactorily resolved in the Labour Green Paper.

... there may still be areas of doubt and uncertainty about the way policies will be implemented ... Scotland will of course retain its existing Parliamentary representation at Westminster.[4]

Labour's *political* as well as constitutional dilemma is clear: as a British party, it cannot afford the removal of its 49 Scottish MPs from London. Yet the intellectual inconsistency of setting up Scottish and Welsh assemblies in isolation is a problem the party must face and is one which is not fully addressed in the party's policy review proposals.[5] The notion that regional assemblies could be set up in England as demand arises smacks of an attempt to appease nationalist sentiment without fundamentally reforming the apparatus of British government. Bernard Ponsonby of the SLD sums up Labour's dilemma:

> (Labour's Front Bench) can't contain the nationalist wing because defeating Thatcher is the number one priority; but they can't embrace nationalism because if they embrace nationalism they give up on the UK strategy.[6]

Labour's record on devolution is not good: in government three times between 1945 and 1979, the party was never able to deliver a Scottish Assembly. It is perhaps the stifling traditionalism of Britsh government which has been a root cause, but accusation of Labour subservience to the English establishment are not new. Tom Nairn wrote in 1977:

> It would be exaggerated, admittedly, to claim that the UK state is yet quite like the Hapsburg Empire or the old Castilian State. But the similarities are notable enough: there is a recognizable composite of archaism, incorrigible economic failure, backward-looking complacency, indurate social conservatism and blind will to survive in the same historic form. Culture has become largely the celebration of these values. The main 'opposition' party, British Labour, is as addicted to them as the overt conservatives.[7]

In considering Labour's stance on devolution, then, two points are worth bearing in mind: that the party represents a broad spectrum of viewpoints and that British socialism has never embraced constitutional politics. Constitutional debate has been almost inevitably tied in with the particular policies of the political parties, with the exception in Scotland of the cross-party campaign for a Scottish Assembly. Chris Ross of the CSA assesses Labour's position vis-a-vis its commitment to a Scottish Assembly:

> I think you have to be very wary of discussing the Labour Party as if it were a monolithic block ... attitudes within the Labour Party vary enormously; I think there is undoubtedly an element of political opportunism and to be fair Labour would be failing in its job if there wasn't.[8]

At most, then, Labour's constitutional thinking seems based on a desire for *partial* or expedient reform. The party recognises a need to stall the rise of the SNP without seeing a need to remove some of the key elements of the archaic British state which have aided and abetted that rise: namely, the excessive power of the executive, caused by a discredited voting system which Labour nonetheless support because 'We're not convinced that it's possible to have strong government under either an STV system or an AV system'.[9]

Such a piecemeal approach to reform would surely threaten the continued existence of the 'regional' assemblies should a less sympathetic government take office. The question of enshrining the sovereignty of a Scottish Assembly is a vital one in any analysis of devolution: in countries such as Spain and the German Federal Republic this is achieved by means of a written constitution. However, this is something which is completely alien to the British political tradition and is not at present on Labour's agenda. Perhaps the key to Labour's thinking on the matter can be detected in their own Green Paper:

> Devolution will strengthen our links with the rest of the country... It will not undermine or destroy, but, in fact, will strengthen our ties with the United Kingdom.[10]

I will return to this question, and to the fundamental contrasts between devolution and federalism after looking at the 'strong devolution' proposals of the SLD. Bernard Ponsonby outlines the shift in emphasis:

> Labour believes in an *Assembly*: we believe in a *Parliament*. It's not a semantic debate; ... an Assembly is effectively a subordinate legislature ... we propose that there is a division of sovereignty and the power (of the Scottish Parliament) would be constitutionally guaranteed.[11]

Where Labour covers a wide range of views on the constitutional question, the SLD present a much more united front, as the inheritors of the Liberal Home Rule tradition. Federalism, the creation of completely independent regional parliaments, the powers of which would be defined and guaranteed in a written constitution, would amount to the most fundamental reform of the machinery of British government ever enacted. Federalism differs from the Labour devolution proposals in the following key areas:

(1) *The Powers of a Scottish Parliament* A written constitution and a Bill of Rights are seen by the SLD as essential components of a modern democracy. As far as the government of Scotland is concerned, a written constitution would play a vital role in the 'division of sovereignty' or enshrining of the respective powers of the Scottish Parliament and the Federal Parliament in London. Any disputes between London and the regional parliaments would be resolved by a Constitutional Court, as in Spain. However, the essence of federalism is to give total independence to the federal regions as far as possible and so a Scottish Parliament would have responsibility in a wide range of areas, with the exception of such all-British concerns as defence, foreign affairs and aspects of macroeconomic policy. The SLD Green Paper sets out these aspects of responsibility as follows: economic affairs, employment and training, the European Community, education, health, housing, social welfare, local government, environment, transport, energy, agriculture and

fisheries, the legal and criminal justice systems and arts and leisure.[12] Perhaps most importantly of all, the Scottish Parliament would have its own tax-raising powers and would thus be able to determine both the pattern and extent of Scottish expenditure. Labour has come to accept this principle since 1979, but the general tone of their devolution proposals is criticised by the SLD as having 'more to do with the history of the Scottish Office than with giving a mature democracy like Scotland the necessary amount of freedom to run its own affairs.'[13]

(2) *Scottish Representation at Westminster* While the SLD's policies on constitutional reform envisage the eventual implementation of a federal structure throughout the UK, it is stressed that the establishment of a Scottish Parliament is not 'dependent upon the creation of a UK federal structure or of Parliaments and Assemblies for the three other nations.'[14] The reduction of Scottish parliamentary representation from 72 to 60 MPs is proposed after the creation of a Scottish Parliament, given that the establishment of such parliaments in England, Wales and Northern Ireland could well take longer. This figure would mean that Scotland had the Westminster representation that its population warrants, and the 60 MPs would not be able to vote on legislation purely affecting the other three nations. Thus, the 'West Lothian Question'—the dilemma of Scottish MPs having control over Scottish legislation while at the same time exercising the right to vote on English affairs—is resolved quite unambiguously.

However, it is quite easy to understand Labour's different perspective on this issue. In the current political climate—with Labour at present drawing one-fifth of its total parliamentary representation from Scottish constituencies—the removal of its Scottish MPs would render a British Labour government quite unable to carry out some of the central planks of its policy programme in England and Wales. It is obvious therefore that pressure from some sections of the Scottish Labour Party is leading the British party into dangerous and previously uncharted territory. The SLD on the other hand, facing low levels of support for their newly established party, can work on building their own policy programme without worrying about such harsh political realities. It is against this background that we must understand some of the key differences in policy.

(3) *Scotland and Europe* As a federal and autonomous European region, Scotland would have its own direct links with the European Community. These would go further than the current 'observer' status accorded to the German *Länder* and would seem to form part of the at present somewhat nebulous concept of the 'Europe of Regions'. In many ways, the European dimension underlines a crucial difference between the two sets of devolutionary proposals: Labour's devolved legislature would have no significant input into European affairs precisely because it would be a devolved assembly and not an independent region or nation within a federal Europe.

Clearly, the establishment of a federal system would require significant changes to the entire UK system of government. Another central plank of the SLD's proposals is a change in the voting system, with a move from the current 'first past the post' method to the Single Transferable Vote system of proportional representation. Yet the intricacies of constitutional and electoral reform on a UK basis have never been central issues in elections, and, with their current standing in the opinion polls, the SLD's chance of achieving these goals seem limited.

All these comparisons, of course, lead to another crucial area in the debate on constitutional reform: why and where do the proposals for a federal Scottish parliament, with its own links with the EC, differ from the SNP platform of 'Independence in Europe'? Given that the continued development of the Community seems sure to lead to a further pooling or erosion of national sovereignties, it seems legitimate to question whether 'Independence in Europe' would truly constitute 'independence'. But for that very reason, it also seems legitimate to ask whether a federal British government would not merely be an additional tier of government in the European context. The SNP's policy document on the subject states:

> Other small nations, such as Ireland, have shown what is possible and have protected and strengthened their national interests while playing a positive role in the European arena. The European institutions are designed in such a way that small nations are able to play a full role.[15]

Yet despite the apparent closeness of thinking on some matters, Graham Lait, the SLD candidate for Strathclyde East in the 1989 European elections, told *The Scotsman*:

> Scotland's economy has been irretrievably wedded to England's for many years. Our businesses are by and large tied in with southern businesses, our physical communications all run south of the Border... The SNP are offering the Scottish people an entirely futile vision of the future and if it was ever obtained it would leave us in a very deep mess.[16]

The key to the whole debate over Scotland's future role in Europe, then, goes far beyond the respective visions of Scotland's political parties: it is a debate about the future of Europe itself. If Europe is to eventually adopt a unified, quasi-federal structure—the basis of the Europe of Regions concept—then the need for any sort of 'British dimension' to Scottish politics would be called into question. However, it is the current British government which has been in the forefront of opposition to the 'United States of Europe' vision, and it seems almost certain that national parliaments will continue to play a highly significant role for at least the next ten years. Should this prove to be so, the SNP will remain quite isolated from the rest of Scotland's mainstream political parties.

Many political commentators believe that the most crucial date in the current Scottish consitutional debate will be the next British General Election. Another victory for Mrs Thatcher's Conservatives—i.e. the fourth straight Labour defeat since 1979—is widely expected to lead to calls for more radical action on the 'Scottish Question', as well as a considerable increase in support for the SNP, with Labour voters disillusioned with Labour's chances of ever again forming a British government.

So where does all this leave devolution, the long-standing solution to all of Scotland's problems?

Scotland's distinctive traditions and distinctive character are in no doubt. First aired in the late 1960s, devolution was originally conceived as a means of appeasing nationalist sentiment while at the same time keeping Scotland inside the United Kingdom. Yet the 1970s devolution debate cannot be compared with the present one for one vital reason: at that time there were pro-devolutionists in all the political parties and the Conservative Party, now staunchly opposed to constitutional reform, had issued its own pro-devolution policy docments.[17] Indeed, the very essence of pre-Thatcherite paternalistic Conservatism was its 'one-nation' approach. Now circumstances have changed: Scotland has quite clearly developed a siege mentality and a growing despair at the implementation of unwanted policies by what is perceived to be a quintessentially *English* government.

The SNP's triumph in the Glasgow Govan by-election in November 1988, therefore, seemed to pose major problems for Labour's traditional Scottish support. Labour's Catch 22 dilemma reveals the true nature of its thinking on constitutional reform. First and foremost, the Labour Party is *British* and *Unionist*, Her Majesty's Loyal Opposition. The Thatcher years have led to an alienation of many Scottish voters and Labour's devolution proposals smack of an attempt to stem the nationalist onslaught. However, Labour cannot afford to devolve too many powers, or to effect too many reforms of the machinery of British government, precisely because its top priority is to form a *British* government. This is quite clear from any analysis of Labour's Green Paper: for Scottish MPs to have seats in both Westminster and Edinburgh parliaments reveals more about Labour's commitment to political power than it does about any commitment to constitutional reform.

The SLD, on the other hand, find themselves in the opposite position: their coherent policy proposals have been tried and tested in other countries but seem incapable of garnering any electoral support. The key difference is that the SLD—and for that matter, the SNP—are willing to fundamentally alter the structure of British government, while Labour—a traditional British party with a substantial number of anti-devolutionists in its ranks—has a vested interest in retaining much of the structure which provides 'strong' government or 'elective dictatorships'. The essence of the devolution debate is to observe where the balance is struck between idealism and political realities. Jim Ross, Under Secretary with responsibility for devolution in the last Labour Scottish Office, summed up the situation in *Radical Scotland*:

> A devolved Assembly would therefore be subject to 'the essential tenor of British political ways' ... The only Assembly acceptable now is one which reflects a change in the structure of the British constitution.[18]

In other words, if Labour wins the next General Election it could pretend to have just pulled off the trick. If not, it will simply have to accept that the past is another country, and they do things differently there.

Sources and bibliography

Interviews were held as follows:
Flora Maclean, SNP Research Officer, at SNP Offices,
6 North Charlotte Street, Edinburgh, on April 4;

Bernard Ponsonby, SLD Press and Policy Officer, at SLD Offices,
4 Clifton Terrace, Edinburgh, on April 6;

Kenneth Ferguson, Conservative Councillor for Morningside on Edinburgh District Council, at work (Ferguson & Partners, 24 Castle Street, Edinburgh) on April 11;

Wendy Alexander, Labour Research Officer, at Labour Party Offices.
1 Lynedoch Place, Glasgow, on April 20;

Chris Ross, Secretary, CSA Edinburgh Branch, at work
(Department of languages, Heriot-Watt University) on April 25,
all 1989.

Policy documents

Conservative Party:	*Scotland's Government*, 1970
CSA:	*Blueprint for Scotland*, 1981
	The Scottish Constitutional Convention, 1984
	A Claim of Right for Scotland—Report of The Constitutional Steering Committee, 1988
Labour Party:	*Labour's Green Paper on Devolution*, 1984
	Scotland Bill Press Briefing, 1987
Liberal Party/SLD:	*Scottish Self Government*, 1982
	Sovereignty And Integration—The Case For A Scottish Parliament, 1988
	Scotland And Europe, 1989
SNP:	*The SNP's Constitutional Policy*, 1984
	Scottish Independence And The European Community, 1989.

Books and articles

Hooper, J, *The Spaniards*, Penguin, London 1987.
Nairn, T, *The Break-Up of Britain*, Verso, London, 1981.
Ross, J, 'A Fond Farewell to Devolution', in *Radical Scotland*, Issue 36, Dec. 1988/Jan. 1989.

Notes

1   *A Claim Of Right For Scotland*, p.1.
2   Source: MORI Poll conducted 28-29 April 1989, published in *The Scotsman* 5 May 1989.
3   *A Claim Of Right For Scotland*, p.9.

4   *Labour's Green Paper on Devolution*, p. 7.
5   Labour's recent policy review proposes the replacement of the House of Lords with an elected second chamber serving the interests of regional assemblies. However, the English assemblies would only be set up as demand required and therefore fundamental questions remain about the structure of representation at Westminster.
6   Interview with Bernard Ponsonby, 6.4.89.
7   Tom Nairn, *The Break-Up of Britain*, p.190.
8   Interview with Chris Ross, 24.4.89.
9   Interview with Wendy Alexander, 20.4.89. STV (Single Transferable Vote) and AV (Alternative Vote) are the two most commonly advocated forms of proportional representation.
10 Labour's *Green Paper on Devolution*, p.7.
11 Interview with Bernard Ponsonby, 6.4.89.
12 *Sovereignty And Integration*, pp.15-19.
13 Ibid, p.15.
14 Ibid, p.12.
15 *Scottish Independence And the European Community*, p.1.
16 Graham Lait, quoted in *The Scotsman*, 23.5.89.
17 The Scottish Secretary Malcolm Rifkind is the best known former Conservative devolutionist. See *Scotland's Government*.
18 Jim Ross, 'A Fond Farewell to Devolution', in *Radical Scotland* 36.

Hungarian Nation, Hungarian Language

Jerry Payne

The story of the tower of Babel tells how hubris led to the world community's fall from grace. Not quite the original sin but one that was to have consequences equally devastating and long-lasting, for God punished the transgressors by 'confusing' their language and forcing them to communicate in 'strange' tongues. People 'fought on account of the many misunderstandings occasioned by this confusion of language' and were 'dispersed over the globe and divided into nations'. At the very least the Babel story is a remarkably early exposition of the link between language and nation. Many centuries later, when modern nationalism was taking root in Europe, Herder restated the link between language and nation, although this time it was seen in an altogether different light. Herder believed that the individual could only find complete fulfilment through the nation and that language was the transmitter of the nation's heritage and values. Diversity, linguistic and national, was a positive ideal and one actively pursued by liberals in search of social and political reform, particularly those citizens of small nations for whom the precondition of such reform was national emancipation: 'The Herderian concept of national character and its role in the destinies of mankind was to have an incalculable effect on the small nation intellectuals of Europe' (Okey, 77). Nowhere was this more true than in Hungary, and perhaps nowhere was language such a critical component in the definition of what constituted 'national character'.

As the Reform Era got underway in the later decades of the eighteenth century, not only was Hungary particularly backward politically and socially, not only did it remain under Austrian suzerainty, but the Magyar language was under threat of extinction or at least perceived by the liberal reformers to be so. For people eagerly seeking to identify their historical roots and in the process construct a sense of national identity Herder's prediction of a dire fate for the Magyar language and people had a traumatic effect: 'Now they are the smaller part of the country's population, among Slavs, Germans, Wallachians and other peoples, and after some centuries perhaps their language will almost have disappeared' (quoted in Barany, 264).

The perceived threat to a language that was in any case 'alien' in its linguistic environment was exacerbated by the circumstance that Magyar was generally not spoken by the 'nation'. Membership of the *natio Hungarica* was confined to the class of nobles, constituting 5% of the population (10% if those of non-Magyar descent are taken into account) and with the exception of some Szeklers, the descendants of the original settlers in Eastern Transylvania, they did not speak Hungarian. 'The attribute Hungarus or Hungaricus ... was not identical with Magyar ... it did not mean a community of those speaking Hungarian, but a ruling class' (Niederhauser, 197). Latin was the official state language, Magyar the vernacular of the serfs.

Kazinczy and the language 'renewers' set about rescuing the language and succeeded in their aim of modernising and making it fit to serve as the national language. In 1770 János Sajnovics published his seminal comparative study of Lappish and Hungarian, whilst in a book published in 1799 Sámuel Gyarmathi examined all the Finno-Ugrian languages. Their work laid the basis for the acceptance of the Finno-Ugrian group of languages 'as a proven fact' (Hajdu, 17). The renewed language and the survival of the 'common' people who had nurtured it through centuries of neglect and oppression were to play a major role in the emergence of Hungarian nationalism, the 'transformation of Hungarian feudal, or estates nationalism into modern Magyar national consciousness' and an 'identification of language and national character' (Barany p. 261). Although the interest the political elite showed in Magyar was, initially at least, more a counter to Germanising attempts under Joseph II than a positive commitment, they deemed its adoption to be essential if they were to exploit and control growing national sentiment. Hungarian was declared the official language of the state by the 1844 Diet. It went on to become a potent instrument in the revolution of 1848, the finest hour of Magyar nationalism, and the subsequent War of Independence against the Austrians.

The failure of the nation to achieve full sovereignty from the Austrians in this struggle and the repeated setbacks to national aspirations since then may account for what appears to an exaggerated concern for the welfare of the language. The prevalence even today of romantic, Utopian speculations about linguistic and national roots, going far beyond the prosaic findings of academic linguists and ethnographers, could be considered a latter-day symptom of the same insecurity that gripped the Hungarians when Herder first expressed his fears for the future. Such speculations, for all their diversity and lack of scientific rigour, represent an alternative, if eccentric tradition in the business of searching for national roots.

Gyula László has produced a fascinating survey of such theories. The following is a very limited selection from that survey (see László, 104 ff.):

Ferenc Kemény (1975) claims that all Eurasian languages developed, like 'pidgin offspring', from English, from one single original Euroasian 'Kultursprache', namely Magyar. The Magyars were also the creators of agriculture in Europe and the original inhabitants of the Danubian Basin.

Adorján Magyar (1977) flatly denies the existence of any evidence to support the orthodox view that the Magyars came from Asia and that they were nomads. This was, he believes, a fabrication put about by the Habsburgs for their own purposes and swallowed by gullible Hungarians.

According to Jenö Csiscáky (1961), who is responsible for developing the Hungarian version of Churchward's 'Mu' theory, on 13 May, 11,542 BC a volcano swallowed up the continent of Mu (=mother land etc) in the Pacific, where lived the first man, the biblical Adam. The inhabitants of Mu were known as 'Magyák'. They taught the people of the world language, writing, agriculture, mining, navigation, arithmetic etc. Despite the intervening 13,000 years the similarity to present-day Hungarian is 'striking', in both lexis and syntax. The most significant of the three Magyák branches that left

Mu went East; after surviving another disaster, namely the sinking of Atlantis in 7,274 BC, they eventually crossed the straits of Gibraltar and settled in prehistoric Europe, where they gave rise to the ancient Etruscans, Armenians etc. From one such tribe there emerged the Hungarians of today.

Bátor Tóth László Vámos (1976) also refers to the Mu theory and demonstrates that most geographical names, of which he provides a list of 1000, are Hungarian in origin, claiming that Hungarian is the 'most ancient of languages'.

Sándor Csöke (1977) asserts that the Hungarian language 'is Hungarian in origin. It was the product of historical chance. It is an original ancient language, emanating from the transcendental depths, of its own accord ... Ninety-five percent of the Hungarian vocabulary is Hungarian in origin ... it is neither Finno-Ugrian nor Mongolian-Turkic in origin ...' The Hungarian vocabulary is Hungarian, there are no such things as Finno-Ugrian languages, they are the 'invention' of linguists and historians.

Tibor Baráth in a three volume work (1968, 1973 and 1974) rejects the conventional view that locates the origins of the Magyars somewhere in the Volga region and identifies eight ancient homelands of the Magyars, ranging from the valley of the Indus to the American continent, all of which contain unmistakably Hungarian place names. He concludes, however, that the Hungarians spread out originally from the 'Ancient East', i.e. Egypt. There, Magyar was spoken and written by the common people as well as religious and state institutions in the millenia before Christ. The Hungarian peoples 'created ... the first high culture in the history of mankind'.

Finally, one of the more widely held theories, the Sumerian. According to it, Hungarian originated in the area between the rivers Tigris and Euphrates (the presumed location, incidentally of the biblical Babel!). Very briefly: the relationship between Sumerian and Hungarian is demonstrated by 60% of words with a common origin. A close ethnic tie is also postulated. Hungarian is considered to be a direct descendant of Sumerian; the Magyars spread towards the Carpathians, where two or three thousand years of settlement is proved by archeological remains and where their advanced culture and civilization served as an example to the other peoples of Europe.

Common to these Utopian theories is the assumption of a type of conspiracy on the part of non-Hungarians and their Hungarian lackeys, be they academics or politicians, to convince impressionable Hungarians that their origins are somewhat less than heroic; they do not properly belong in Europe, their rights to be where they are (or would like to be!) are less well-established than those of other nations, particularly the Germans and the Slav peoples. In short, the argument is that the Finno-Ugrian theory was an invention designed to put the Magyars in their place and to deny them their birthright. László quotes one such observation made by an adherent of the Sumerian theory: 'Nobody has yet written the history of the contribution made by the Hungarians to the shaping of Europe, therefore it was necessary to squeeze them into the humiliating confines of the theory of their Finno-Ugrian origins' (László, 138). As he arrives at the end of his survey Gyula László is at pains to reassure his readers and reiterates the conventional wisdom of academic linguists and ethnographers, namely that Hungarian is indeed a member of the Finno-Ugrian family of languages and that the origin of the Magyars is to be sought in the Volga region.

Karl Deutsch wrote that 'A nation ... is a group of people united by a common error about their ancestry'. On the strength of the theories outlined above one might be tempted to assume an unusually highly developed sense of national identity among Hungarians. This is anything but the case. The Hungarian psyche is marked by insecurity. There is a strong and persistent conviction among Hungarians that they have had a rough deal from history. That interpretation of events is roughly as follows: St Stephen's Christian kingdom was ravished and devastated by the Mongol invasions from the East, then attacked by the Ottoman Turks from the south, dismembered and occupied by them and the Austrians. The reward for the decades when Hungarian blood was spilled in the defence of Christian Europe against the Turk was incorporation into the Austrian Empire. The glorious revolution of 1848 and the struggle for independence from Austria was quashed by Tsarist armies. Even the 'Compromise' of 1868, which saw a settlement with the Habsburgs and a division of the Empire between Austria and Hungary, was deemed to offer something considerably less than full Hungarian autonomy. The only real period of full independence, the interwar years, was blighted from the beginning by the *diktat* of Trianon, which deprived the Hungarian state of two-thirds of its territory and more than a half of its population, leaving considerable Hungarian minorities outside the frontiers of the truncated state. Reaction and irredentism under the Horthy regency were fuelled by an unfeeling and disinformed *Entente*, which failed to recognize legitimate Magyar claims, with the result that Horthy and his clique concluded a Faustian pact with Nazi Germany. The price for the partial return of lost territory in the Vienna Awards was the loss of sovereignty and eventually occupation by the Germans in 1944. After the war the recently reacquired territory and populations were returned and Rákosi proceeded to impose a particularly vicious brand of Stalinism on the country. The Revolution of 1956 was crushed by a mixture of Soviet tanks and Western indifference.

It has taken the wave of present liberalization in Eastern Europe for a radical reappraisal of Hungary's position in the Soviet sphere to become possible, in particular of the significance of the 1956 Revolution. Only now does Hungary appear to be entering another period of real independence. Unfortunately, the condition for greater autonomy, the Soviet withdrawal, is at the same time likely to increase instability in Eastern Europe, thereby creating an uncertain environment for the development of national aspirations. In addition, any renewed sense of national self-confidence today is inevitably marred by the concern for the fate of Hungarian minorities in surrounding countries, especially in Romanian Transylvania, where an approximately two million strong outpost of Hungarian language and culture is under virtual siege.

The term 'Hungarian' in Transylvania is primarily a linguistic one, in other words it relates not to ethnic origins but to the language spoken, covering not only Hungarians proper, but also Szeklers, Jews and Gypsies. The 1956 census gave the Hungarian population as being 25% of the total, a considerable decline since the first decade of the century when the figures showed the Hungarians in a slight majority (*The Hungarian Observer*, 2-4). Although awareness of the current Transylvanian problem in the Western media only developed relatively recently, in particular in connection with the coverage given to Ceausescu's policy of 'systemisation', Hungarians have long been conscious of the plight of their compatriots. Hostile exchanges at an official level between the two socialist countries are now a commonplace and a historical dimension has been added to the dispute by claims and counterclaims regarding the history of Hungarian Transylvania. The Hungarian leadership now openly claims that the Romanian government is pursuing a systematic policy of discrimination against the Hungarians in Romania, denying them ethnic and cultural rights. Forty refugees are now reported to be crossing into Hungary each day, with 6,490 having crossed the border illegally in 1988. The Hungarian authorities are ignoring the extradition agreement existing between the two governments. In short, Hungary, which traditionally has lost emigrants to the West, has become a recipient of immigrants from the East, a situation made more ironic by reports that Hungarian border guards have started to dismantle the fence running the full length of the frontier with its non-socialist neighbour Austria. The *Hungarian Observer* sums up the conditions in Transylvania as follows:

> ... ethnic Hungarians feel they are subject to a conscious policy of assimilation: under-provision of culture and schools; employment discrimination (members of the Hungarian intelligentsia find it hard to get jobs in Hungarian-speaking areas); linguistic discrimination ... and most recently the policy of erasing villages, which will have devastating social and cultural effects on the rural population, particularly if they belong to an ethno-linguistic minority.

The Transylvanian problem is part of a complex historical legacy, a malaise that has plagued the Hungarian nation since the first stirrings of a Magyar national consciousness in the latter half of the eighteenth century. Formulated briefly, the malaise was rooted in the lack of identity between 'historical Hungary' and the Magyar nation. Demographic developments in preceding centuries meant that by the mid nineteenth century the country which Kossuth and his fellow revolutionaries aspired to emancipate from foreign domination and endow with the democratic freedoms had a non-Magyar majority of Croats, Serbs, Slovaks, Ruthenes and Transylvanian Romanians. Mihály Károlyi claimed that the nationalities problem was ultimately responsible for the failure of 1848, Kossuth's fear of Slav nationalism moving him to sacrifice the interests of the non-Magyar nationalities to the cause of Magyardom (Pálóczy-Horváth, 8). The words Kossuth used to state his case suggests that even for him legitimate national claims had degenerated into something far more messianic. 'I shall never, but never recognise, under the Holy Crown of Hungary more than one nation and nationality, the Magyar' (quoted in Barany, 269). His difficulties consisted, as they did for the German liberals at the same period, in reconciling the conflicting claims of national emancipation and social and political reform.

The 'Compromise' of 1867 was more than a compromise between Austria and Hungary, it also represented a compromise of many of the ideals of social and political reform which had inspired 1848, just as Bismarck's united Germany in 1871 represented a retreat from the ideals of the liberals of the Frankfurt Parliament. What was worse, independence from Austria was to be repeatedly exposed as being less than full. An illustration of the underlying tensions that continued to bedevil relations was the bitter struggle the Hungarian leadership had in asserting the use of Hungarian as a language of military command in the Hungarian half of the Empire (see Stone, 167). The affronts to national pride from the senior partners in the Dual Monarchy were all the more deeply felt in the context of the strenuous efforts that were made to redress the balance of the nationalities in Hungary and to secure Magyar ascendancy.

In the mid nineteenth century the Hungarian leadership had embarked on a programme of Magyarisation in an effort to encourage or force the use of Hungarian by the non-Magyar nationalities. Language became an instrument of policy and for the Magyarisers the predominant criterion of national allegiance. As has already been stated, demographic developments had produced an ethnic mix in which the concept of a 'Magyar nation' defined in strictly ethnic terms had become extremely problematic. The ethnic origins even of many of the major figures in 1848, including the poet-statesman Sándor Petőfi and Lajos Kossuth himself, were non-Magyar, and among the most fervent nationalists later in the century were many whose Hungarian roots were shallow indeed: Szterényi (formerly Stern), Vázsonyi (formerly Weissfeld), Irányi (formerly Halbschuh) and Zsedényi (formerly Pfannenschmied) (Stone, 164). Later attempts by extremists to equate 'Magyardom' with a Magyar 'race' were therefore totally unconvincing. To be Magyar was to profess allegiance to a linguistic/cultural community.

The main Magyarisation drive started in earnest after 1867, although the first measures were introduced in the 1840s, once Hungarian was declared to be the official state language. The chief instrument of Magyarisation was education. Magyar leaders advocated the 'spreading by law of Magyar culture ... they believed that by teaching Hungarian in the schools they would achieve the universal acceptance of Magyar as the state language' (Deak, 44). Legislation was introduced to make possible the imposition of Magyar in the schools, with Hungarian becoming compulsory in primary schools in 1879 and Magyar language and literature similarly becoming obligatory subjects in the upper forms of all secondary schools shortly afterwards. Other laws required every place in the country to have an official Magyar name. In addition, it was made easy for the bearers of non-Magyar names to exchange them for Magyar ones. Officials were strongly urged to do so and as Seton-Watson points out in one of his (relentlessly anti-Magyar) publications in the interwar years such people were known as Crown Magyars because the cost of Magyarising one's name was so slight (Seton-Watson, 33).

Magyarisation was undoubtedly motivated by a not unnatural anxiety for the survival of Magyardom in the multinational state:

> For the recognition that the population of Hungary consisted of more than Hungarians alone became widespread at this time, whilst also forming a source of anxiety. The simplest solution was to Magyarise all the national minorities. They could share all the benefits of the new bourgeois future. (Niderhauser, 207/208)

Mixed with this anxiety, however, was a large measure of arrogance and the desire for supremacy in the lands whose occupation by the Magyar tribes a millenium earlier was celebrated with conspicuous pomp and ceremony in the closing years of the century. For the Magyars the 'Magyar character of the state was axiomatic, and the conduct of the nationalities in and after 1848, and the attitude of Vienna towards them had only confirmed their conviction that the very survival of the Hungarian state depended on the maintenance of its Magyar character' (Macartney, 183). This overriding imperative was pursued at the cost of political and social reforms, thus the Magyar response to liberalising pressures from Vienna was invariably obstructive: 'Reforms can only be fitly and wisely introduced if, as in England, they are brought about gradually ... and such reforms must in no way prejudice the Magyar national state, as it is above all our duty to preserve the predominant character of the Magyar race' (Prime Minister Kálmán Széll, quoted in Stone, 180). As the World War approached, nationalism became increasingly chauvinist, an extreme form represented by Jenö Rákosi's 'primitive linguistic nationalism' and his call for a nation of 30 million Magyars as a defence against pan-Slavism and pan-Germanism (Barany, 283). The interwar years saw a revival of the 'old myth about "historic" Hungary and her mission in defense of Christianity, this time against the Bolshevik danger' (Barany, 291) and the espousal of openly racialist policies, with the development of a 'Ural-Altaic' version of Hitlerian racialism well before the occupation of the country by the Germans, into whose camp the irredentist logic had pushed the country years earlier.

According to Macartney, by the end of the nineteenth century the whole state apparatus was 'exclusively Magyar in feeling and practically so in speech' (Macartney, 185). There were dramatic successes, for example the Magyarisation of the towns. To cite one instance, Budapest was three-quarters German-speaking in 1848, but by the turn of the century when the overall population had increased threefold, it was 79.8% Magyar. Magyarisation of the Germans was 'complete and sincere' (Macartney, 190). Successes such as this, however welcome to the Magyarisers, were highly regrettable to others who considered themselves no less patriotic. A large proportion of the Austrian officials who had been brought in to administer the defeated country in the post-1849 Bach era stayed on and assimilated. In a populist interpretation of Hungarian history, in which he sees the Hungarian malaise chiefly as a product of a social, economic conflict between the 'lords' and the 'common people' and unequivocally identifies with the 'people', Pálóczy-Horváth dismisses this Austrian assimilation as skin-deep and opportunistic:

> ... since they had by this time lived for nearly twenty years in Hungary, had estates there and spoke some Hungarian, they started to change their names. ... Naturally these new Hungarians, these tens of thousands of Habsburg officers, civil servants, police agents and what not, had to make a very loud noise to prove that they were Hungarians. They preached chauvinism ... they became more Hungarian than the Hungarians (Pálóczy-Horváth, 84/85).

Like the many German landowners who also Magyarised their names 'they Germanised them back under Hitler'. Even Gömbös, the 'strong-man' of Hungarian right-wing politics in the 1930s, was, Pálóczy-Horváth reminds us, not Hungarian, but German, his real name being Graner. 'His mother could not speak a word of Hungarian.' He goes on to talk about 'illiterate Swabian petty criminals becoming leaders of true Hungarian culture'. The military who gained the upper hand in the country in the later years of the Horthy regime were 'the generals of German origin who now bragged in their German mother tongue' (123 ff). Although Pálóczy-Horváth recognises the severity of the problems posed by the country's mixed population, he places the ultimate responsibility for them squarely at the door of the 'lords': 'If our lords had not chased us eastwards out of the country for eight hundred years and westwards between 1890 and 1914 [a reference to emigration to the United States, which was approximately 1,500,000 in that period—JP] there would not have been a mixed population problem in Hungary.' (93). It was their unwillingness to surrender their class privileges and to promote real Magyardom that led to the 'Hungarian tragedy': 'Our lords wanted St Stephen's Hungary, we wanted Hungarian Hungary. That was the difference' (112).

To return to the overall effects of the Magyarisation policy, however, the statistics made grim reading for the Magyarisers, the net effect with respect to the avowed aim of radically redressing the imbalance in the country being thoroughly disappointing. Macartney concludes that the 'effect of all the efforts on the ethnic map of Hungary, regarded in broad terms, was practically nil' and points out that a study conducted in 1902 found that of all the nationalities, the Ruthenes had been the biggest losers, then the Magyars, then the Serbs, whilst the greatest gains had had been made by the Romanians, the Slovaks and Germans in that order (Macartney, 187).

The failure of Magyarisation to achieve its aim of assimilating the non-Hungarian nationalities can be ascribed at least partly to the existence of alternative nationalisms with which they could identify and, after Trianon, of nations which they could join. The position of the Jewish population, however, was different and in their case the evidence points to a high degree of assimilation and acculturation.

Large-scale Jewish immigration coincided with the Magyarisation drives between 1840 and 1914, the numbers of (unbaptised) Jews reaching 900,000 by 1910. According to Seton-Watson they were the 'willing instruments' of

Magyarisation (Seton-Watson, 34). Already in the 1840s Eötvös is reported to have trusted in the Jews developing 'their own healthy version of Magyar nationalism' (Deak, 114) and Kossuth to have been ready to receive them with 'open arms' (Deak, 45). Indeed, Jews were emancipated in 1849 as part of Kossuth's belated attempt to reconcile the non-Magyar elements of the population. The emancipation decree was reinforced in 1867. Jews were later to constitute an extremely significant element in Hungarian life and to exercise considerable influence in the professions and industry and commerce. The position they achieved in Hungarian society was stronger than that of the Germans, and even stronger in some fields than that of the Magyars themselves. William McCagg, who provides an extremely comprehensive account of the situation of Hungarian Jewry in the late nineteenth and early twentieth centuries, found as many as 302 Jewish nobles listed in the *Lexicon of Hungarian Jewry*, published in 1929 by the Pest Israelite Community (McCagg, 18). The degree of assimilation was such that Deak talks of the 'aggressive' Magyar nationalism of the Jews at the time of the War of Independence. He also quotes a certain Rabbi Ignác Einhorn writing in 1851 of the,

> common Asiatic origins, the great similarity in the destinies of the Jewish and Magyar peoples, the conspicuous lexicographic and grammatical affinities between the Magyar and Hebrew languages ... (Deak, 115).

This identification is paralleled a century later by a Jewish Hungarian, Móric Rosenberg, resident in the United States after escaping the Hungarian Holocaust, in which an estimated 600,000 Jews were murdered. The parallel is notable for the emphasis placed on a sense of linguistic integration:

> The good Lord saved me then as he had done so often before. I was condemned to live. Yet the monstrous tragedy that was being acted out before our own eyes was not mine alone. This was a tragedy of the whole Hungarian people, of those who, at the command of the Germans, shed their own blood with their own hands. Who can deny that our blood was Hungarian? ... and one day I should like to return to the country of my birth, to the great swamp country. They say that the village houses have two storeys now. But I'm right, aren't I? The Hungarian spoken there is still pure, isn't it? (quoted in Reviczky, 403 ff).

The situation of the estimated 200,000 Jews who survived the Holocaust and remained in the country after 1945 was problematic. They did what society expected of them, namely to deny their Jewishness and become 'true' Hungarians. If they tried to preserve their culture and liturgical language or exercise their religion they were persecuted. One of the consequences of the new openness in present-day Hungary is the lifting of the taboo surrounding anti-semitism and the cultural allegiance of the Jewish community. Jewish consciousness is reported to be growing and increasing numbers of Jews rediscovering their roots (see *Hungarian Observer*, 9). The removal of obstacles to free association have resulted in the creation of the *Cultural Federation of Hungarian Jews*, its aim being to foster Jewish 'culture, consciousness and identity'. One member is quoted as stressing the compatibility of a Jewish consciousness with a feeling of Hungarian identity: 'The words Hungarian and Jew in the name of our organisation are equally important ... We believe that Hungary's Jewish culture is an integral part of Hungarian culture' (*Hungarian Observer* p. 9). However, there is disagreement in the Jewish community over whether legislation on ethnic minorities (which now constitute a very small percentage of the total population) should also cover Jewry or whether the Jewish community should consider itself purely as a religious denonimation.

Whether it was historical accident, a malign fate or, as Pálóczy-Horváth suggests, a hopelessly reactionary ruling class that created the nationalities problem for 'historical Hungary', postwar Hungary has accepted the same national frontiers that were so utterly unacceptable to Horthy's Hungary. These frontiers have secured a 'Hungarian Hungary', in the sense that the overwhelming majority of citizens are now Magyar speaking. And yet, despite the new openness and optimism within the country, the continuing persecution of Hungarian minorities beyond the frontiers is a reminder that the nineteenth century nationalists' dream of an identity between state and nation has not been fully realised and that the nation is still incomplete.

References

Barany, G, 'Hungary: From Aristocratic to Proletarian Nationalism', in *Nationalism in Eastern Europe*, edited by P. Sugar and I. Lederer, Seattle, 1969
Deak, I, *The Lawful Revolution*, New York, 1979
Deutsch, K, *Nationalism and its Alternatives*, New York, 1969
Hajdu, P, *Finno-Ugrian Languages and Peoples*, London, 1975
Gyula, L, *Östörténetünk*, Budapest, 1983
——*The Hungarian Observer* Vol. 2, No. 4, Budapest, 1989
McCagg, W, *Jewish Nobles and Geniuses in Modern Hungary*, New York, 1972
Macartney, C A, *Hungary: a Short History*, Edinburgh, 1962
Niederhauser, E, 'The Emergence of Eastern European Nationalities', Budapest, 1981
Okey, R, *Eastern Europe 1740-1980*, London, 1982
Pálóczy-Horváth, G, *In Darkest Hungary*, London, 1944
Reviczky, A, *Vesztes háborúk, megnyert csaták*, Budapest, 1985
Seton-Watson, R W, *Treaty Revision and the Hungarian Frontiers*, London, 1934
Stone, N, 'Constitutional Crisis in Hungary, 1903-1906', in *The Slavonic Review*, Vol. 45, pp. 163-82, London, 1967

Babel Reversed in Glasgow

Rainer Kölmel

Unlike any other historical event, the Holocaust—the systematic attempt to destroy a people and a culture—has left scholars puzzled and in disagreement. Extensive research has not brought us any closer to explaining why it happened, and why it happened in Germany. On the contrary, opinions have become more divided the further away we move from the events. The passing of time has led the Germans in particular to overcome their 'amnesia' and the 'collective silence' with respect to history and there is now a move towards a redefinition of German identity. It is being carried out partly with the support of the present German government, and suggests the historical relativity of the Holocaust. This revisionist historiography, which became the focus of the Historians' Debate of 1986, does not question the irrefutable evidence of the Holocaust. It does, however, with the aid of comparative historical analyses, attempt to relativize it. A partial denial of the reality of the Holocaust does not help the redefinition of a German identity. It contrasts with the need for a critical appropriation of the past which was supported until recently by almost all Germans.[1]

One of the aims of this paper is to continue the now unfashionable process of enlightenment by looking at the experience of the Holocaust survivors and at the same time to point to humanistic, cultural and left-wing traditions which have remained alive everywhere in Europe throughout the twentieth century and which have built the bridges essential for the survival of a culture and a people. The temporary unity which came about between German-speaking Jews, German-speaking gentile political refugees and members of the receiving culture—in this case that of Scotland—before, during, and shortly after the war, may be seen as a valuable component of a collective European identity. We have no right to relativize the Holocaust but we do have good reason to focus our attention on historical developments which Germans, Austrians and Scots can be proud of.

This article deals with the response to the threat of National Socialism and with the efforts made to help the refugees from racial and political persecution, and with their attempts at self-help. It also deals with aspects of the political and cultural climate at the time, which provided a catalyst for the relief work and international cooperation which occured. It is a case study which focuses on the developments in Glasgow. What happened there was in many ways typical, even though Glasgow and Scotland were fairly far removed from events in Germany; and London, of course, played a much more important role as a haven for mass emigration from Nazi-Germany.

More than 70,000 refugees from Nazi oppression found refuge in Britain, of which only two thousand or so ended up in Scotland—not necessarily of their free choice. They came because there was no room for them elsewhere.

Most of them settled in Glasgow, partly because the city already housed the largest Jewish community in Scotland and also because at the beginning of the war the East coast was declared a *protected area* and the refugees, as enemy aliens, had to move west.

It is probably fair to say that, although they proved to be excellent hosts, most of the Scots had at the beginning little idea of precisely who their guests were. When the first news of racial persecution in Germany reached Scotland some well-meaning Scots suggested that the victims be settled in the Highlands—after all there was plenty of space there! But it is important to recognize that not all Scots were so naive and that there was a strong minority who very early on warned of the dangers of National Socialism and started campaigns to increase the awareness of the impending threat to fellow Jews and to political allies.

The Scottish Jews played a prominent part in enlightening the Scottish population about the way the situation was developing in Germany. They were the first to appeal to the public directly on this issue. The situation was discussed for the first time in the *Jewish Representative Council* in Glasgow on 16 March 1933, and on 27 March the calling of a protest meeting was suggested.[2] From this time onwards, the Jewish community bore the main, if not the entire, burden of refugee relief work. The work undertaken by Glasgow Jews in particular was related to the nature of their community. This had grown enormously following a large influx of immigrants from Eastern Europe at the turn of the century. The shared experience of antisemitic persecution in Eastern Europe represented an enduring link between the Glasgow Jews. They also gathered valuable experience at the time of their own immigration, experience, which was later to benefit German-Jewish refugees.

It was some time before the Jewish community in Glasgow became fully aware of the dangerous position of the Jews in Germany and of the consequences for the whole of the Jewish community. This is not surprising, for the German Jews themselves only gradually became aware of the implications of National Socialist racial policies. Even though the Glasgow Jews were sensitized towards anti-Semitism because of their experiences before emigration, they had experienced hardly any anti-Semitism once they had settled. This was despite the existence of a small Fascist party in Scotland, which was, however, more anti-Catholic-Irish than anti-Semitic.[3] In addition, the Glasgow Jews were predominantly Eastern European in origin and did not feel particularly close to the German Jews. But prominent members of the Glasgow Jewish community maintained contact with Germany through their international trade connections, and therefore had a direct interest in what was taking place in National Socialist Germany. It was these people who were later to lead the protest movement and who initiated the relief measures which followed.

The relief work will not be analysed in detail but it has to be said that the financial burden was difficult to bear because of the economic climate of the time. The economic differences generally apparent between the north and the south of Great Britain were even more accentuated in the case of the Jewish communities of Glasgow and London.[4] Against this background one would expect a certain reluctance to help, in particular as the government emphasised very early on that immigrants could only be admitted if their settlement in Britain was consonant with the interests of the country, and that these interests must predominate over all other considerations,[5] and by 'interests' was meant above all the preservation of the jobs of British citizens.

Because of the strong Zionist leanings, the Jewish community in Glasgow in particular saw one solution to the refugee problem as being the preparation of the refugees for settlement in Palestine. Accordingly, they earmarked their refugee fund subscriptions for Palestine.[6] This was not done with the aim of shirking responsibility. When it finally became clear that refugees would arrive in large numbers directly on their doorstep they did everything they could to alleviate the refugees, plight in spite of the limited resources available to them.

For many Jews from Germany and Austria, particularly for those who had no contacts other than those provided by the voluntary relief organisations, the success of their flight from Germany and Austria depended on the efforts of these organisations to find people prepared to adopt child refugees, to offer apprenticeships in agriculture or industry for young refugees, to find jobs for domestic servants[7] and to provide finance for the continuation of their journey in cases where only transit visas had been granted.

The first to arrive were not a burden on the Scottish and the British population, as the restrictive immigration policy of the British Government proved successful and only those who had sufficient means entered. There were some exceptions, in particular students and academics who received help from the *Academic Assistance Fund*. Most of them had come either to continue their studies or to acquire British qualifications. Medical students in particular favoured Scottish universities, because they could take the final examination of the Triple Qualification Board after only one year, which contrasted with the more restrictive policy of the English colleges.[8]

By 1938 refugees were arriving in larger numbers. By then the political climate had definitely changed. National Socialist racial persecution reached its first cruel high point in the *November Pogrom* of 1938 and as a reaction to it the doors to Britain were opened a little wider. Official policy towards Germany, however, remained the same. Even in the late 1930s invitations to parties in the German Embassy in London were highly sought after in establishment circles.

There were of course also some Scots who saw National Socialism and anti-Semitism as some sort of German disease, which would pass with time. These Scots found it hard to become excited about the suffering of the persecuted Jews and political opposition in Germany.[9] But a majority of Scots, and in particular Glaswegians, had gone through an education which had taught them all about the class enemy and about Fascism. The radical movement which found its expression in the powerful Scottish Labour movement and the parties which represented it made people receptive to the dangers of Fascism. From no other part of Britain did so many young people leave to fight against Franco as from Glasgow. When they returned they became influential elements in a socialist culture concerned to enlighten people about the fascist threat and to unite them against it.

Very important for the thesis of this article is the fact that the 'radical and humanitarian traditions (...) have been largely assimilated by Glasgow Jewry'.[10] One of the most important Jewish social centres in the Gorbals was the Workers' Circle. At the Workers' Circle, above a bakery in Oxford Street near Gorbals Cross,

> ... at almost any hour, in clouds of throat-catching cigarette smoke, men sat and reshaped society, as children tirelessly experiment with plasticine or clay. The Circle was a social and political club, union supported, a gathering place for immigrant Jews. (...) In bookshelves fixed to one wall were rows of revered source books—Mill, Spencer, Marx, Engels, Keir Hardie, Lenin, Kropotkin, de Leon, Kautsky. Heaps of socialist and anarchist papers and pamphlets, dog-eared and tea-stained, lay on a table nearby.[11]

For most of the Glaswegian Jewish immigrants from Russia the revolution was the dawn of human betterment and some of them felt so strongly about it that they decided to return.[12]

Their socialist theory was anti-nationalist. The Jews in the Gorbals were 'cosmopolitan socialists' not essentially of their own choice, but also because of their minority status in the society in which they lived. But they were not isolated in their 'cosmopolitan socialism'. Even though the Labour Party and the ILP had a strong commitment to Home Rule for Scotland at the time and stood up for the independence of India, they were anti-nationalist in regard to Scotland. This also applied to a large extent to the Scottish Communist Party. Although there was more Yiddish spoken in the Gorbals than English, there was nevertheless a unity with the outside world, a link created through socialism.

Jewish immigrants in Glasgow were part of a Socialist counter-culture, which more and more clearly turned against the enemy outside. It was therefore not surprising that almost at the same time as the *Glasgow Jewish Institute Players* put on Clifford Odets' *Till the Day I Die* it was also performed by the *Glasgow Workers' Theatre Group* and the *Clarion Players*. This development of the Socialist Theatre in Glasgow formed an important backdrop for the arrival of the refugees from Nazi-Germany and Austria. It was a very obvious indication of the cosmopolitan outlook of people in Glasgow concerned with the arts. These amateur groups drew from all sorts of international influences. They all aspired to the Stanislavskian ethos. There was an appreciation of the Constructivist achievement in Soviet theatre and an interest in the non-naturalistic side of drama, including the agit-prop of the 1920 *German Workers' Theatre.*

Undoubtedly, however, the strongest influence was the *American Workers' Theatre* and Lee Strasberg and Elia Kazan's *Group Theatre*, who first performed Clifford Odets' plays in the United States. *Till the Day I Die* tells the story of communist underground resistance in Nazi Germany and spells out a strong anti-fascist message. One can assume that several thousand people in central

Scotland saw this and other plays with a similar message put on by the socialist amateur drama groups which included the *Jewish Institute Players*. There can be no doubt that such productions had a strong influence on the awareness of ordinary people in Scotland, as they not only provided entertainment but also a message which fell on fertile ground. In addition, the activities of these groups were not restricted to stage performances. One form of performance was the Living Cartoon. An active participation in all political demonstrations and May Day processions was part of it. Political figures of the day were caricatured, such as May Day 1938 with Hitler as 'The Butcher of Austria' or on May Day 1939 when the theme was 'The Slaughter of Albania and the Enslavement of Abyssinia'.[13]

When the refugees first arrived they were strangers and in no way better off than other refugees before them. Contact with the indigenous population was direct in the first instance, because they were of course largely dependent on their hosts, particularly in the case of those who arrived after 1938 and did not have sufficient means to support themselves. This applied very clearly to the children, who came in large numbers through the efforts of the *Movement for the Care of Children* from Germany. More than 300 children were put in the care of the *Glasgow Jewish Refugee Children's Aid Committee*. As not enough foster parents could be found some of them were put up in hostels.

This and other forms of segregation were to last throughout the war. Even though on the surface the atmosphere was ideal there were of course many reasons why newcomers would feel different and would stay different for the time being. First of all they had gone through an experience of persecution, which even the well-meaning Jews and socialists in Glasgow could not understand. They had left family, possessions and a culture behind. They were uprooted and felt utterly and totally insecure. Most of them did not speak the language. They experienced culture shock which even today can be shared by people who come from the continent to Glasgow for the first time. They entered another world and they experienced alienation without the Glaswegians wanting to be alienists.

> I arrived at Central Station at the time and it was awful. To us it looked dirty. I was shocked the way the shops were. Food was handled by hand, which was not done in Germany at the time. The way they washed the dishes; all in one dirty water. ... We were dressed differently. You could spot us a mile away and we continued to dress in the continental style because we could not afford new dresses and we had brought tons of them from Germany because that was about all we could take out. One large suitcase even arrived during the war and I don't know how my father got that away.[14]

A similar indication of the alienation of the newly arrived refugee is given by Chaim Bermant, who tells us in great detail stories about his contacts with young Jewish refugees from Germany. He points out:

> On the other hand, as we observed with envy, there was little that was 'green' about the refugees, and certainly anyone brought up in Berlin or Vienna, or even Karlsruhe was unlikely to be overawed by Glasgow Jewish society. Indeed,

they were hardly in it before they took the measure of it, and were out of it. They were widely read, cultivated people and where they remained part of the community enriched it immensely, but in the main they kept to themselves.[15]

And they did indeed found their own organisations in Glasgow at an earlier stage than in London. The *Austrian Jewish Club* was founded in summer 1939 in the University Union and the *Society of Jewish Refugees* followed in early 1940 to be supplemented by *Glasgow Refugee Voluntary Help, Lend a Hand*, later to be called *Refugee Mutual Aid Society* and still in existence today. The foundation of these organisations met with some initial resentment on the part of the Glasgow Jewish community; indeed there were acrimonious arguments between the two groups for several years.[16] The Glasgow Jewish community demanded unity with their co-religionists. In the end it was appreciated that the newcomers needed a period in which they could give each other mutual support because of the common experience they had gone through.

The alienation of the refugees was not exactly alleviated by the introduction of the internment policy. Refugees who had just started to settle down were rounded up overnight and taken to internment camps, most of them on the Isle of Man. If there was any danger of a 'fifth column'[17] operating in Britain, the British created the conditions for it with internment. But it was a fifth column of a different kind. Refugees became very close. Lasting friendships were formed. They saw themselves under pressure to express opinions. Young people who up till then had no idea about politics were now exposed to some of the most politically aware men and women on the island. When they were released they had a much clearer idea of their position in the host society. They joined the war effort, became politically active or created social circles which gave them protection in an alien culture. Many of the refugees immediately joined the British Forces.

One of these new centres of refugee activity was opened in Glasgow immediately after the first Germans and Austrians were released from internment. The *Austrian Centre* in London, which had been founded on 16 March 1939 and had as its first president Sigmund Freud, served as a model. In fact the *Association of Austrians* became the core of what was to be called the *Glasgow Refugee Centre* and later the *Scottish Refugee Centre* and it remained affiliated to the *Austrian Centre* all through the war.

The *Scottish Refugee Centre* was a truly international centre, located right in the centre of the city in a large house in Sauchiehall Street.[18] It was international in the sense that it was open to all refugees from all countries under Nazi rule and that it was also visited by Scots. Only refugees from Nazi oppression could become ordinary members, but every British subject could be a guest. The impression remains therefore that there was something exclusive about the centre. According to its constitution its aims were to enrich the cultural and social life of all refugees from Nazi oppression living in Scotland; to organize self-aid among them and to strengthen the links of friendship with the Scottish people. It was also stressed that the Centre was a 'completely unpolitical club'.

What links of friendship were created with the Scottish people and how unpolitical was the club? Refugees leave no doubt about the great warmth with which they were received by the Glaswegians. They were poor but prepared to provide the financial help without which the Centre could not have functioned.[19]

There were numerous activities directed at Scottish audiences which made contact with the Scottish population possible. Concerts and plays were put on and craft shows were organized and in that sense the centre's activities did not remain exclusive. Apart from that the continental cafe and restaurant in the Centre were open to guests. This on the surface was propably the most important feature of the Centre's activities.

Below the surface there was more. The Centre was possibly unpolitical only in the sense that it was an unpolitical umbrella under which all kinds of political people and organisations met.[20] And in any case how could the refugees have been unpolitical in war-time Glasgow? Their status as such was political. There were a number of refugees, though not many,[21] in the Centre who had come because they were part of the political opposition to Hitler. One would assume that they represented the core of the Centre, in particular those who had occupied such prominent positions in Weimar Germany such as Hugo Graef, a former communist deputy of the *Reichstag*. He did in fact give the impression of running the Centre, but probably mostly because he was there all the time, keeping a little office on the second floor.

More central were the activities of the *Youth Club of Czechoslovak, German and Austrian Refugees*. The young people were most in need of each other's company and above all in need of solutions which could be offered in their search for a future. They were deeply involved in discussions about how Hitler came to power, how the war started, and about socialism as an answer to it all. They felt a tremendous hunger for knowledge, most of them having been deprived of any formal education long before their departure. They organized seminars and discussion groups and a kind of Youth University, consisting of various educational classes, such as Literature, Music, Economics, The Jewish Question, English Language, Shorthand, etc. Henry Wuga remembers: 'it was intellectually very stimulating. The discussions were fairly high powered and ranged from philosophy to medicine and from art to music. Our elders were very educated academics. It was a hotbed of information and very stimulating indeed.'[22]

With a number of activities they turned to the outside world. And these activities are the most interesting because they had to be delivered in a form which was comprehensible to the Glaswegian population. This meant that music and the theatre were the most obvious. By using these art forms they could also avoid having to make any clear political statement, which was not asked for from Austrians and Germans even if they had a history of persecution. Even the Labour-run Glasgow Council was reluctant to openly support the *Refugee Centre*.

But it was different when these young people showed their commitment to the war effort, by organizing 'Dramatic Evenings' to which the Glaswegian population was invited. The first one took place on 28 February 1940 at Glasgow University under the patronage of Sir Hector Hetherington and the second on 31 January 1941 in the Glasgow School of Art under the patronage of Sir John Richmond, K.B.E. Up until mid 1941 the *Refugee Youth Club* had arranged about 30 smaller performances in churches, halls, cinemas, and under the auspices of such societies as the *Society of Friends* or the *Burns Society*.[23] They also left Glasgow and travelled right up to the north of Scotland,

> ... where we took songs from Czechoslovakia, songs from the Spanish War, from Germany and then we had *Sprechchöre*, but we did not only do that, we wanted to let the Scots know how much we appreciated living here. We recited Burns at them with rather strange accents and they bore with us with a great deal of pleasure and even more tolerance.[24]

They also participated in May Day parades and showed banners which read: 'Austrians for their Homeland fight on the Danube and the Clyde'. Particularly active was the Centre's campaign for a second front as part of which young speakers from the Centre addressed union meetings and rallies. There was a passionate belief that the Soviet Union should not carry the burden of the fight against fascism alone. The young refugees themselves wanted to fight on this second front.

Through all these activities the young refugees made contact with Glaswegian groups which had been involved in similar forms of agitation for some considerable time. There were of course formal contacts with the ILP, the CP, the Labour Party, the Scottish Co-operative Society, and the STUC. Some of these contacts were sealed through sponsorships, others through a solid common foundation in theory.

But much more important were the informal contacts which arose during those war years between refugees from the Centre and Glaswegians. The Centre was situated in a part of town which was dominated by the School of Music and Drama, the Art College which was in Renfrew Street immediately behind the Centre and by the University. Quite a few of the younger refugees lived in the Garnethill Synagogue Hostel, others in Bath Street and Hill Street. When war broke out the various progressive theatre groups mentioned above came together as the *Glasgow Unity Theatre*. *Glasgow Unity Theatre* was 'no symbolic or political name. ... It was the result of amateur theatre in crisis due to members being called up, the halls they used being requisitioned, lighting problems, scarcity of theatrical materials and so on.'[25] The new rehearsal rooms of the *Unity Theatre* were in Scott Street just around the corner from the Centre. The place in Scott Street was not just a democratically run theatre but also a political entity, held together by a common anti-fascist aim. But not just the theatre and its political aims characterized this place. There were also discussions on music and painting and it is easy to discover an affinity with the *Refugee Centre*. Consequently contacts between the two establishments were numerous and intensive. The lack of male actors in town led to refugees participating in productions not only on stage but also backstage in all sorts of functions.[26]

There were other contacts with the art world. Glasgow had become the home of two prominent Polish artists, Josef Herman and Jankel Adler, who had both escaped from Poland before the German invasion and by some coincidence ended up in Glasgow where they found support from the Glasgow Jewish Community, which organized their first exhibitions. Josef Herman who lived in Glasgow between 1940 and 1943 made a particularily strong impact. Close contacts with Benno Schotz, the head of sculpture, one of the few teachers at the college open to outside influences, with Helen Biggar, Joan Eardley and Tom Macdonald were established. Here we again find a link with the theatre, as Herman spent much time in and around the Unity. Visits to the Refugee Centre are not recorded, but must have been frequent. 'There were other memories too. Memories of singing voices, abstract memories, memories of the splendor of the Yiddish theatre (that theatre, by the way, was my strongest influence) and memories of early readings.'[27]

Unity was upheld for a long time in the Centre. As late as 1943 different political groups still mangaged to pool resources for a massed 'Unity Concert'. That kind of cooperation was unheard of in London at the time. It must have been the supportive mood of the city which kept them all so close together. But the news about the Holocaust did in the end prove tragically divisive. All the political groups in the centre had worked towards a return to Germany and Austria after the war but when it dawned on the Jewish refugees what had really happened to their families and friends, they realized that there was nothing to go back to. Humanity had committed the ultimate sin.

Almost all of the 150 or so members of the *Refugee Youth Group* were Jewish. They had received a thorough political training, some of them had become members of cadres of the Austrian Communist Party. They had to realize that the Party was not a representative body of Jewish Refugees. This was one of the reasons why the *Society of Jewish Refugees* had kept a distance from the Centre throughout the war. Some of the younger refugees now also realized that their Jewish identity after all needed more expression than it had received in the Centre during the war years. They left the Centre. Only very few returned to Austria and Germany.

The spirit of unity did however survive the war years, albeit more in its artistic expression. When the *Scottish Refugee Centre* closed at the end of 1945 and the Unity Theatre appropriately took over the premises they inherited something of the Centre's atmosphere. People could now discover the *Unity Theatre* and Wiener Schnitzel at the same time, as Frau Alexander was still running the restaurant.[28]

But the impact which the influx of German and Austrian Refugees had on Glasgow was certainly more than just that. They had brought with them a social atmosphere of their own which by the end of the war was easily absorbed by those who were open to this continental influence. And it so happened that these people were also open to the refugees' political aspirations. There was a very lively communication between local left-wing groups and the Centre. Both Scots[29] and young Austrian and German Jews received formative political and humanistic schooling in the Centre. For Scots and refugees this spirit of unity across political barriers was also important. The fact that this unity was of course enhanced by the war effort and the common enemy is another matter. There was a unity on a very subtle cultural basis, one which united the Scottish sculptor with the Polish painter and the Unity Theatre player with an Austrian dancer. Against a background of left-wing politics and the war effort there was something of a cosmopolitan culture developing in Glasgow which was unique for Britain. And it was possible not only because of special conditions at the time. It was also possible because of the nature of the city and its people, best described by Josef Herman:

> I walked the streets of that gaunt Scottish city and all I could see was what memory wanted me to see: a fabric of distant life which was nonetheless part of me; men and women in the refinement of a unique spirit. Most of them poor, certainly, but I saw them in an aura which I can only describe as enchantment.[30]

Notes

1 Norbert Kampe, 'Normalizing the Holocaust? The Recent Historians' Debate in the Federal Republic of Germany'. In: *Holocaust and Genocide Studies*, Vol.2, No.1 pp. 61-80, 1987

2 Minutes, *Jewish Representative Council*, Glasgow, JRC Archive

3 Tom Gallagher, *Glasgow the Uneasy Peace*, Manchester 1987, p. 157

4 In 1936 more than 50 per cent of the Glasgow Jews lived in the Gorbals, a slum area. Many of them were unemployed and themselves dependent on assistance from the welfare organisations of the secular and religious communities. Ralph Glasser paints a very sypathetic but also gruesome picture of the Gorbals in the twenties and thirties:'Malnutrition was rife in the Gorbals, exacerbating any abnormalities from birth. Rickets was common.' Ralph Glasser, *Growing up in the Gorbals*, London 1987, p 2

5 A J Sherman, *Island Refuge: Britain and the Refugees from the Third Reich, 1933-1939*, London, 1973, pp. 27-8

6 *Jewish Echo*, 20 January 1939

7 A 'Domestic Bureau' had been established on the initative of the Quakers and was responsible for the placement of women and married couples as domestic servants in Scotland. A total of more than 1200 cases were processed by the Domestic Buereau, but the Home Office only granted work permits for half of them. *Minutes*, 27 November 1939, G1/3/41, Strathclyde Regional Archives, and *Jewish Echo*, 9 May 1941.

8 Kenneth E Collins, 'German Refugee Physicians in Scotland 1933-1945', in *Remembering for the Future*, Theme I: Jews and Christians during and after the Holocaust, Oxford 1988, pp. 283-295.

9 *The Scotsman*, 10 April 1934, quoted in A Sharf, *The British Press and the Jews under Nazi Rule*, London 1964, p. 64

10 Chaim Bermant, 'Does Glasgow speak for the Jewish conscience?' *Jewish Chronicle*, 30 September 1988

11 Ralph Glasser, op.cit., pp. 6-7

12 Flora Leipman, *The Long Journey Home*, London 1987

13 Douglas Allen, 'The Glasgow Workers Theatre Group', in *New Edinburgh Review*, No. 40 1978, pp. 14-17

14 T. G. *Interview*, 28/12/88

15 Chaim Bermant, *Coming Home*, London 1976, pp. 49-50

16   Rainer Kölmel, 'Problems of Settlement', in *Exile in Great Britain*, edited by Gerhard Hirschfeld, Leamington Spa 1984, pp. 266-270

17   Peter and Leni Gillman, *Collar the Lot, How Britain Interned and Expelled its Wartime Refugees*, London 1980, pp 109-110

18   It was first founded on 24 January 1941 and located at 189 Pitt Street. In February 1942 it moved to 358 Sauchiehall Street.

19   A number of donors were mentioned in the 1941 report of the Centre's activities, such as private individuals including Sir Daniel Stevenson, Dr M Anderson and her sister W Anderson. The Society of Social Service payed the rent for some period of time, The Kinning Park Co-operative Society gave a grant for the purchase of furniture and decorations. The Scottish National Council for Refugees, based in Edinburgh, gave a grant, which was used to pay water, gas, electricity and coal bills. The Churches and Co-operative societies gave money. Some money was collected at concerts and plays performed by the Refugees. *Report of the Glasgow Refugee Centre* Glasgow 1941, p. 4

20   Most of the important political exile organistions were started in Glasgow at about the same time as in London. There were branches of the Free Austrian Movement, the Free German Movement, Free German Cultural Union, Free German Youth.

21   There were about thirty political refugees in Glasgow, most of them were Communists, only two were Social Democrats.

22   Henry Wuga, *Interview*, 1988 BBC Scotland Archive

23   *Report* 1941, op. cit., p. 14

24   Interview with Edith Prais, 1977, p. 6

25   Willison Taylor, 'The Unity Theatre Years', in *Tom Macdonald, 1914-1985* Glasgow 1986

26   Peter Kramer, London started his career in theatre lighting with the Unity Theatre in Glasgow during the war. *The House on the Hill* BBC Scotland, 27/2/89

27   Josef Herman, 'Notes From A Glasgow Diary: 1940-1943', in *Scottish Art Review*, Vol XIII, No. 3 (1972)

28   Edward Boyd, 'A Word on the Blackboard', in *New Edinburgh Review*, No. 40, 1978

29   Jenny Buchan, MEP, claims to have had her political outlook formed in the Centre during the war. *Glasgow Herald*, 11 August 1988

30   Josef Herman, op. cit.

I want to thank Karl Blau, Janey Buchan, Geoffrey Cameron, Ernst Fettner, Vincent Flynn, Trudy Galetzka, Bet Low, Kenneth Miller, and Ida Schuster for helping me find valuable new evidence.

Concepts of Proletarian Literature in France from the Turn of the Century to the Popular Front

Andrew Hunter

For many, the most obvious divisive barriers which persist in our global society as it approaches the twenty-first century continue to be race, culture and language. However in the industrial democracies, the barrier of class has played a not insignificant role in heightening social tensions. Class has always been a subject of debate among ideologues on the one hand attempting to create or destroy political myths, or social scientists on the other, reaching for definitions likely to encompass the complex interrelationships which operate within society. Many of these arguments are well rehearsed and commonplace but while they may be fascinating in their own right, if only because of the constant process of mutation to which they are subject, they do not concern us here in their most direct form. It is rather a tangential by-product of class awareness which is the subject of this study which aims to show that cultural tensions arising from class awareness did, for a brief period in France, produce creative writing of a kind which had hitherto been unknown in any developed form. It is not inappropriate in the context of this volume to consider how the notion of class found expression in art and specifically literature in many western countries as the spread of literacy towards the end of the nineteenth century through the establishment of compulsory elementary schooling provided the enabling factor. France has been chosen because of the intensity of debate which has always surrounded the arts in general and committed art in particular.

Jules Ferry's educational reforms of 1881 and 1882 carried with them their price; the inculcation of republican values, which although comparatively liberal, were preponderantly middle-class in essence and hardly likely to inspire working class youth in their efforts to define self with respect and assurance. In all probability the little bit of culture that was transmitted only served to underline, from the recipient's point of view, the amount of culture he did not possess and his limited opportunities of doing anything further about it. Respect for culture and respect for the possessors and creators of that culture could even, under these circumstances, be viewed as a means of effecting class control. Certainly the long working day and general fatigue experienced by the industrial proletariat did little to encourage the pursuit and development of culture after the period of compulsory schooling. It is not surprising that statements by workers on culture did not really appear in France until around the First World War when the first beneficiaries of the Ferry reforms were reaching maturity and able to benefit from somewhat rare workers' evening classes. These statements will be considered in due course but it is important to appreciate first of all the background established by the liberal intellectual debate centred on culture and the proletariat which had been going on at least since the 1840s in France.

There was a genuine fear of the labouring masses in nineteenth century France. Stendhal and Balzac give eloquent expression to the animal nature of the mob which was subsequently reinforced by Zola and the other naturalists. Ever since the Revolution of 1789, the nations of Europe had been listening carefully to class rumblings in France and it is not unusual to find reflections in British journals throughout the nineteenth century on the state of France. In the following excerpt from an article which appeared in translation in a Glasgow Music revue of 1844 describing the civilising (if not disarming) effects of culture on the Parisian masses, one can detect the fear of social revolution referred to above in the earnest if not patronising desire to soothe the savage breast with 'Culture'.

> Governments which seek to secure the affections of the masses will do well to attract their confidence by procuring for them, as far as power lies within *their* hands, work, education, and amusement. Let the industrious poor, when assailed by the solicitations of the factories, be able to reply—'We too, have our share in the distribution of the social enjoyments; that share is adapted to our simple tastes and proportioned to our scanty leisure. With it we are content; and, far from striking at a social condition of things in which we hold an honourable place, we are ready to defend it against every species of attack.[1]

The historian Michelet was one of the first French intellectuals to make a plea for a more human understanding of the working class. But Michelet was no ordinary middle class intellectual but rather the son of a printer in whose workshop he had worked as a boy. He was specifically concerned by a process of class alienation which worked in two directions. In his work Le Peuple (1846), Michelet warned against dehumanising stereotyped views of the masses as entertained by the bourgeoisie;

> There are no more contacts with the masses. The bourgeois' only acquaintance with them is through the Police Gazette. He sees them in his servant who steals from his and mocks him. He sees them from behind windows; the drunk man down there, shouting, falling and rolling in the mud. He does not realise that the poor wretch is more honest than the retail and wholesale poisoners who have put him into this sad state. The future of our country is in your hands, rich people of France, but you will have to rid yourselves of your fear of the masses, you will have to get to know them and cast aside these fables which have nothing to do with reality. You must get on with each other, you must open up your hearts and speak to each other as fellow human beings.[2]

Michelet was convinced that art and in particular drama had a vital role to play in this rapprochement of the social classes,

> Theatre is the most powerful means of educating and bringing men together; it is our best hope for the regeneration of our society.[3]

In so saying, Michelet was returning to the republican tradition of didactic drama of the Revolution (of which there are countless examples) all extolling revolutionary and republican ideals. The audio-visual advantages contained in theatre as an art form obviously made it a most attractive pedagogical device.

These observations were made two years before the bitter popular revolt of 1848 and the institution of the IInd Republic. When Romain Rolland devoted a whole treatise to the problem of the masses and theatre in 1903,[4] the Paris Commune had engraved itself in the revolutionary consciousness of the people whilst the Dreyfus Affair had driven intellectuals into opposing ideological camps. Michelet's conciliatory theories lacked credibility in a more and more divided French society. Rolland did not believe that the role of the generous liberal bourgeois intellectual should be to introduce the grateful proletariat to the world's great classics, but rather that both could and should unite in the struggle for the realisation of a better society in which cultural alienation would cease to exist together with all the other forms of alienation;

> We are not bringing culture to the People, we are calling on the People to help us bring about Culture.[5]

The overtones of the strength of class collaboration in a common ideological cause as exemplified by the Dreyfus Affair are unmistakably present in these sentiments. But Rolland believed that before the proletariat could be expected to make its contribution to universal art, its own condition had to be transformed which put the whole question of art and the proletariat squarely into the political arena;

> You want a People's art? First you must have a People intellectually capable of enjoying it, a People with leisure time, liberated from poverty and which doesn't swallow all the superstitions and fantasies of Left and Right. A People controlling its own destiny and triumphant in the struggle which is going on at the present time.[5]

Jean Jaurès echoed these sentiments in that he deplored any theory of art which was class based be it bourgeois, proletarian or otherwise. In his opinion, true art was classless and could only be created and communicated fully in a classless society. It was the task of the socialists to achieve that society

> It is we who will create human art for the first time ever; until now there have only been shreds of human art because humanity itself has been in shreds.[6]

In the meantime, it was accepted by intellectuals of the left that art could be enrolled in the service of the socialist struggle; Rolland was not alone in believing that art could have a role to play. Jules Valles, the popular intellectual hero of the Commune and editor of the *Cri du Peuple* wrote many articles to this effect and similar writing was going on in other left-wing journals such as *Le Peuple*, *Le Mouvement Socialiste*, and *La Petite République*.

The Naturalist Paul Alexis, writing in the *Cri du Peuple* in 1883 had this to say with regard to the natural alliance between socialists and naturalists;

> What are the naturalists doing? Without jumping to premature conclusions and using analysis as a tool, they are preparing the socialist "ground" by identifying some fragments of truths which will be useful in creating a future society which will be more equitable . . . Naturalists are socialists in the realm of ideas while socialists are naturalists by their very deeds.[7]

Robert Caze writing in the same publication that same year made an even more dramatic claim for the effectiveness of naturalist writing in the cause of socialism;

> The proletariat understands *L'Assomoir* better than Karl Marx's *Das Kapital*.[8]

Thus far, all the theory concerning the proletariat and culture had come from middle class sources. By the end of the First World War new strands of thinking about art and the proletariat were emerging from genuine working class intellectuals. It is not surprising that the revolutionary syndicalists should have been the most ardent champions of a possible proletarian art, which should not, of necessity, be enlisted as a propaganda weapon in the class struggle, but should be the artistic expression of the working class experience and condition. In other words, the proletarian writers claimed as much right to reflect their own lives and experience as bourgeois writers. This independent stance, independent of political parties and middle class literary coteries (the proletarian writers were particularly wary of the populists), was to provide a source of much friction and debate in the inter-war years as the French communist party, acting on the orders of the International sought to impose revolutionary policies on the socialist and syndicalist left. The situation was further complicated in that within the French party there existed a variety of opinions on the matter which did not necessarily reflect the Moscow line.[9]

But what was the intellectual itinerary of French 'écrivain prolétarien'? Henry Poulaille, son of a carpenter and a chair caner, orphaned and apprenticed to a pharmacist at the age of twelve, is one of the most striking examples of this school of writers. He was recognised by his contemporaries as the leading figure in the grass roots proletarian school. He launched an important revue, *Le Nouvel Age Littéraire*, contributed to other publications such as Henry Barbusse's *Monde*, and generally led the way in a literary movement which had more to do with the tenets of anarcho-syndicalism than any other body of political theory of the reovlutionary left. Poulaille was not a priori against bourgeois intellectuals and indeed recognised his debt to those who gave of their time to teach in the 'universités populaires'; for example he pays unstinted tribute to the Université Populaire of the Faubourg Saint-Antoine and in particular to the philosopher and writer, Han Ryner;

> I remember the first time, it was when I was coming out of a lecture given by

Han Ryner at the Faubourg Saint Antoine Universite, I had accosted the old man just as he was getting ready to leave . . . I asked him some questions to which he replied and then he asked me a few in turn, I had the impression that a real dialogue between fellow human beings was taking place and it lasted a good ten minutes. He shook me by the hand . . .[10]

Poulaille was fifteen years of age at this time. He was to become the most prolific and influential of the proletarian writers.

Poulaille collaborated closely with Marcel Martinet, son of working class parents, who, thanks to the republican meritocracy eventually graduated from the Ecole Normale Superieure, became a most articulate defender of la littérature prolétarienne, and for a short period, literary editor of l'Humanité. Martinet and Poulaille believed in an anarchist interpretation of proletarian culture which had to be (a) based on authentic first-hand experience of life and (b) the fruits of one's labour. This was indeed a broad church reflecting the work-based ethos of anarcho-syndicalism which in theory could transcend purely class based limitations. Thus Poulaille considered Edouard Peisson, a ship's officer as being a 'proletarian' writer because his writings were based on his professional life. Similarly the writing of Louis-Ferdinand Céline was admired by Poulaille because it contained elements reflecting Céline's professional life as a doctor.

The relationship between the PCF and the anarcho-syndicalist inspired proletarian writers was one of great tension as the Party sought to discredit and eliminate all competition on its left. Such policies were difficult for some communist intellectuals to take; especially those whose socialism had been nurtured by the old French humanitarian traditions of the French revolutionary left. One of these was the novelist Henri Barbusse whose novel Le Feu published during the First World War depicted so courageously (he narrowly escaped being tried for treason) the terrible conditions confronting front line soldiers. In his novel, Barbusse projects himself as the spokesman of the martyred poilu and there can be no doubting of this middle-class intellectual's affection for, and commitment to, the proletariat. Barbusse's sentimental attachment to the working class cause disposed him kindly towards Poulaille and his fellow-writers to the extent that they were given space in the review Clarte, the journal of the pacifist movement of the same name organised by Barbusse. Barbusse's soft-centred socialism which caused him to maintain open house to all who seemed interested in changing society, eventually cost him his review as it was infiltrated and taken over by the surrealists. This was particularly galling to the PCF since funding for the review had been provided by the Comintern. The next publication with which Barbusse was connected was the weekly pacifist newspaper Monde. This publication was also financed by Moscow on the understanding that Barbusse would allow it to become a platform for proletarian art and literature. However Barbusse's definition of proletarian literature and that of Moscow did not coincide. Whereas in the first few years following the October revolution, Lenin welcomed the principle of bourgeois 'fellow travellers', the accompanying proletcult or worker based movement in the USSR, eventually began to distance itself from the middle-class intellectuals becoming very left-wing in the process. The proletcult 'writers' were fiercely committed to the October revolution, whereas the French proletarian writers were deeply suspicious of any group or organisation which limited their freedom as artists. Barbusse continued during the rabid years of the Comintern's 'class against class' policies to show sympathy to the indigenous French proletarian writers. It was therefore not without some irritation that the French Party saw Barbusse allowing a platform to the mostly anarchist proletarian writers in the form of a whole page in which they could air their theories, publish reviews etc.

In 1930, two years following the foundation of *Monde*, a special congress of the International Association of Revolutionary Writers (a Comintern organisation of proletcult tendencies) was held in Kharkov in the Soviet Union. Barbusse although summoned to attend, did not do so claiming ill health. Two French Party members, albeit lacking official invitations, did make the journey; the film critic Georges Sadoul, and the surrealist Louis Aragon. It was obvious that Barbusse was to be severely censured by the Societ proletarian writers which may explain why he did not attend in person. A statement from Barbusse was read out in which he defended his policy of offering a platform in *Monde* to the French proletarian writers. This was greeted by a severe reprimand from the Soviet delegation in which Poulaille was described as a 'social fascist'. At this point Aragon jumped to his feet and made the following statement;

> I think it is abundantly clear that his [Barbusse's] base is nothing other than an upstart grouping of some petty bourgeois who are using the theme of the proletariat in their novels and think they have done enough to call themselves paid up members. This school of writing has to be purely proletarian under the control of the avant garde of the proletariat and its best defender i.e., the communist party. It has to develop quite apart from bourgeois literature; if there is the slightest contact, it will be harmful. The only concrete work which merits the name of proletarien literature in the context of the class struggle in France at the present time is that of the worker correspondents. According to the different sections of the Comintern their movement has not developed uniformly throughout the world but it cannot be denied that the only basis for a proletarian literary movement should, nay must, be in the work of the rabcors.[11]

This surprise attack on Barbusse, even if it did reflect proletcult policy was badly received by the delegates who rounded warmly on this renegade surrealist and bourgeois degenerate. But to what proletarian policy was Aragon referring and who were the 'rabcors'? Herein lies one of the sources of tension in France since within *l'Humanité*, there were elements who wished to apply Soviet cultural policy directly (and somewhat mechanistically) to France. Whereas in *Monde* a French definition had been found for 'culture proletarienne' it seemed to owe more to anarchism than Marxism.

The rabcors (worker correspondents) were created by the Soviet cultural shock troops sent out into factories and the countryside in the years immediately following the October revolution. Their task was to spread literacy and to procure from the workers, statements about their hopes and aspirations as well as cameos of their working lives. The objective was to fill Pravda with their work and at the highest point of this campaign it is said that three pages of the newspaper were being filled each day. By giving over a page of *Monde* to the French proletarian wroters, Barbusse could be said to have been following the Moscow line. Of course these writers were more sophisticated than their Soviet counterparts, and were actually writing novels, auto-biographies and collections of poems; in other words, Barbusse had interpreted the line in terms of the situation as it existed in France. Unfortunately for him, *l'Humanité* had adopted the Moscow line and was publishing work from French 'rabcors'. The French effort began in 1927 and was intended to mark the 10th anniversary of the October revolution. Four hundred letters were received following the first appeal for material; most of these praised the USSR and its communist regime. Continuing response showed that many workers were eager to have their letters published in the Party daily. The number of registered correspondents from 15 March to 15 June of that year increased from 351 to 648; by September there were 866. The number of letters received by the editors of *l'Humanité* over the summer period was just over one thousand. Some 60% of these came from workers, 10% from peasants and 15% petit-bourgeois; only 0.5% were from women. The standard was disappointingly low with many letters descending into tales of personal grievances between workers and foremen or just plain repetition of political commonplaces. One correspondent in the review *Correspondance Internationale* (financed by and dictated to by the International), pointed out that the French rabcors had little or no understanding of the current ideological issues as defined by the International; in short their letters did not contain attacks on the 'reformist' trade unions or the social democratic parties, the true enemies of commumism;

The pathetic utterances often conceal a great lack of clariry.[12]

It was obvious therefore that the rabcor experiment had failed in France to the extent that it had become a source of embarrassment for the Party. Against this somewhat tense background of the failure of the proletcult ideal to meet French Party tastes, Barbusse insisted on promoting a broader concept of revolutionary literature in which the proletarian writers of Poulaille's and Martinet's stamp were deliberately included. In August 1928, he organised an enquiry into the nature of revolutionary art and solicited responses from over fifty members of the literary and philosophical community. Of course this was a well tried method to induce famous figures to make public statements on their ideological commitment; the replies constitute a precious record of prevailing attitudes. Some fifty responses were published with not a few famous names included such as Jean Cocteau, Han Ryner, André Breton, Miguel de Unamuno and Upton Sinclair. The questions were simple but revealing and designed to illicit a response to current and classical Marxist dialectic as applied to artistic production.

1. Do you believe that artistic and literary creation concerns purely the individual?

2. Do you believe that there are such things as art and literature which express
the aspirations of the working class? What, according to you are the main
examples?[13]

André Breton's response to the first part of the question rejected as mech-
anistic this over-simplified mixture of ideology and sociology of literature.

> Under these conditions, to say that that artistic production could or should be
> the reflection of the great currents which determine the economic or social
> evolution of society would be to pass pretty impoverished judgement implying
> a purely circumstancial theory of thought. It would be selling short its fun-
> damental contradictory nature which is at one and the same time uncon-
> ditioned, utopian and yet realist, self-justifying yet desirous to do nothing but
> serve.[14]

His response to the second question was even more devastating in so far
as it promoted Trotsky's theory that proletarian art would never be realised
in either (a) pre-revolutionary society since it would be bourgeois art which
would prevail, nor (b) in the post-revolutionary society since the dictatorship
of the proletariat would be so short that there would not be time to produce
art in its name.

Poulaille chose to ignore the first question. On the other hand the second
afforded him the opportunity of reiterating his belief in proletarian literature:

> I believe in the existence of a literature and art forms which express the
> aspirations of the working class. Almost inevitably, art expresses and is rep-
> resentative of, social class. Until recently only the idle rich has written, at least
> this is the only class we have any knowledge of in France. For too long, writing
> has been one pastime and reading another.[15]

Undoubtedly, *Monde*'s enquiry was a success in that the subject was well
aired and a fair ideological profile of a number of prominent artists and writers
put before the readership. It had also served to sustain the debate surrounding
proletarian literature and its claims to authenticity.

However, even at this time events in the Soviet Union were beginning to
point towards a reassessment of the theory and role of literary and artistic
production. From 1930 onwards a systematic denigration of the proletcult
was carried out prior to its definitive replacement by the Writers' Union in
1932.

The French communists still continued to pay attention to the proletarian
writers some of whom they believed could be won over to a greater commitment to 'revolutionary' art than they had hitherto exhibited. In October
1932, Paul Nizan one of a new transfusion of brilliant young intellectuals to
enter the Party, was invited to report on 'revolutionary' writing in France.
He went out of his way to disabuse any who might have thought of the
proletarian writers as revolutionary:

In France there have been some singularly amusing debates on "proletarian" literature. We know that they were the product of the populist movement, the New Age movement and some books. The proletarian literature movement is not the literature of revolution. Some like Henri Poulaille have betrayed a great faith and real talent just to justify this identity. Proletarian literature, if I understand it correctly, is literature written by members of the proletariat for the proletariat. Obviously, such literature is not necessarily revolutionary and in any case, its champions are quite content to describe it as merely 'human'.[16]

From July 1931 onwards, Barbusse had been writing a series of leading articles in *Monde* explaining the need to forge new theories of revolutionary writing. This culminated in 1933 in the ousting from *Monde* of a group of intellectuals sympathetic to the aims of Poulaille and Martinet. Furthermore a new international organisation of revolutionary writers (the A.E.A.R.) was formed by the International and the stage set for the launching of a new Soviet artistic theory; socialist realism. It should be said that the pre-war version of socialist realism bore little resemblance to that subsequently elaborated in the Soviet Union during the Cold War. The initial socialist realist theory was meant to present the broadest possible front so that as many intellectuals and artists as possible could subscribe to it. Even for those who did not, it was not made a condition of membership of the front against fascism organised by Barbusse and other Party intellectuals. Communist intellectuals such as Nizan, Henri Lefebvre and Georges Politzer were actively encouraged in the field of the development of Marxist inspired research in their various fields; non-communist intellectuals such as Gide and Malraux made public appearances and statements against the rise of fascism.

Although some of the proletarian writers went over to the communists, others such as Poulaille and Martinet remained suspicious and even hostile to the Party. Martinet's reaction to the new departure in Soviet cultural policy was to republish in 1935 a collection of articles on proletarian culture published in the period 1918-23, a defiant gesture reiterating the claims of the proletarian school as the only authentic artistic representation of the working class. Given that the new Soviet policies stressed the anti-fascist nature of the new realism, Martinet was quick to confirm the anti-fascist credentials of his own school, for indeed the proletarian writers were being systematically attacked for their apparent apathy towards the anti-fascist cause. In his foreword Martinet makes an impassioned plea for the humanitarian and therefore anti-fascist nature of the proletarian school. But he feels strongly the danger of the freedom, spontaneity and authenticity of the worker writer being subsumed in another totalitarian ambition, i.e., that of the French communist party:

> Propaganda! There is a lot of talk about culture today. It would seem that all propaganda which works up and fanaticises the masses, the great lumpen proletariat, according to varying party lines put out by the infallible 'centre', the infallible 'head', is the only valid culture, the only useful culture possible today.
>
> Any kind of understanding or compromise however prudent or tentative with

such a concept of revolutionary action and theory regarding the role and destiny of the proletariat and not a resigned proletariat but a revolutionary proletariat, is quite out of the question. Given such a conception one should not mince one's words or avoid the issue behind a dilettante or sceptical stance—We must not be afraid of exposing this for what it is—it is monstrous, criminal, stupid, anti-proletarian and counter-revolutionary.[17]

Thus we see the proletarian writers becoming involved in the most major issue of the decade, the attempt of the French communist party to orchestrate the opposition against fascism from the centre, having hitherto attempted to destroy all enemies on the left. It is not difficult to understand their bitterness and deep seated suspicions.

The advent of socialist realism saw an end to the disruptive debates concerning the rabcors and the Party, the non-communist French proletarian writers and the communist establishment. The first interpretations of socialist realism were maintained as loose as possible in order to attract as large a body of bourgeois intellectuals, to the anti-fascist cause as possible. In this was the intellectual popular front initiated.

The importance of the national cultural heritage was stressed in order to demonstrate that the Party was the true custodian of this heritage and would defend it at all costs against the fascist aberration.

Within this context the French proletarian writers sensing an even greater attempt to attract individuals and groups into the sphere of influence of the communist party, became more and more isolated as they put artistic creation and artistic freedom as vital to the defence of their class interests before all else. Those who could afford to suspend their intellectual judgement in order to join the struggle against fascism, those who had the intellectual room for manoeuvre to do so, were for the most part, bourgeois intellectuals. (Some like Gide and Malraux were unable to sustain unequivocal support for too much longer and joined Martinet in the denunciation of the totalitarian implications of Stalinism; but they were notable exceptions.) Most intellectuals and artists who rallied to the intellectual Front, did so out of the conviction that they were joining the only effective opposition to fascism available at the time. The proletarian writers, mostly from an anarcho-syndicalist background, who refused categorically to subscribe to the line of the International, did so because their commitment to their class was so precious to them that any intellectual compromise would have been to deny everything that their access to culture had brought them. Class therefore, and its attendant ideological ramifications, was the most important motivating force behind this uncompromising stance. The tragedy was that Poulaille and Martinet were only too aware that one day the genuine proletarian writer would cease to exist as educational opportunity and social reform removed the cultural barriers to create conditions in which the proletarian stance would be an anachronism. The points of view expressed by Jaurès, Trotsky and Nizan had a sad ring of truth to them in that the proletarian movement was indeed short-lived disappearing as it did within the new and more democratic French society of the IVth Republic.

The fragile little movement set up by the self-taught and the cultural underdogs of the lumpen-proletariat, was to enjoy but a brief existence. However the tenacity with which it was defended despite the hostility of the major political force of the left in its day, remains as a monument to the right of expression. The novels, poems and plays of the proletarian writers may not meet bourgeois standards of artistic production, but they do bear witness to conditions of life and to the indomitable nature of the human spirit; it was the first time in France that such a concerted effort had been made by members of the proletariat to express themselves in their own terms.

The movement did not survive the Second World War.

Notes

1   *The British Minstrel* p. 132 Vol 1. William Hamilton, Glasgow 1844.
2   Michelet, Jules, *Le Peuple*. Didier, Paris 1946.
3   Michelet, Jules, *L'etudiant* (Cours de 1847-48).
4   Rolland, Romain, *La théâtre du peuple*. 1st edn 1903, revd edn 1913. Albin Michel, Paris.
5   Rolland, Romain, op. cit. p 49, and p 169.
6   Jaurès, Jean, 'L'art et le socialisme', in *Oeuvres de Jean Jaurès*. Vol 2, p. 153. Reider, Paris 1933.
7   *Le Cri du Peuple*, 8.11.1883.
8   Caze, Robert, in *Le Cri du Peuple* 15.11.1883.
9   For a detailed analysis of these issues see Bernard, J-P A, *Le parti communiste français et la question littéraire 1921-1939*. Presses Universitaires de Grenoble. Grenoble 1972.
10   Poulaille, Henry. 'Mon ami Calandri', p. 10 *Spartacus*. No 37-A, April 1970.
11   In *La Littérature de la Révolution Mondiale*. Vol 5, 1931.
12   Paul, E, 'Les correspondants ouvriers de *l'Humanité.' l'Humanité* 23.6.28.
13   *Monde* 4.8.28.
14   Breton, André, *Monde* 8.9.28.
15   Poulaille, Henri, *Monde* 27.10.28.
16   Nizan, Paul, *La Revue des Vivants*, p 393, parts 9-10. September-October 1932.
17   Martinet, Marcel, *Culture prolétarienne* p 49. Librairie du Travail, Paris 1935.

Artur Dinter's Anti-Semitic Trilogy[1]

J M Ritchie

A recent volume of essays under the title *Im Zeichen Hiobs*[2] set out to deal with the problem of the German-Jewish dialogue and German literature 1870-1940 and to this end assembled an impressive collection of studies of a broad range of famous names: Arthur Schnitzler; Else Lasker-Schüler; Karl Wolfskehl; Karl Kraus; Alfred Döblin; Franz Kafka; Max Brod; Lion Feuchtwanger; Arnold Zweig; Kurt Tucholsky; Franz Werfel; Nelly Sachs; Ernst Toller; Joseph Roth; Elias Canetti; Paul Celan. Valuable as such studies of German-Jewish literature are, they do perhaps suffer from one defect, namely that they give no idea of what anti-semitic literature was like or even that such literature existed, though it is true that the extensive and extremely well-researched introduction by the editors does give an excellent survey of the 'symbiosis' and 'dialogue' between German and Jew as regards the various developments characterising the period from 1870 to 1940. According to this kind of approach however, the standard of literary presentation of Jews was set for a long time by the society novel Georg Hermann developed in *Jettchen Gebert* and *Henriette Jacoby*, though such works have not enjoyed great critical acclaim. Instead literary studies have tended to focus on the presentation of Jews in better known writers like Freytag and Raabe, indeed it has been the standard approach among literary scholars to look for social and racial stereotypes in such examples of literary realism in the nineteenth century and the early twentieth century.[3] So far, however, critics have been unwilling to descend from the heights of high culture to the depths of low culture to consider what outspoken anti-semitic literature looked like, where its roots lay, and what effects it aimed for and achieved. As a result Artur Dinter is granted only one passing reference in *Im Zeichen Hiobs* as the author of a 'Novel-Pamphlet', *The Sin against the Blood*. This is seriously to underestimate a major figure from the sub-culture of modern anti-semitism, one whose 'Novel-Pamphlet' provided the Nazis with a slogan which they converted into legislation leading to the holocaust, one who enjoyed alarming success in his own time.[4]

The career of Artur Dinter can be rapidly sketched, though it has to be said that his literary successes were in some senses greater than his political endeavours. Born in 1876 in Alsace Dinter was, by his own account, proud of his academic background and training. He studied philosophy and science at Strasbourg and Munich and never lets his reader forget this, indeed he packs his literary works with long philosophical discussions and extensive, quasi-learned footnotes to show his erudition. In the context of his treatment of the Jewish problem he clearly feels such learned references to be important, because he is intent on producing not only a 'metaphysic of race', but one which has 'scientific' argument on its side. Hence the hero of his novel *The

Sin against the Blood is a university chemistry lecturer, the hero of one of its sequels an engineer. Such buttressing is intended to give the arguments of his central figures the force of apparent reason. Dinter himself became a teacher for a time, and teaching is another element clearly present in his works which are blatantly didactic; however, he gave up this profession for the theatre. The list of published work he appends to all his books reveals not only a preponderance of scientific and pseudo-scientific works, but also the titles of plays which were probably little known at the time and are certainly totally forgotten today. He did nevertheless succeed in setting up an *Association of German Stage-writers* and this indication of organisational ability also became evident in the political sphere when he became active in the *Deutschvölkischer Schutz- und Trutzbund*, of which indeed he was one of the founders.[5] After the failure of the November 1923 *Putsch* in Munich he joined Esser and Streicher in the move to join the emerging Nazi party. By 1924 he was a member of the Federal State Diet in Thuringia and when Hitler re-established his banned party Dinter proclaimed his absolute allegiance to the man who was to become the *Führer*.

While Dinter's anti-semitic views were doubtless echoed by Hitler, the latter was more cautious in his political and diplomatic manoeuvering vis-à-vis the established churches than Dinter was prepared to be, and so by 1928 Dinter was in trouble for making impossible statements like 'the Hitler party is a Jesuit party which conducts Rome's business under the nationalist flag'. Dinter was expelled from the party for this and for similar statements in the journals *Der Nationalsozialist* and *Geisteschristentum*, which he edited, but he still remained close to the party and worked closely with it in its attempts to bring the Church under centralised state control.[6] After 1945 he was clearly unaltered in his views and formally charged in the courts with agitating for a racist *People's Church*. In 1947 the journal *Aufbau* published a 'j'accuse' reminder of Dinter's guilt by association with the sins of the Nazi past:

> We accuse former party-member number 5, *Gauleiter* of the Nazi Party in Thuringia, founder of the former fighting association German People's Church, author Dr. Artur Dinter of being guilty of active participation in intellectually brutalizing and spiritually poisoning our people, of being guilty of promoting national arrogance and political stupidity in our people, such as found expression in the dictatorial regime of the National Socialists, of being guilty of causing deprivation, misery and suffering for our people in most recent times and at present and of being guilty of defaming the German people and the good name of Germany throughout the world. We accuse him of being guilty of continued and deliberate racial provocation, guilty of continued and deliberate undermining of respect for democracy and guilty of bringing into contempt all human feelings and all striving for humanity in our people, and therefore of being guilty, as the main instigator, of thousands upon thousands of crimes against humanity, crimes committed over the last thirty years in the name of Germany against millions of Jews, foreigners, or those of a different race and different political creed.

Dinter was not further pursued by the courts and died in 1948 at the age of 72.

The fervour with which Dinter pursued his 'campaign against Rome' and his advocacy for a new Reformation was so great that it almost overshadowed his campaign against Judaism. This campaign gives some indication of where the roots of his ideas are to be found. The dedication of his 'Novel for the Times' *The Sin against the Blood* to 'the German Houston Stewart Chamberlain' puts the matter beyond any doubt. The frequent references in the multiple footnotes not only to 'literary' works like Chamberlain's *Goethe*, but also to the essay *Race and Nation* further reveal what it was that attracted Dinter to Houston Stewart Chamberlain. That the latter was *not* German but English did not deter Dinter in any way, but only inspired him to a lengthy post-script in which, his eyes having been opened to the race question by Chamberlain, the Germanic Englishman, he details his further reading in these matters starting with the ancient Indian epics and continuing by way of Plato to Mommsen, Treitschke and Gobineau. Evidence of the far from random racial reading is in any event liberally scattered throughout the pages of his novel, though the lengthy passages of Hebrew which he also likes to present as evidence from Jewish sources, in order, as he sees it, to condemn the Jews with their own evidence, are fortunately restricted to the some fifty pages of footnotes.

No reader who lays great store by literary style should be tempted to read Dinter's novel, for the prose is of the most banal. The style is indeed so banal that it was almost too bad for Robert Neumann, the famous parodist, to imitate, though the page or so of quasi-Dinter prose he produced is almost bad enough to be genuine:

> But quick as a flash Teut Kämpfer wrenched aside the door-curtain and shouted 'Desist, Jew!' An almighty slap across the rake's face. Then Teut lifted the unconscious maiden up in his arms and proceeded with firm tread to the door. At the threshold of the same, he turned again and said, 'know this, I have gone through your records. This virgin is the two hundred and fortieth you have violated this year. Your secret Book of Laws is also known to me, wherein (see footnote 823) this kind of thing is made your bounden duty. In your devilish Talmud it is written, and all this has been skillfully translated as follows, by good German men and true, that is to say, men who have not been suborned by the Wise Men of Zion, your supreme Council of Criminals, or by the Free-masons, or by Fellow traveller-type Jews you have made your subjects. This is what it says, "for three hundred, six and and forty days in the year shallt thou rape Christian virgins, but ye on Easter Day shallt thou slaughter them!"'
>
> 'As for now, do not dare to follow me, scion of Judas', he thundered at the pasty-faced seducer, 'or else I shall go straight to the District Attorney and tell him a tale ... of how you get to be a Commercial Councillor!' And with that he slammed the door shut behind him, leaving the racial intruder slumped broken on the carpet...[7]

If the style is bad the plot of a Dinter novel is even worse and the charac-terisation almost non-existent—or rather it relies on the most basic of estab-lished stereotypes. What is important in the analysis of a work of this kind is to identify what gave this piece of literary garbage appeal to such a vast readership. Estimates of print runs vary, but its popularity with a certain public was beyond question. As the biographer of H.S. Chamberlain has put it:

> It would merit little notice had it not become *the* best seller in Germany at the end of the war. By 1922 some 200,000 copies had been sold and some estimates have placed Dinter's readership as high as 1.5 million. Some teachers, it was claimed, had read it aloud and recommended it to their students. A sequel, published in 1921, also sold more than 100,000 copies in the first year.[8]

In fact there was more than one sequel: there were two, but neither *The Sin against the Spirit* nor *The Sin against Love* was ever as successful as the first volume of the Trilogy.

The hero of Dinter's tale *The Sin against the Blood* is a scientist, bearing the telling name Dr. Hermann Kämpfer (*Kämpfer* = fighter). He is fortunate in having not only pure German blood, but a father with roots in the soil. Unfortunately this peasant father has been deliberately embroiled in debt by a Jewish money-lender, and has accidentally killed the Jewish money-lender, when he throws him out of the house. The result of all this is that father goes to prison, where he hangs himself following the death of his wife, the family scatters, the daughter has a baby and dies. Hermann the son manages despite all this to take his school leaving certificate and be admitted to university, where he does well in chemistry, the queen of sciences. As the novel opens he is a dedicated researcher on the brink of a major break-through, though filled with doubts that, like Goethe's *Faust*, he may have taken on too much. The second chapter already brings the first of what are to be many quotations from Goethe, warning against analytical reason which vainly tries to fathom the unfathomable. So Dinter's 'Faustian' Kämpfer fears he has dedicated ten years of his life to science, thereby missing out on real life. Dinter's novel is not only replete with such aspirations to high culture and advanced science, it is also deeply sentimental and oblivious to the dangers of kitsch. Hence when Hermann the 'struggling soul' frees himself from the laboratory to find peace in nature in the form of a winter-landscape, he is quickly transported in his mind back to the world of the German fairy-tale, to the aura of a German family Christmas. With the appropriate verses in his head and Kant's 'starry sky above him', Hermann the German wanderer on skis makes his way to a modern hotel where by contrast to the family circle he finds the international haute volée well installed. He also catches sight of the temptress who will enthrall him, the innocent who has never touched a woman! Just like his father Hermann is about to become embroiled with a 'diabolic' Jewish man of money, indeed one bearing all the tell-tale signs, 'an ugly loosely hooked nose, a thick-lipped mouth, hands covered with black hair and speech patterns involving *Mauscheln* and phrases like *Kesch daun* (=Cash down!).' Despite unconscious awareness that this is the 'race enemy' in person, Hermann agrees to abandon his academic career and help solve this Councillor's technical problems.

It will come as no surprise to hear that in this novel filled with coincidences and fateful meetings, the flirtatious woman who first catches his attention at the International Christmas Party, turns out to be the councillor-businessman's daughter, or that a Jewish colleague Dr Siegfried Salomon takes all the notes the brilliant Hermann had left behind in the laboratory and claims all the credit for his work. Before Hermann leaves the place where he had worked for long he enjoys one night of love, with the chaste Germanic daughter of the house who has admired him so much for so long:

> He had entered unnoticed. When she discovered his presence, she at first tried to speed past him to the door. He caught her in his arms. Without a will of her own she let him cover her with his burning kisses, and that last night brought both of these young and passionate people the fulfillment they had for so long resisted so resolutely.(120)

Needless to say the until then so pure Rosele will be soon forgotten by the till then so pure lover Hermann who is distracted by the daughter of the dastardly Jew. This Elisabeth is on the point of entering upon 'a modern marriage' with an assimilated Herr Baron von Wertheim. Neither of the two (as Elisabeth explains) believes in the empty life they lead, the roles they play. Elisabeth's rejection of this 'modern' life also extends to modern art:

> All that insipid talk about Max Reinhardt and Richard Straus, Max Liebermann and the Secession, about monism and futurism, Wedekind and Strindberg, and then in one and the same breath all that enthusing about Bach and Beethoven, Lissauer and Sternheim, Puppchen and Goethe, it's enough to make you sick. (86)

Elisabeth does not know it, because she has not yet been enlightened to the fact that she is the offspring of a mixed marriage between her Jewish father and a Protestant mother or that the divided nature she consequently feels is the result of the racial struggle within herself, a Hitlerian *Kampf* which is the main feature of the whole book. Just as there was a Faustian struggle going on within Hermann, there is a similar battle going on between her good and bad halves. Hence she is attracted by the sturdy Germanic Hermann and rejects her Jewish suitor. Her father (like all Jews according to Dinter) is attracted to everything German and surrounds himself with blond people. Even Elisabeth's mother, once an innocent girl, has been drugged and abused by the Jew who marries her only when forced to do so. But the mother cannot explain to her daughter either the 'unbridgeable, racially conditioned chasm yawning between Old and New Testament' (102) or the facts of the blood and the soul and of many thousands of years of history which cannot be washed away. The whole problem of the *Old* and the *New Testament* is one to which Dinter in this novel and elsewhere returns again and again, for it is essential for his purposes to divorce Christianity from any suggestion of Jewish roots, indeed to prove that Jesus was not a Jew! At the beginning of the novel, however, he is concerned to demonstrate through mother and daughter what happens when 'German blood' is 'soiled' by 'foreign, impure blood, sprung

from the darkest chaotic intermingling of races'. So the love-story demonstrates the struggle within herself when she, the spoiled scion of a mixed
marriage, catches sight of her blond hero, her 'dream vision'. Within Hermann too a similar struggle is taking place:

> His scientifically schooled, methodically thinking reason was battling with his
> impulsive temperament, his instinctive feeling, which usually got the right
> answer regardless of all rational calculations, something which was often
> especially the case when all rational reasons seemed to demand the opposite.
> (117)

Hermann's struggle is not only a personal one but typical too of the conflict
in the novel between reason and instinct. According to the National Socialist
Weltanschauung rationality is critical, negative and 'destructive', only thinking
with the blood can arrive at positive solutions. For Dinter the same arguments
will apply when it comes to proving the case for a 'positive' Christianity
without Jewish elements.

In his mental struggle Hermann finds his path through his darkness by
reading Plato, a philosophy linked in his mind with the New Testament which
he understands in his own way: 'How dreary schoolmasters and dull priests
had stifled the living feeling for the Word of God when he was a boy!' (113)
When he does become more closely involved with Elisabeth their strange
preliminary conversations revolve round unlikely subjects of this kind, just
as they do over the question of *Geist* (spirit), a problem much discussed by
the intellectuals of the time, but which Hermann reduces to a rejection of
'materialism' of the scientific kind argued by Darwin, Häckel and Ostwald.
The Jewish Baron von Wertheim is needless to say a defender of such materialism, while Hermann emerges as the triumphant defender of Kantian idealism.
It is little wonder then that the second part of Dinter's trilogy will be called
The Sin against the Spirit, though this will involve very special pleading for
Geist as spirit leading to Spiritualism. The battle for Elisabeth is fought out by
argument between Hermann and the Baron, with Hermann presenting at
great length the case for *Kultur* as distinct from *Civilisation, Geist,* the *New
Testament* and Plato, as against Jewish materialism. The final argument pre-
sented as absolutely decisive is racial:

> Just as a sloe-tree always bears sloes and never apples or pears, so too the
> delicious teachings of Jesus could never have grown from Jewish roots. And in
> fact there is a whole series of indications, one might even say proofs, indicating
> that Jesus was not a Jew, but an Aryan, or what comes to the same thing, that
> he was Indogermanic. He was only a Jew by upbringing and religion, never,
> but never by race. (164)

It is about this point in the novel that the argument moves from the narrative
to be continued in the footnotes, because for Dinter such matters cannot be
satisfactorily resolved by discussions between fictional characters, but must
be fought out by reference to heavy-weight philologists, theologians and
others. Certainly what is left in the text is not very convincing, e.g., the nature

of Jesus's larynx, his *Kehlkopf*, which is supposed to indicate that he was racially incapable of pronouncing Hebrew! The battle over Elisabeth continues over many pages, many marked out by sections in capital letters to give maximum effect to the arguments presented. What Hermann is arguing for is the appearance of a new Luther, who will complete the deeds of the first, free Christianity from the Jews and Judaism and make some kind of purely 'German' Christianity a reality. Here Dinter was being prophetic yet again, for not only was the title of his novel *The Sin against the Blood* to become, as *Rassenschande* (racial disgrace), a punishable offence in the National Socialist state, but the same state would also attempt to nationalise Christianity in order to produce a nation of 'German Christians'.

The 'Sin against the Blood' which characterises Elisabeth's background and origins is mentioned explicitly in the seventeenth chapter. Nothing Hermann undertakes to counter the social factor can have any success. He maps out a course of study for her, taking her through the *New Testament*, Plato, Dante and Kant, he gets her to read Homer and the *Song of the Nibelungen*, he follows this up with Keller, Storm, Raabe and Fritz Reuter, he makes her listen to Bach and Beethoven, while her art education is completed by the study of Dürer and Rembrandt, complemented by those masters of the Italian Renaissance Michelangelo and Leonardo da Vinci who, as he explains, were also of Germanic blood! The sensationalism of 'modern' theatre and opera are meanwhile avoided.

For a time it looks as if Elisabeth under Hermann's instructions can be rescued from the empty meaningless existence she led before, and even the father seems to be not averse to Hermann marrying his daughter, despite financial considerations favouring Baron von Wertheim as a more suitable husband. After all there is talk of a war and the businessman, who has his 'feelers out in all countries in the world', needs as much support as possible to ensure that Germany is *not* victorious in such a war! Many signs and inner voices, even that of Goethe, who according to Chamberlain's interpretation had early been aware of the Jewish menace, warn Hermann against an alliance with the lovely Elisabeth, but he ignores them all. At first everything seems fine on the surface and the couple are idyllically happy together, away from the distractions of frivolous society life. Once married everything changes: 'Her father's chaotic blood begins to assert its true nature'. Elisabeth begins to reject everything 'German' and longs for society life again. At first Hermann fails to understand the reasons for this sudden change in behaviour. According to Dinter, he makes the common mistake of assuming that the Jewish problem is religious and not racial in essence. The birth of his first child is what wakens him from his fundamental ignorance! The birth itself is an easy one. The child is a boy. But when Hermann looks at the child for the first time he sees: 'Something not in any way human, with dark skin and crinkly, jet black hair'. The explanation offered by the doctor is a simple one: atavism, that is, a throw-back to an earlier generation. The word is enough to set Hermann off on yet another quest: 'the scientist in him was suddenly reawakened' and the reader has to follow him both in the novel itself and in the footnotes as he discovers the manifold literature of race and eugenics.

The 'scientific' truth which he uncovers is of a kind familiar from such racial literature: the Jews who constitute one per cent of the population control the money-market, the press, politics, science and the arts. The 'Sin against the Blood' is for a German to marry a Jew, for regardless of anything else a Jew cannot change, a Jew remains a Jew. This 'racial doctrine' is hard and apparently unchristian but according to the insights Hermann gathers, it explains *everything* in the world from the Fall of Rome to the state of Germany in the modern age!

What Hermann also comes to believe in (and this is developed in the sequel *The Sin against the Spirit*) is 'the problem of the soul's effect over a distance', the *non*-scientific force of *Geist*. His baby, he discovers, *looks* like the Baron, because the thought of the Baron has been in Elisabeth's mind, indeed 'in her mind she has sinned with the Baron'. This is as hard for the reader to believe as it is for Hermann; however, he challenges the cowardly Jew to a duel and shoots his ear-lobe off. When the baby's birth-mark proves that he *is* the physical father of the child, he determines to start an experiment to determine whether nature or nurture, race or education determine the character and spiritual qualities of a child. At first his wife refuses to have a second child for such an experiment and suggests that he find a racially pure Germanic mother with blond hair and blue eyes, but in the end she agrees. Prenatally he surrounds her with *Geist*, things of beauty and the music of Beethoven. Unfortunately she dies giving birth to the second child which is very attractive despite its semitic features. The child too does not survive the mother. In fact the death of the mother is brought on because of the scandal caused by the death of her father, for despite all that Hermann does to conceal the truth from her, she discovers that her father, the Commercial Councillor, has been systematically poisoning the German race by keeping one hundred and seventeen blond mistresses in order to breed blond babies from them! The case becomes public and when Elisabeth gets to know of the scandal the effect is to bring on the premature birth of her child. The mother in fact dies when she sees that she has given birth to another Jewish child.

While the lustful behaviour of the stereotype Jewish businessman may stretch the credulity of the reader to the limit, Dinter has still a few demonstrations of the power of *Geist* to impose upon the reader's patience, for suddenly at this point, following the death of both his wife and her father, Hermann hears from his long lost Rosele. From her death-bed her spirit has called to him and following up her death-bed letters he finds that he has a son by her. Now the novel is able to demonstrate the instinctive behaviour of his two sons—one by Rosele, one by Elisabeth, two boys of about the same age. Their development follows racial as distinct from educational or social patterns, Elisabeth's Jewish son being prepared even to lick the boots of his schoolmates for a few pence. Not surprisingly in a novel of this kind, both boys suddenly die; the cowardly Jewish boot-licker Heinrich falls into the water and the brave Germanic brother jumps in to save him. The coward in his terror clings to his rescuer and both drown. Father Hermann meanwhile has been trying to clear up the mess left by the sudden demise of the Councillor and it is only in doing so that he becomes aware of the world-wide ramifications of the Jewish conspiracy. 'The existing body of letters and cables covered the whole globe ... like a big fat spider he [the Commercial Councillor] sat in his Berlin office, sucking the very marrow out of the body and soul of all these people by means of his wireless messages.'(275) Here once again Dinter has recourse to page-long footnotes in order to reinforce this stereotype of the spider at the centre of the financial web, controlling the destinies of the universe, with details and statistics drawn from all sorts of sources. Hermann is caught up in this web when he tries to determine fairly the fate of all the wealth that has suddenly become his. The universal Jewish Conspiracy leaves him impoverished.

His last experience is yet another involving the 'Spirit working over a distance'. In hospital following an accident he meets a nurse: 'a well-built, blue-eyed, blond, luscious woman of about thirty', a person obviously ideal for his breeding purposes. He pursues her and marries her, although she confesses that she has had a child which died in childbirth. When they marry and have a child it turns out to be Jewish, but how was this possible?

> The mystery was soon solved when Hermann discovered the following: it is a significant racial law, one well known, particularly when it comes to breeding animals, that a throughbred female becomes useless for breeding purposes for ever, if she is even once impregnated by a male of inferior race. (350)

What this means is that one 'bad crossing' was sufficient to taint for ever all subsequent offspring of the female. Geoffrey Field in his biography of H.S. Chamberlain gives further details of this phenomenon of 'telegony' or 'remote impregnation'.

> Explained in many textbooks, including the writings of Spencer and Darwin, this doctrine was largely applied to animal breeding, but racists soon appropriated the notion to apply to Aryans and Jews.[9]

This was exactly the kind of belief later propagated by Walther Darré, a pig-breeder who popularised theories of Blood and Soil so successfully that he rose to become Reich Farmer's Leader and Reich Food Minister. In Dinter's novel the doctrine is used not to glorify the healthy German peasant but to show the consequences for the German race if year after year Jewish boys are seducing thousands upon thousands of German girls. The lustfulness of the Councillor fades into insignificance compared with this vision of the destruction of the Germanic race by mass racial pollution. Hermann immediately takes action. He finds out who it was who had seduced his wife years before, proceeds to the barracks where this Jewish officer is to be found and shoots him. When he returns he finds his child dead from a morphium injection and his wife dead with the same needle stuck close to her heart. Only a war, Hermann has earlier stated, can awaken the German nation to the racial peril and this is how the novel ends with Hermann dying as a hero for his sacred Fatherland, not before he has been recognized as the *Führer*, 'for long desired, ready at last to take up the struggle against these deceivers and poisoners of the people'.(368) Hitler, who admired anti-semites like Dinter and Streicher, was to emerge as the Führer in this role.

Clearly it would be very difficult for any sequel to match the heights or depths achieved in Dinter's first novel and it has to be said at once that *The Sin against the Spirit* falls short on every count. The hero, it is true, is a dashing one, a famous 'Cavalry Officer and Fighter Pilot', a blond-haired holder of the *Pour-le-mérite* no less, and he does save an aristocratic maiden from drowning in the first chapter. Unfortunately the love-story, such as it is, becomes entangled in the hero's discovery of spiritualism and her failure to follow this path. The time of the action is 1919, that is immediately after the war at the beginning of the Weimar Republic, which such people bitterly rejected and resented:

> Germans who had lost all sense of decency, who had been befuddled to the point of madness by foreign-blooded seducers and exploiters, had set up the Republic and put their names to that disgraceful and disgusting peace treaty. (10)

The Republic has left the dashing Cavalry Officer without a role in society, for the revolution is lacking in moral motivation, being only the false construct of the Jewish-inspired leaders of the working people: 'Salvation could only come from the German national movement'. While statements of this kind promise a novel of social conflict, the plot in fact drifts off into discussions of Kant (yet again—this time his 'Dreams of a Spiritualist') though the implications become serious when such anti-materialism involves the mastery of true Germans over Jews 'in effect by purely legal means, involving the exclusion of all Jews in practice'.[10] When the National Socialists came to power that was precisely what happened. Elimination of the Jews always followed apparently legal routes and involved the promulgation of progressively strict legislation. In addition to Kant, Socrates and Plato, Goethe is once more over and over again called upon to provide evidence for the 'spiritualist teaching' which fascinates our hero. That this also involves anti-semitism goes without saying, since the point of the exercise is to produce an anti-materialistic 'metaphysics of racism'. That our Cavalryman also propagates the removal of the 'Judaeo-Roman institution of interest slavery', something which was to reappear as point eleven of the twenty-five programme of the NSDAP, is also worthy of note, though what is perhaps even more interesting is that the officer's main antagonist proves to be a reactionary aristocrat, namely his beloved's father. This was exactly the kind of conservative 'reaction' which was attacked by the NSDAP in its early stages, vestiges of which are still to be found in the Horst-Wessel Song. These are the conservative 'reactionaries' who fail to see and accept the 'revolutionary' nature of the NSDAP. The same is true of the aristocratic Gerhilde's 'Sin against the Spirit', a sin which cannot be forgiven: 'she has declined to accept knowledge which could have been so beneficial, and has willfully acted against knowledge she knew to be true.' Even more damning is the sin which leads on to the third part of the trilogy: 'She has sinned against love, she was not true to you'. This kind of 'sin against love' is a little hard to grasp, because it involves metempsychosis and the experience of souls over the centuries.

Turning for further explanation to the final volume of the Trilogy, the reader will discover to his dismay that he is expected to digest a volume of some five hundred or more pages, with the author's own admission in the post-script that he has had to rewrite completely the first edition and that the second edition is still not complete, but needs the complementary reading of the author's *197 Theses on the Completion of the Reformation*, the *Restoration of the Pure Teaching of Our Saviour* and of his journal *Christentum*, plus his edition of the Gospels! Like the previous volumes this one is also richly provided with sections in especially heavy black print for emphasis and many footnotes. The plot, however, is much reduced, involving this time an engineer and a revolutionary uprising at a country estate. After this lively beginning the novel abandons action for the discovery of messages received through table-tapping and a medium, progressing finally to lengthy messages received and recorded from the other world. The essential message of this wordy non-novel is, however, a 'worthy' one quite explicitly stated:

> If politics, religion and race form one indissoluble unity, only then will the German people prove capable of fulfilling the earthly mission God has placed upon them.(400)

That Dinter saw himself as the 'new Luther', the *Führer* who would bring this fusion about by his own brand of 'Spiritualist Christianity', his trilogy of novels has made clear. Reality, however, was to provide a different solution and Germany found another Führer.

Notes

1 Books of the kind discussed here are not readily available. The editions which have been used are *Die Sünde wider das Blut. Ein Zeitroman von Artur Dinter.* Achte Auflage 51.-60.Tausend. Leipzig: Verlag Matthes und Thost und Hartenstein in Sachsen 1920; *Die Sünde wider den Geist. Ein Zeitroman. Erste bis zehnte Auflage 1.-50. Tausend.* Leipzig: Verlag Matthes und Trost 1921; *Die Sünde wider die Liebe. Ein Zeitroman.* 26.-30.Tausend. Leipzig: Verlag Ludolf Beust 1928. Page references in the text will be to these editions. While the first volume of the trilogy is dedicated to Houston Stewart Chamberlain, the third volume is dedicated to the memory of Paul de Lagarde.

2 *Im Zeichen Hiobs*, Jüdische Schriftsteller und deutsche Literatur im 20. Jahrhundert, ed. by Gunter E Grimm and Hans-Peter Bayerdörfer, Königstein/Ts: Athenäum 1985.

3 See, for example, the essay by Hans Otto Horch, 'Judenbilder in der realistischen Erzählliteratur. Jüdische Figuren bei Gustav Freytag, Fritz Reuter, Berthold Auerbach und Wilhelm Raabe', in *Juden und Judentum in der Literatur*, ed. by Herbert A Strauss and Christhard Hoffmann, Munich: Deutscher Taschenbuchverlag 1985.

4 One chapter is devoted to Dinter in the French study by Pierre Angel, *Le Personnage Juif dans le Roman Allemand (1855-1915). La racine littéraire de l'antisemitisme Outre-Rhin.* Paris: Didier (1973). The period which immediately fol-

lows is taken up in Margit Frank, *Das Bild des Juden in der deutschen Literatur im Wandel der Zeitgeschichte*. Studien zu jüdischen Gestalten und Namen in deutschsprachigen Romanen und Erzählungen 1918-1945. Göteborg: Diss. Deutsches Institut (1985). Contemporary reviews of Dinter's novel are hard to find, though some discerning ridicule deserves note, for example: from the pen of Rudolf Olden in *Das Tagebuch* vol. 2 (1921), p.410: *The Sin against the Blood!* Excitement in Glauchau. The novels of the Aryan author Artur Dinter are published in editions of a kind only Courths-Mahler [the all-time top of the German best-seller lists] ever experiences. It is worthy of note that Rudolf Olden has decided to read one of these novels from beginning to end.' However, it was clearly dangerous to tangle with Dinter. When Olden continued to ridicule Dinter's novel he was taken to court by the author and fined 20,000 DM, even though the court agreed that Dinter's novels were artistically and scientifically worthless as well as morally flawed. Olden reports this example of Weimar Justice in *Das Tagebuch*, vol.4 (1923), pp.422-23.

5   Uwe Lohalm, *Völkischer Radikalismus* Die Geschichte des Deutschvölkischen Schutz-und Trutzbundes 1919-1923. Hamburg: Leibniz Verlag (1970).

6   Lohalm describes the Dinter wing of the Schutz- und Trutzbund as 'the followers of the spritualist Christianity proclaimed by Artur Dinter, a totally unnatural Aryan-Germanic, spiritualist Christianity, based exclusively on the Gospel of John. This 'spiritualist Christianity' was supposed to contain the totally Aryan-Germanic teaching of the Saviour, Dinter got by combining his spiritualist doctrine with a form of Christianity purified of any association with the Old Testament and 'Judaeo-Pauline dogmatic rubbish'. This was a form of Christianity which basically no longer deserved the name', pp.172 and 392.

7   Quoted here from Robert Neumann, *Dämon Weib oder die Selbstverzauberung durch Literatur, samt technischen Hinweisen, wie man dorthin gelangt*. München: Kurt Desch (1969) pp. 97-8.

8   Geoffrey G Field, *Evangelist of Race. The Germanic Vision of Houston Stewart Chamberlain*. New York: Columbia University Press, (1981), p. 403.

9   Geoffrey G Field, op.cit., p. 221.

10 Already in the first volume of this trilogy Dinter had adumbrated legislation, which was in fact to be brought in by the National Socialist regime: 'No Jew may any longer be a teacher of a German boy or a German girl. No Jew may any longer be a professor at a German college or a German university! No Jew, no matter whether baptized or not, may sit in judgement over a German... No Jew may ever again hold public office!' ... *The Sin against the Blood* p. 363.

The Tower of Babel: Reflections on Elias Canetti's Auto-da-Fé (Die Blendung)

Noel Thomas

The *Tower of Babel* was the title which the American translator supplied for *Die Blendung* (*Auto-da-Fé*) when it was published in New York in 1947. The French followed this example in 1949 with *La Tour de Babel*. An earlier English translation which appeared in London in 1946 bore the title *Auto-da-Fé* and this title has been retained in subsequent English editions of Canetti's novel. The two different titles stem from the difficulty in translating the words *Die Blendung*, which according to Wahrig covers three meanings: *the blinding, being blinded* and also *a small dug-out*. The English word *blinding* would reflect effectively only the first meaning, whilst Canetti, one must assume, would be equally keen to include the second meaning, i.e. the state of suffering from blindness which could be caused by external forces or be induced from within. The third meaning of *Blendung* is also not without significance for the novel, in that each of the main characters seeks protection in his or her own private dug-out: Peter Kien retreats into his library, Pfaff conceals himself in his guard room and regards the world through his spy-hole, Fischerle takes refuge under the bed, Georges Kien is enclosed by the walls of the mental asylum and Therese confines herself largely to the kitchen.

The existence of three titles helps to confirm in some measure Detlef Krumme's[1] approach to Canetti's novel. He suggests that the novel can be viewed in terms of four or even more *reading models*, an expression which stems from Arno Schmidt. Such models or interpretative approaches may coexist and may be the reflection of the reader's personal interests. Detlef Krumme leaves it largely to the recipient to decide which reading is felt to be most appropriate. He seems reluctant to emphasize that such interpretations may be complementary. Detlef Krumme suggests that *Die Blendung* may be regarded as a warning against specialisation, or as a demonstration of the lack of communication between human beings who speak only their own private language, or as the story of a paranoiac who, unable to cope with reality, drives himself into insanity and suicide, or, finally, as a grotesque illustration of the big city environment. The titles of which we have been speaking do not correspond either in content or quality with those of Detlef Krumme, they merely lend credence to the view that different emphases may be permissible in the interpretation of the novel and may still retain their validity.

Canetti's novel is certainly a salutary reminder to the academic of the dangers which confront him or her in the world of learning. Canetti makes it quite clear in *Fackel im Ohr*,[2] that the category which he confers upon Peter Kien, the main character of the novel, is that of bibliophile. It is equally relevant to mention the fact that Canetti originally named his hero Kant, thus arousing philosophical associations, at least until Hermann Broch[3] dissuaded him from using this name. Canetti[4] also explains the origin of the main character and the central event by referring to the burning of the Palace of Justice on 15 July 1927 in Vienna and how on this occasion he encountered a man who was more alarmed by the loss of the documents than by the death of ninety people who were involved in the accompanying demonstration.

Canetti is equally convinced of the harm which may be caused by specialisation and in a conversation quoted by Franz Schuh,[5] Canetti refers to specialisation as 'nothing short of using men as tools'. In *The Human Province* Canetti[6] produces a similarly critical remark about the fragmentation of learning:

> My whole life is nothing but a desperate attempt to overcome the division of labour and think about everything myself, so that it comes together in a head and thus becomes one again. I do not want to know everything, I merely want to unify splintered things.

Peter Kien, the bibliophile whose life and death Canetti describes in *Die Blendung*, certainly conforms to the mode of thinking apparent in the remarks of the bystander on the occasion of the burning of the Palace of Justice. At the same time he embodies all the dangers inherent in the academic mind. He confuses books with human beings and consequently is insensitive to human suffering, as David Roberts[7] indicates. The library in which Kien works is emblematic of his remoteness from the concerns of other people: its windows have been walled up and the room is open only to the insubstantial expanse of the heavens. People serve only to distract him from the ethereal realm of the mind. As the title of the first part of the novel indicates, he is 'a head without a world'. People just as much as furniture, are superfluous, only books matter: people are an obstacle to learning. His attitude is summarised in the following quotation:[8] 'You drew closer to the truth by shutting yourself off from mankind. Daily life was a superficial clatter of lies' (p. 13). As is stated elsewhere, he has not the slightest desire to notice human beings and hence he keeps his eyes down or looks above the heads of people (p. 13).

Peter Kien's link with the external world is established through the medium of books. They constitute the criterion by which those few impressions which stem from the outside world may be assessed. The qualities of pigeons or roses, for example, are verified in relationship to the written word: 'He took the roses from Fischerle's hand, remembered their sweet smell which he knew from Persian love poetry, and raised them to his eyes; it was true, they did smell' (p. 226). Equally well, his critical talents, which are presented as being considerable, operate exclusively within the world of books: 'a scholar's strength consists in concentrating all doubt on to his special subject. Here he must let doubt surge over him in a ceaseless and unrelenting tide; in all other spheres and in life as a whole he must accept current ideas' (p. 60).

Even within those areas in which he engages his critical faculties, he is selective in the way he employs them: 'Ignoring is in the blood of learned man. Learning is the art of ignoring' (p. 356). The two quotations indicate the dangers which his detachment from the world presents both for himself and for others. His concentration on the things of the mind leads to passivity and blindness in the face of the real world. In fact he makes blindness into one of the fundamental principles in his life quite consciously and yet with no understanding of the implications of such a decision.

> Blindness is a weapon against time and space; our being is one vast blindness, save only for that little circle which our mean intelligence—mean in its nature as in its scope—can illumine. The dominating principle of the universe is blindness. It makes possible juxtapositions which would be impossible if the objects could see each other (p. 63).

On reading such statements and on learning of Kien's incapacity to understand or handle other people, it is not difficult to realise why Canetti should have chosen the title *Die Blendung* for his novel.

As we have already seen, Peter Kien isolates himself from the world by withdrawing into himself and into a mind which is dominated, so he thinks, by reason—at least this is the *Blendung* of which he is a victim. By cutting himself off from the world, he detaches himself from the realm of feeling and also from the realm of sexuality. His emotional and sexual needs are ignored and as a character he remains stunted and unbalanced. His brother, Georges Kien, approaches the world through the medium of feeling and fails equally well to find a state of equilibrium. In Georges's estimation the two of them are complementary:

> Artists have this—a memory for feelings, as I'd like to call it. Both together, a memory for feelings and a memory for facts—for that is what yours is—would make possible the universal man. Perhaps I have rated you too highly. If you and I could be moulded together into a single being, the result would be a spiritually complete man (p. 402).

However, even though Georges Kien is a psychiatrist and is ostensibly more in contact with people than his brother, his judgment is just as defective as that of Peter and though wishing to help his brother he does not cure his insanity and hence prevent his suicide. In fact it is Georges Kien who suggests the possibility of setting the library on fire (pp. 398/99).

The forces of unreason which Peter Kien is at pains to suppress re-emerge in the dreams which thrust their way from his subconscious into his conscious mind. On one occasion he dreams that a man is being attacked by two jaguars, that books cascade from a wound which is inflicted on him, and thereby catch fire (pp. 34-35). In another vision he imagines a gigantic library building perched on a crater of Vesuvius which is about to erupt (p. 132). Peter Kien also dreams of a fire breaking out in the Theresianum, the enormous pawnshop (p. 351) which does indeed catch fire in the closing stages of the book and thus provokes Peter Kien's act of arson and suicide (p. 411). Other nightmares and distortions of reality which he experiences have as their common element the exercise of violence (e.g. p. 142, pp. 239-40, pp. 277-8). The mental imbalance which is linked with Kien's blindness fosters his destructiveness and converts into reality the very things he had feared most, i.e. the burning of his books.

In the light of the above remarks, the title of Salman Rushdie's[9] essay *The serpent of scholarship twists and turns, consumes its own tail and bites itself in two* seems to be totally appropriate as an indication of the self-destructiveness which the blindness of the bibliophile unleashes. It is just as easy to accept Salman Rushdie's assessment of Kien as a warning of the dangers of scholarship. At the same time one might even feel tempted to propose a further title for the novel, i.e. *The Ivory Tower*, if one wanted to accentuate this aspect of the book.

The reader would also be inclined to agree with Salman Rushdie in thinking that *Die Blendung* has a strangely prophetic quality. The book was completed in 1931, two years before the burning of the books in Nazi Germany, this being the prelude to the destruction of those cultural and humanitarian values which German intellectuals had failed to defend. Salman Rushdie reminds us also of Heine's[10] equally devastating prophecy: 'Wherever books are burned, men also, in the end, are burned.'

However, one is perhaps less inclined to share Salman Rushdie's enthusiasm for *Auto-da-Fé* as the title of the English version, for example, in preference to *The Tower of Babel*, whilst agreeing in some measure with his reservations about *The Blinding* as a possible translation. *Auto-da-Fé* with its secondary meaning of the public burning of forbidden books—at least according to German sources—clearly does fit as the title of the novel. The primary meaning, i.e. the burning of a heretic, may well lead to greater resistance on the part of the reader, since it suggests the imposition of a sentence of death by an external authority upon an individual. Admittedly Friedberg Aspetsberger[11] does view the novel precisely in these terms: 'The novel is the public act, the celebration of punishment, an 'act of faith' of a lay judge who feels himself responsible for humanity and against whom Kien emphatically turns in the novel...' The concept of a lay judge is difficult to accept, firstly, because there is no such source of authority within the novel and, secondly, because Canetti himself does not intervene in the course of the narration. It is rather that the figures themselves reveal and denounce themselves through the medium of the interior monologue. There is no resident judge. Certainly there is a reference within the novel to the Inquisition (and Friedberg Aspetsberger quotes it in attempting to substantiate his proposition):

> Learning ought to possess its own Inquisition Tribunals, to which it surrenders its heretics. One ought not thereby to think immediately of death by fire. The legal independence of the priest caste in the Middle Ages has much to recommend it. If only the scholars of today were as well treated! As a result of some small, perhaps necessary offence a scholar whose work was invaluable, would be condemned by laymen (p. 406).

There is, however, in spite of this reference to the Inquisition, no suggestion in the novel that the world of learning pronounces its verdict and takes its revenge on the heretics. It is rather that Kien's suicide is brought about by his own intellectual shortcomings, even though the individuals with whom he is in contact foster the idea of self-destruction by aggravating the unhinging of his mind or even by introducing him, as is the case with his brother, to the idea of suicide. Canetti neither condems nor punishes; he presents and implies. In this sense Canetti's novel has much in common with Günter Grass's *The Tin Drum*. In neither case is judgment pronounced upon the characters.

It is also difficult to know in what way Peter Kien may be regarded as a heretic. One possibility might be to suggest that Kien thrusts himself into the role of Christ by claiming to be the saviour of books rather than men (and in any case fails in his mission). In this purely religious sense Kien may be said to have blasphemed the name of Christ and hence to be a heretic. In another sense it could be claimed that Kien is heretical in betraying the world of learning and wishing to deviate from accepted forms of belief, for example, in wanting to dispute the existence of blue as a colour. Aspetsberger's idea that *Die Blendung* is an act of punishment meted out by a judge is in any case at variance with other critics. David Roberts, for example, speaks of Kien's death as a symbol of the volcanic forces in the individual and in society (p. 201). Karl Markus Michel[12] produces a statement which is much in line with Salman Rushdie's view: 'Kien stands paradigmatically for the unworldly intelligentsia of our century, for its capitulation to political reality'. Claudio Magris[13] describes *Die Blendung* as the 'highest modern parable of the intelligentsia which does not feel itself equal to the chaos of life and destroys itself in a delirious defensive mechanism'. In none of these analyses does the idea of punishment or judgment occur.

In his essay entitled *Revoking the Fall* Gerhard Neumann[14] produces arguments which allow the reader to think of *The Tower of Babel* as a viable alternative to *Auto-da-Fé* as the title of the English-language version of Canetti's *Die Blendung*. The essay in question is an attempt to identify the nature of Canetti's aphorisms, concentrating primarily, of course, on *The Human Province*, since at the time the second volume of aphorisms, i.e. *The Secret Heart of the Clock*,[15] had not yet been published. Gerhard Neumann's argument proceeds from a quotation from Canetti's[16] first book of aphorisms:

> The fact that there are *different* languages is the most sinister fact in the world. It means that there are different names for the same things; and one would have to doubt that they are the same things. All linguistics hides the striving to reduce all languages back to *one*. The tale of the Tower of Babel is the tale of the second Fall of Man. After losing their innocence and eternal life, human beings wanted to grow artificially to the heavens. First they had tasted of the wrong tree, now they mastered its ways and grew straight up. In return, they lost what they had managed to retain after the first Fall: the unity of names.

Gerhard Neumann then explains, as does Canetti, the fall from grace as taking place in two stages: the first stage, i.e. eating from the tree of knowledge brings with it the birth of language as a result of the confrontation with sexuality and death, and the second stage involves the fragmentation of language yet again as a consequence of God's displeasure with man. The sinfulness of the world—what Canetti[17] refers to as *disintegration* in his essay *Die Blendung*—has thus been caused by man's twofold transgression and the accompanying double curse of God, 'by the loss of innocence and eternal life' on the one hand and 'by the loss of authentic language' on the other hand (p. 183, Neumann). However, the awareness of evil presupposes the existence of good, the condemnation of Adam presumes the existence of the second Adam, and the fragmentation of the language points to the possibility of linguistic reintegration. The fall foreshadows redemption, healing and the bridging of the division.

The number of occasions when the word *Turm* (tower) occurs in the text is not large. It is, however, used to describe the piling up of books. Even when Peter Kien as a young boy has himself locked in the bookshop overnight, he considers the possibility of building a tower of books (p. 12). This statement could be regarded as anticipating what does in fact happen later on when he migrates each night from one hotel room to another. He carries large quantities of books around with him and each night arranges them in neat piles on the brown paper which he lays out on the floor. The books, however are imaginary, having been 'purchased' in the various bookshops in accordance with non-existent booklists:

> 'The books built themselves up (*'türmten sich'*) higher and higher, but even if they fell they would not be soiled for everything was covered in paper. Sometimes at night when he awoke, filled with anxiety, it was because he had most certainly heard a noise as of falling books. One evening the piles of books were too high even for him; he had already acquired an amazing number of new ones. He asked for a pair of steps. (p. 150)

Each evening he unloads these books from inside his head. When Sancho Panza in the shape of Fischerle enters the service of his Don Quixote, he humours his master by arranging the books in towers, allowing them only a limited height, presumably in keeping with his own limited stature (p. 176-77). The building of these towers of books is a visible sign of Kien's increasing insanity at a point in time when he has been expelled from the heaven of his own library by the machinations of a woman. It smacks of the self-same arrogance which in the building of the Tower of Babel (Genesis, chapter 11) provoked God's chastisement. In this sense it may be regarded as the 'Second Fall of Man'. David Roberts refers to the three parts of *Die Blendung* as 'the progressive destruction of Kien from the Fall of Man via the expulsion from the paradise of his library to the headless world which ends in the fires of hell'. This description of the novel fails to encompass the twofold aspect of the fall from grace: the act of original sin involves not only eating from the tree of knowledge but building the Tower of Babel.

As Dieter Dissinger[18] states, the dialogue between the figures in *Die Blendung* emphasize in grotesque manner the inability to communicate one with another, and suggests 'a Babylonian linguistic chaos caused by specialisation, the self-delusion ('Blendung') of man'. However, this failure to communicate does not set in after Kien's second fall from grace for it has existed from the outset even whilst Kien was still living in the protective environment of his own library. Kien shows not the remotest understanding of Therese Krumbholz, his housekeeper—even after drawing on the advice of Confucius, and his misunderstanding prompts him to make an offer of marriage. He erroneously imagines that she will be the best means of keeping his library in order (p. 42) The gulf between them is equally wide when they discuss financial matters, especially their respective wills. However, their non-communication does reach a meaningful climax: 'A few moments later they had understood each other for the first time' (p. 131). The naming of names is just a prelude to Kien's expulsion from his home and 'the paradise of his library'. From the moment in time when Kien begins to build his towers of Babel the lack of communication is total: Kien and Fischerle fail to understand each other and Georges Kien's inability to help his brother is also a clear-cut sign of a breakdown in communication. Linguistic chaos prevails.

The Babylonian confusion of language within the world as portrayed in *Die Blendung* is caused, as has already been stated, partly by specialisation and by the fact of the individual figures' inability to communicate. In effect they speak different languages, each one being separated from the other because the individual has his or her private myth. Canetti[19] refers to this aspect of the novel in a conversation with Rudolf Hartung in making the following statement:

> That each person has a dream which recurs again and again, which becomes most important, by which he is motivated, which distinguishes him from other men—one might call it his private myth ... and I was very concerned in *Auto-da-Fé* to create figures which clearly express even such private myths, in other words to leave out much else which otherwise belongs to a figure in a novel. It was important to me to show how the private myth of a person impinges on that of another.

Elsewhere Canetti has spoken of the *acoustic mask* which each figure possesses and both terms, Kien's *private myth* and the *acoustic mask*, emphasise the distinctiveness of each individual's mode of speaking and mode of thinking. The private myths create unbridgeable gulfs of misunderstanding and much of the humour, usually of a grotesque nature, stems from this basic situation. Canetti[20] has commented in one of his essays upon human beings as totally separate linguistic units:

> I realized that there is no greater illusion than the view that language is a means of communication between people. Rarely does anything penetrate into the mind of another person and when this does take place, then something which is incorrect.

The figures in *Die Blendung* suffer precisely from this illusion and in their blindness even pride themselves on their capacity for probing the minds of their fellow human beings. After imposing an image upon Fischerle Peter Kien summarizes the situation: 'Never before had Kien felt himself enter so deeply into the mind of another man' (p. 170). Such a conclusion allows Kien to surrender himself totally into the arms of a person who systematically tricks him out of the possession of his money. His brother Georges is no better in his assessment of character, failing to comprehend in succession Therese, Pfaff and his brother. Nevertheless he persists in thinking of himself as a great student of men (p. 392). In the light of these observations it is easy to share the opinion of David Roberts: 'Society has become the tower of Babel of the modern city' (p. 126).

In his *Lectures on the Philosophy of Religion*, Hegel[21] speaks of the division of the world into good and evil as a result of man's eating of the tree of knowledge and states in particular: 'The higher explanation, however, is that by this Adam the second Adam, i.e. Christ, is to be understood. Knowledge is the principle of intellectuality, which, however, as has been said, is also the principle of healing the damage caused by division.' If one reviews Kien's life in the light of this statement, a pattern emerges suggesting that he has eaten of the tree of knowledge, been expelled from the paradise of his library, indulged in the building of the Tower of Babel and thus contributed to the decimation of language which resulted from God's curse. Peter fails to make good the damage which proceeds from division. He refuses to come to terms with his own sexuality. His fear of women leads to the suppression of his body and devaluation of all life. He lives in one half of himself. Rather than trying to overcome death, he takes refuge in death. Ostensibly he pursues matters of intellectual concern but finally succeeds in betraying the very values he wishes to protect. In a perverse sense he destroys the humanitarian principles to which his mind should be attached. He converts Heine's prophecy into reality. He builds towers, fails to counter the linguistic chaos which such spiritual arrogance produces, and is unable to bridge the gap between himself and others. He is unintelligible to others and they are unintelligible to him. He does not rescue his own tongue. He is unable to undergo that change which would allow him to combat the consequences arising from the Garden of Eden and the Tower of Babel. He is incapable of recognising, and falls victim to, those power structures which exist both inside and outside himself. He denies in his life those principles which Canetti himself upholds. The linguistic confusion in Kien's mind does not allow him to recognize his own situation. Babel triumphs. And in this sense *The Tower of Babel* as the English translation of *Die Blendung* is just as appropriate, or even more appropriate, than *Auto-da-Fé*.

References

1   Krumme, D, *Lesemodelle, Elias Canetti, Günter Grass, Walter Höllerer*. Munich/ Vienna: Carl Hanser Verlag (1983), p. 84.
2   Canetti, E, *Die Fackel im Ohr, Lebensgeschichte 1921-1931*. Frankfurt am Main: Fischer Taschenbuch Verlag (1982), p. 339.
3   Canetti, E, *Das Augenspiel, Lebensgeschichte 1931-1937*. Frankfurt am Main: Fischer Taschenbuch Verlag (1988), p. 44.
4   See note 2, p. 341.
5   Schuh, F, 'Blendung als Lebensform'. *Elias Canetti, Blendung als Lebensform*, F Aspetsberger and G Stieg (eds), Knigstein/Ts: Athenäum (1985), p. 41

6   Canetti, E, *The Human Province*, London, Picador Edition (1986), p. 34

7   Roberts, D, *Kopf und Welt, Elias Canettis Roman, Die Blendung.* Munich: Carl Hanser Verlag (1975), p. 25.

8   Page numbering refers to the Picador edition of *Auto-da-Fé*, London, Pan Books Ltd (1978).

9   Rushdie S, in *Hüter der Verwandlung, Beiträge zum Werk von Elias Canetti.*Frankfurt am Main: Fischer Taschenbuch Verlag (1988), pp. 85-89. (This article appeared originally in *The Listener*, 3 December 1984).

10 Heine, H, *Almansor* (1820-1), l. 245.

11 Aspetsberger and Stieg, p. 107.

12 Michel, K M, *Neue Rundschau.* (1964), p. 310.

13 Magris, C, 'Ein Schriftsteller, der aus vielen Personen besteht', in *Hüter der Verwandlung.* (See note 9), p. 267

14 Neumann, G, 'Widerrufe des Sündenfalls', *Hüter der Verwandlung* (see note 9), pp. 182-204.

15 Canetti, E, *Das Geheimherz der Uhr*, Munich: Carl Hanser Verlag (1987).

16 Canetti, E, *The Human Province*, London, Picador Edition (1986), p. 7

17 Canetti, E, *Das Gewissen der Worte.* Frankfurt am Main: Fischer Taschenbuch Verlag (1981), p. 249.

18 Dissinger, D, Der Roman Die Blendung, in *Canetti, Text und Kritik.* Munich: Heinz Ludwig Arnold (ed) (Sept 1982), p. 33.

19 Canetti, E and R Hartung, *Selbstanzeige. Schriftsteller im Gespräch*, edited by Werner Koch. Frankfurt am Main (1971), p. 34

20 *Das Gewissen der Worte*, p. 48

21 Hegel, G W F, *Werke 17, Vorlesungen über die Philosophie der Religion II*, Vorlesungen über die Beweise vom Dasein Gottes. Frankfurt: (1969), p. 258

'Die utopischste aller Utopien'—Language after Babel. Interpreting Christa Wolf's Störfall[1]

Karin McPherson

'And the whole earth was of one language and of one speech', I read, and it seemed as if I were reading this ancient text for the first time. 'And they said, Go to, let us build a city and a tower, whose top may reach unto heaven...' THE LORD seems to be very sensitive on the subject of hubris. He descends promptly and speaks: 'Behold, the people is one, and they have all one language; and this they begin to do; and now nothing will be restrained from them, which they have imagined to do'. At which point he confuses their tongues and thus prevents the building of the tower, as we all know. Interestingly enough, he uses the same means in the case of the megalomaniac Emperor Nimrod: he, too, has a tower built, a shining symbol of his presumption, a tower so high already 'that it took an entire year before the slime and the bricks did reach the mason at the top'. But while they were building,

> they shot arrows into the heavens, and the arrows fell back bloody. And one did speak to the other: Now we have killed all that is up above. But this was the work of the LORD that they be confounded and wiped off the face of the earth. And this he did by confounding their language that they may not understand one another's speech.

How seriously THE LORD takes language. How he makes certain that it does not become an instrument which serves his subjects to join forces against him. We, on the other hand, all understand the basic language with which we build our towers, I couldn't help thinking, but that doesn't do us any good; and we all recognize the technological voice coming out of a machine, and we join in the countdown when it sends that other machine, the rocket-powered tower, into the sky, which is no longer called the sky, by the way, but the cosmos: five-four-three-two-one-ZERO! Only sometimes the towers come crashing down, with their bloody cargo...(84/85)

In this passage, taken from Christa Wolf's latest work, to date, *Störfall* (1987), translated as *Accident*, a narrator's voice, authenticated as a woman, a writer, an 'I', which it is difficult to imagine as being anyone other than Christa Wolf, gives us, the readers, a fresh reading of a 'very old text', quoting from *The Old Testament*.[2]

By putting the biblical images into the context of modern technology, Christa Wolf performs the task of the interpreter; juxtaposing, as she does, the language confusion after Babylon with the contemporary unified 'basic language', the computer speak, she demonstrates how we have become conditioned to receiving news through the modern media, of our contemporary *Babel*: the Challenger disaster at the American Space Centre in

January 1986 and the explosion of Reactor IV at Chernobyl in April 1986. In this way, the narrator/writer finds herself in a new situation of having to interpret, to acquaint herself, her readers, who act as silent listeners, with a rapidly changing language, with a host of new terms, a new jargon from a highly sensitive, coded technical area: these are measured against a rich, varied traditional language of idiomatic expressions, idiosyncratic sayings, quotations from and references to fairy-tales, poetry, prose—especially *Old* and *New Testament* language.

Although writing in retrospect, the narrator relates her thoughts and experiences of one particular day in early May 1986 as if it were the immediate present, and speaks from a position of isolation, left to her own judgement, as an interpreter might be, in the isolation of a booth; hers, however, is a voluntary retreat in a house in the country.

Her isolation puts the narrator into the position of a passive recipient of speech, as one might expect of an interpreter; she (the narrator) receives radio newsflashes and commentaries, becomes addicted to them ('a certain wanton desire for those evil news reports every hour' (54) as the friend puts it to her), to the point of carrying her small Japanese (!) portable radio with her everywhere. Only much later towards the evening, the addiction is trans-ferred to the television set and finally carried to an absurd level, when the narrator spends part of the evening switching constantly between different channels to watch two 'old films' simultaneously.(103/104)

Secondly, she depends on the telephone for receiving 'news' of a very different, personal kind: about the outcome of her brother's operation to remove a brain tumour, from her sister-in-law with whom she shares the silent fears for her brother's physical and mental survival; about her children, and more specifically, about her grandchildren who are a major source of joy and deep human concern to her, indeed her most 'real' link with life; the telephone also brings unexpected joy ('the bright red telephone, God bless it,' (32)), when her friend, like her a woman writer, chooses this particular day to tell her that she is fond of her. By contrast, the voices and faces of the media remain impersonal and belong to men:

> They put some gentlemen in front of the cameras who, solely on account of their nicely tailored gray or bluish-gray suits, (...) their prudent choice of words and the whole official capacity of their posture, radiated a soothing effect— quite in contrast to the handful of young, bearded, sweater-clad individuals who, on account of their agitated talk and manic gesticulations, aroused the suspicion that they had unlawfully commandeered the microphones (...)(100).

As the day progresses, the isolation of the narrator is disrupted by human presence, as neighbours pay unexpected visits, telling her stories from their past lives and present problems, thereby putting the narrator's own fears and preoccupations into perspective without, however, alleviating them.

For the narrator, the day is punctuated also by a number of loud and silent communications with herself: not only in the form of thoughts and reflections, as 'inner monologue' but also as an audible, seemingly alien voice emitting from her, which speaks, cries aloud, laughs, shouts, even bursts into song (Beethoven's/Schiller's *Ode to Joy*—that old all-German favourite), and finally, as a scream of terror wakening her out of a sleep fitful of nightmares. (108/109)

The most persistent feature of communication occurs in the form of addressing a silent 'thou', a 'brother'. The 'Du, Bruder' runs as a leitmotif through the narrative, both as extension and opposite of the 'I'. It is to this 'thou' that the narrator addresses most of her thoughts, reflections and silent communications. For him she acts as interpreter and chronicler of the events and words which this particular day produces and which do not reach his consciousness, since he is anaesthetized. 'Brother' obtains a wider meaning than that of a sibling, or, more specifically, of Christa Wolf's own brother who plays a significant role in the earlier narrative, *Kindheitsmuster* (1976); through the use of 'brother' the narrator appeals to her fellow human beings.

At a deeper, more sinister level, the 'brother' motif is linked to those regions of the subconscious which harbour murderous instincts, and references to the biblical story of Cain and Abel serve as proof (52/53). Proof of another kind is found in Grimm's fairy tale of *Bruederchen und Schwesterchen* (Little Brother and Little Sister), from which the narrator quotes at length, recalling childhood experiences shared with her brother.[3]

The major part of the narrative consists of thoughts, memories and reflections, intricately interwoven into the fabric of faithful reporting and relating of 'facts'. A relatively new feature of Wolf's fiction—always a debatable term in relation to her prose—is her frequent and persistent recourse to scientific data and speculative theories derived from such data. The narrator makes reference—albeit tentatively and selectively as outsider and newcomer to the field of evolutionary and psychoanalytical theories—to physiological data (especially the workings of various parts of the brain and their—known and unknown—functions), to nuclear physics and ecological factors, bound up with the so-called 'peaceful' use of nuclear energy, and to research into atomic weapons.

It would, however, be a misreading of the narrator's/author's intention if one regarded those excursions into the realms of science and technology purely as the explorer's curiosity, and as an end in itself; as always with Wolf, they are intrinsically bound up with the whole process of the search for truth, made more urgent in a situation where the extinction of mankind through its own devices has moved one step closer to self-destruction.

> 'I read that the connection between murder and invention has been with us as long as agriculture itself. Cain, tiller of the soil and inventor? The founder of civilization?'(60/61)

If interpreting is being impartial, reducing the self to a fine instrument of understanding and relating (transmitting) words, sentences, facts in their literal meaning in a specific context, then this narrator lacks the essential skills; if, however, we take interpreting in its philosophical sense, as understanding, explaining, relating meaning in its moral significance, we are closer to understanding the intention behind Wolf's latest book and the position of the central, indeed, the only 'real' character. The philosophical, extra-factual dimensions of the book may be fully gauged by investigating the frequent, underlying references to language: '*Sprache*' as 'motif' and theme; words and their semantic connotations, speaking (*Sprechen*) and silence (*Stille, Schweigen*), including a variant of dialogue with self (*Selbstgespräch*); the location of language-motivation in the brain, the role of language in the evolution of the species, language and the subconscious, the 'blind spot', language as suppression of the darker areas of emotion and instinct, leading to language-rejection ('*Sprach-Ekel*'); finally, the written language: '*Schreiben*', intrinsically bound in all aspects of language, is being put to the most stringent and severe test by the writer, in the process of facing up to a completely new situation in which she finds herself and the world around her.

One important aspect of this whole process is the way in which language features as the narrative itself, reflecting not only the constant transition between the written and the spoken word, but also incorporating a process of selecting or rejecting a whole range of new words, or old words in the entirely alien, new context.

In this process of 'testing' whether language is still usable as the writer's tool, the narrator/author is not afraid to move from the sublime to the ridiculous. Belying any notion that as a socialist, she might be an agnostic (a ghost of her past, laid to rest at the very latest in Wolf's penultimate work, *Kassandra*), the narrator in *Störfall* has no inhibitions in addressing a spiritual being within herself, in the natural world around her: '(...) and I intimidated to that authority who had begun early on to watch me alertly from a very distant future—a glance, nothing more—, (...)' (4)

> Simultaneously, wordlessly, at a deeper level of my consciousness, I assured the Lord of the Nettles, or whatever spirit of nature is responsible for more all-encompassing contexts, that I was not intending to wage war against all nettles;(26) 'That inner authority, which has been surfacing in me with ever increasing regularity, has begun, unasked, to calculate at what age the late sequelae of the last days' meals will catch up with me, should those meals contain radiating substances (...)(56)

Nor does she refrain from addressing God and his authority, albeit in the more distancing rendering of Luther's translation as THE LORD in her references to Babel.(84)

Elsewhere, the narrator quotes verbatim from a religious broadcast on the Ascension of Christ:

> Our preconceptions of time and space pale before the all-encompassing reality of God. This Christ went to the Father. That means he rules over us. The lords of this world go, our Lord cometh. Jesus Christ is the Lord. He shall come again. He shall render the world complete.(49)

She adds her own sceptical comment; distancing herself from the narrow Lutheran notion of blind subjection to authority implied in the broadcast (an ironical twist to her claim that the media rely on the word and image of '*Herr*', to transmit the notion of authority). She warns of the fatal consequences for the individual and for mankind, worshipping the 'wrong' gods in a god-less world of ideas and idols:

> Fine, I answered the radio. But it wouldn't have had to be all that blunt. If, in fact, the need for rule and subordination is so pressing in us from early on that it must form the basis of the invention of our gods—that we (...), should be capable of freeing ourselves from the compulsion to worship gods, are prey to the compulsion to submit to people, ideas, idols (...).(49/50)

The scepticism and irony of the passages cited above contrasts sharply with the tone in which the narrator refers to passages from *The Old Testament* quoted at the beginning. In this way, she admits a need for a metaphysical being beyond fallible human understanding, which would remain unscathed where human language falls apart.[4]

At the other end of the scale, Wolf does not refrain from inserting apparently trivial and seemingly contrived thoughts and phrases into the flow of her text, bringing it down to the level of everyday speech, frequently in asides, as one would if speaking to oneself: a fact for which she has been criticised by a number of Western reviewers, who regard this book as unworthy of the standard of writing to which they are accustomed from her previous works.[5]

The scale and scope of her concern with language, emerging, as always, from the closest reading of her text, does, however, refute this notion, as the present article hopes to show.

One striking feature of the text is a frequent change of narrative tense, which may indeed be seen as setting *Störfall* apart from such highly polished and rounded narrative works as *No Place on Earth* (1979), *Cassandra* (1983), or the earlier *The Quest for Christa T.* (1968). When one takes into consideration Wolf's essayistic work, her travelogues and diaries in the *Four Lectures* leading up to *Cassandra, the Story*, the difference in style and diction to *Störfall* narrows considerably.

In terms of changes in the narrative mode, the applied linguist or the philologist (an expertise to which the writer of this article cannot lay claim) may indeed have a field-day. The narrator's preferred mode is the perfect, used almost consistently throughout, a mode normally associated with spoken language, but also often used in fairy-tales. At crucial points to which the narrator wishes to draw attention, she switches to the future perfect, the pluperfect and, occasionally, the conditional, but inserts also passages in the present or in the imperfect tense.

Occasional examples of drawing attention to stylistic *faux pas* ('four nots in one sentence'(61)), betray that for Wolf the whole process of using language has become a highly self-conscious part of her self-scrutiny as a writer. Language in its most elevated, the literary form, has reached a point of no return, or rather, of turning against itself and its own purpose of having a civilizing effect on mankind.

> But what does that mean, can any, even the most appropriate, formulation still have meaning, so much has already been said and written, the cordon of word nausea becoming ever denser, I never would have thought it possible, dear brother, for the time being I'm only telling this to you growing older means: all that one would never have thought possible comes true, and how should I have foreseen that first the words, and then my words, would nauseate me, and how abruptly the turnabout into nausea at oneself can take place I wouldn't have thought either (...).(98)

Language, writing can change from a pleasurable to a destructive medium within the self-eliminating process of civilization.

This does not mean that the author absolves herself from her responsibilities, on the contrary; it forces her to subject her own established frame of literal reference to the strictest scrutiny. This she states clearly in the first sentence of the text:

> On a day about which I cannot write in the present tense, the cherry trees will have been in blossom. I will have avoided thinking 'exploded', the cherry trees have exploded, altough only one year earlier I could not only think but also say it readily, if not entirely without conviction. The green is exploding. Never would such a sentence have been more appropriate in describing the progress of nature this year (...)(4)

As the narrator 'unlearns' meaning, she gains a new kind of unwanted freedom with it, she loses her motivation towards a future utopian goal, her 'vision'.

> Free to do and, above all, not to do as I pleased. That goal in a very distant future toward which all lines had run till now had been blasted away, was smoldering, along with the fissionable material in a nuclear reactor.(4)

The effect of the newly gained freedom may best be gauged from the search for the 'blind spot' which runs throughout the text, as the second leitmotif. At first it is seen as intricately connected with the analysis of the human brain, but soon leads into the 'darker' regions of the human mind, where pure sicence is out-of-its-depth and psychoanalysis takes over. The narrator/writer finds herself somewhere between those two disciplines, moving, as we shall see, towards the latter. She proceeds from the beneficial scientific use of the term, denoting the function of the eyes, which are able to compensate for the 'blind spot', to the deficiency in human nature, with its inability of compromise in the same way:

> Now we're getting close, very close, to our blind spot after all. (...) Speedy consolation. Our other eye is said to compensate for this minimal gap in our perception. But who or what can help us fill that gap in our perception which we inevitably inflict upon ourselves through our special way of holding our own in this world?(89/90)

The special situation in which the narrator finds herself after the *Accident* at

Chernobyl opens up a new and terrifying dimension: the blind spot becomes 'der glühende Kern', as the smouldering crater of the burning Reaktor IV, an image of the mind's eye since it occurs underground, out of human sight, comes to stand for the depth of human subconsciousness, the darkest hidden regions of unresolved crime and human guilt, from its beginnings (Cain's murder of Abel) to its most recent past, the Holocaust, from the collective to the individual sin:

> Original guilt. The original crime, which can be committed only against the brother, the sister. (...) force the passions leading to the tough, embittered battles with the brother down into the crater in our selves, which has developed early enough as the final disposal site for unbearable radioactive feelings. (...) The blind spot. The heart of darkness.(89)

Facing up to her personal guilt leads to the question of individual responsibility and quite specifically to her use of language, expressed in a series of increasingly rigorous questions:

> That sounds good, but something in me remains dissatisfied. Where, I thought, would be the blind spot have to be situated within me, in my brain—should it be possible to localize it, after all. Language. Speaking, formulating, articulating. Would not the center of greatest desire have to be located in close proximity to that darkest point? The peak alongside the crater?(89/90)

Evolution, far from freeing humanity from moral responsibility, is seen as intricately bound up with the whole process of culture and civilization. It leads the narrator/writer towards even more fundamental scepticism with regards to the humanizing, civilizing powers of language:

> The light of language has pushed into the dark entire regions of my inner world, which may have lain in twilight during prelanguage times. I do not remember. At some point, or many points, we have had to include that savagery, folly, bestiality in civilization, which was created only to tame the untamed. (90)

Caught between the Scylla and Charybdis of culture and evolution, the narrator, as a last resort, turns to the psychoanalyst, who speaks to her in the 'friendly', but sober human voice of her daughter over the telephone (Wolf's own older daughter is indeed a practising psychoanalyst and Jungian).

> The telephone again. My oldest daughter sounded tired, I still pounced on her [my emphasis] with the question: What do you consider our blind spot?(3)

Brushing aside the notion that it acts as a kind of self-protection, the narrator probes further and asks for a clear directive from her daughter:

> Whether, in her opinion, one should nonetheless endeavour to penetrate to our blind spot. In your profession? she said. Absolutely. But one couldn't go it alone (...)(3)

The above passage stands out in the context of the text as a whole, not only as the most genuine dialogue between two people who are very close, but also as the most 'authentic' one, as it brings us closer to Wolf's own experience, than her imagined dialogues with the unconscious brother. Free from digressions, fears and reflection, it may be read as a possible 'way out' of her dilemma, as leading her into facing up to herself, with the help of (Freudian or Jungian) psychoanalysis, breaking down barriers of self-censorship:

> (...) while asking her where she would set the boundaries in the experiment of dismantling our protective boundaries, and she answered as I had expected: There was no boundary, no stopping, once one had seriously begun. (94)

The political poignancy of the narrator's choice of imagery is transparent, not only for readers in the GDR, but equally to all Europeans whose awareness of the 'border' and all its implications is continually refreshed through the media. The special situation of *Störfall*, with the presence of a mobile radio-active cloud over all Europe, shows the absurdity and fallability of man-made 'protective' barriers, (the narrator frequently ponders to which part of Europe she wishes to count herself, as the cloud moves around). Painful as it may be, facing up to the 'blind spot', the darker regions within each individual's self-perception is a first, but decisive step towards creating the conditions under which it would be possible to go on writing.

> And once one had let them in, the depressing pressure would relent and the courage to act would grow—a painful process, to be sure, but also a pleasurably exciting one.(94)

Taken to its most rigorous consequences, this way not only holds the promise of reward for the individual, but also shows a possible future for culture, and the continuation of humanity. The dialogue between mother and daughter breaks off, as the narrator, speaking to herself once again, tentatively suggests a possible future vision:

> That wasn't her department, she said, but why shouldn't there be a chance for an entire civilization if as many of its members as possible can dare to look their own truth in the eyes without fear? Which did not mean to burden the outside enemy with the threat, but to leave it where it belonged, in one's inner self. Whether this wasn't the most utopian of utopias, I asked myself, not her. (94)

In the wake of the Chernobyl incident, the narrator had lost all confidence in her own writing, as part of the self-declared loss of a future 'utopian' goal. Her script on her desk no longer conveys any meaning to her; she now sees it as a mere pre-text, the letters already fading under the influence of radiation; but, in contrast to the method of deciphering secret documents with X-rays, her script does not reveal a hidden message: 'I sat down on my swivel chair, looking through the pages, reading individual sentences, and found that they left me cold. They, or I myself, or both of us had changed (...)' (23)

Consequently, the writer had given herself a 'holiday', promising herself not to write 'another word' on this particular day:
'Relieved, if that's the proper word here, I gave myself some time off. No words today.'(24)
As the day draws to its close, however, she discovers words by another writer to whom she feels suddenly drawn, as if through the shared experience of having progressed through deepest despair. In Joseph Conrad's *Heart of Darkness* which she begins to read when the media have shut down, she finds the 'secret writing' revealed in a way that speaks directly to her:

> And this also has been one of the dark places of the earth. Finally, after all this time, I once again felt that thump against my heart which I feel only when a writer speaks to me from the depths of self-experience. (...) How he managed to free himself from concepts such as 'device', 'effect'—the hardest thing of all. Enough for today. That writer, he knew the meaning of sorrow. He set out right into the heart of the blind spot of that culture to which he also belonged, and not in thought alone. Fearlessly into the heart of darkness.(107/108)

As Wolf's own text draws to the close, we cannot help wondering whether, in *Störfall*, we witness the emergence of her own 'secret writing', revealing itself through her confrontation with the darkness within herself. How else are we to read the final section of the text, a gruesome, uncoordinated outburst of vision and sound, arising from her in a state between dream and wakening? Among the images, a repulsive, decaying, rapidly sinking moon, a photo of her dead mother, enlarged to inhuman dimension, words also emerge, in a foreign language, from a disembodied, distant voice: 'A faultless monster'.[6]

These words, her language, have moved far beyond any interpreter's reach, as they are taken out of any recognizable context and frame-of-reference. If, as an afterthought, Wolf's latest text is to be read, not only as the severence of self from language, under the shock of *system failure*,[7] and its repercussions experienced by the writer/author/narrator, but also as a search for a possible continuation (as her final line might suggest), a future for language and words, it leads into the regions of the psychological depth, in further search for the 'blind spot'.

Notes

1   Wolf, Christa, *Störfall. Nachrichten eines Tages*. Aufbau Verlag, Berlin und Weimar 1 (1987). Luchterhand Verlag, Darmstadt und Neuwied 1 (1987). *Accident. A Day's News*. Translated by Heike Schwarzbauer and Rick Takvorian. Farrar. Straus. Giroux. Virago, New York and London 1, (April 1989). Page references are to the Virago Edition.
2   *Genesis*, 1 Moses, Chapter 11 (V.4ff) and 1 Moses, Chapter 10, (V.8ff; cf. V. 10, King of Babel). I am greatly indebted to my colleague, Mr Malcolm Burnett, for his research into various possible sources for Wolf's unacknowledged references to this, and other passages from the *Old Testament*, from which she quotes freely.
3   cf., p. 71-74. The deep-rooted envy and guilt between siblings rivalling for parent's

love plays an important part in Wolf's autobiogaphical novel *A Model (of) Childhood*.

4   Hardy, Beverley, 'Christa Wolf and Weltseele', in *GDR Monitor*, No. 9, Summer 1983, pp. 10 ff. This article first drew attention to the role of the metaphysical dimension in Wolf's work, establishing her link with the Romantics.

5   For the most comprehensive review to date, see Winnard, Andrew, 'A Case of Disruption. Christa Wolf's "Störfall"'', in *GLL* 41, October 1987, pp. 73ff.

6   cf., p. 109. The term 'monster' is used by Wolf earlier in the text to describe self-destructive models created by Science; in parallel, the narrator asks whether her own generation has not created similar 'monsters' in the early stages of Socialism which often led to blindness towards their own mistakes.

7   An inspired translation of 'Störfall' by my colleague Dr Fiona Elliott, more convincing than the title *Accident* for the translation of the book. The language confusion became obvious to the writer of this article when trying to reach agreement on an appropriate translation; among the terms offered were: moment of confusion; momentary chaos; state of emergency; incident; disorganization; out of control; flat spin; malfunction; meltdown; 'A Case of Disruption' (A Winnards, see above). *Collins Dictionary*, German/English, 1980, p. 663 gives 'Störfaktor' as source of friction, disruptive factor. A colleague, Dr Andrew Barker, suggested an association with 'Störenfried'.

Literature in a Language Degree: the Middleton Hall Seminars

Stewart Paton

The Historical Background

Until about twenty years ago and the appearance of new courses at the new British universities it had been a matter of tradition that the main, if not the sole, purpose of studying a modern foreign language at university was to read and study the literature written in that language. In his 1967 book *Foreign Language Teaching in the Universities* F.G. Healey was clearly not concerned in the first place with literary studies. However he could not avoid considering the general question of the balance between language and literature in British foreign language degrees and in a refreshingly candid description stresses the subordination in the vast majority of courses of linguistic to literary studies:

> that part of a department's work which is concerned with actual language teaching, a not infrequently unhappy Cinderella at present, [is] often shunned for the more exciting, to say nothing of the more professionally rewarding work of research and teaching in literature or philology.[1]

As Healey points out, it is not difficult to understand the historical reasons for this situation. In order to encroach on the preserves of classical studies the modern languages departments had to show firstly that the cultural wealth of modern European literatures was as worthy of study and research as that of ancient Greece and Rome and secondly that the teaching and learning of such languages offered as rigorous a mental training as the classical languages. This last requirement led directly to the close imitation of the methods used in teaching the classical languages so that, even within the time allowed for language study, reading and writing the language were more important than aural/oral comprehension and performance. The great 'reform movement' in the study and teaching of modern languages gathered pace in the inter-war years and, although in the post-war period it had begun to affect practice in secondary schools, had hardly touched on language teaching methods in British universities and had had virtually no effect on the overwhelming literary content of most courses. Not altogether unjustly, therefore, the traditional 'literary' modern languages courses became associated with the 'conservative' approach to language teaching using principally written 'prose' translation and essay work, with the consequent downgrading of the oral component.

However understandable from an historical standpoint this type of development of language teaching at British universities might be, it did not tend to produce in students an awareness of the normal usages of the living language. But if the language course had defects these were bound to affect the literary component of the degree.[2] Healey touches on this problem in the following passage:

> .../ there is a comparison possible between language teaching in universities today and the situation of the Third Estate in France just prior to the Revolution. Like the Third Estate, the study of language, in most conventional university departments of language and literature, is, in a real sense, everything, in that all else really depends upon it, while in another, and equally "real" sense, it is almost nothing if we judge its importance by the number of teaching hours usually devoted to it, as compared to literature and philology, and by the attention which it has received, at university level, as a subject of research.[3]

If (in any real sense) 'the study of the language (...) is (...) everything, in that all else depends on it', then the basic question must relate to the linguistic competence of the students: are they well enough trained in the language to read with some fluency the more difficult texts in the foreign literature, Gogol and Dostoyevsky for example, as well as the linguistically easier Tolstoy or Turgenev?[4] It is not my impression that many traditional courses addressed themselves seriously to this question. The tendency was (and I suspect often still is) to assume that the competence was there and I cannot but feel that the literary component of the degree suffered certain distortions because of the inattention to the linguistic performance of the students. Two aspects of this problem strike me now as being worthy of mention.

The first is possibly only an indication of the inevitable corrections needed at a later stage to the language acquired principally through the reading of literature. Only some years after my graduation and after residence in Germany when I re-read some novels by Thomas Mann did I realise that I had seriously failed to appreciate precisely the *literary* quality of his writing, since my acquaintance with normal, non-literary German had been inadequate. It is always with a sense of shock that one feels the force of the obvious: that for a native speaker the process is to move from the 'normal' language to the literary, and that the literary method of acquiring the language reverses the natural order of events.

The second difficulty has its origins in the burden placed on students by a heavy reading programme. Since the whole teaching operation (lectures, discussions and essays) was more often than not carried out exclusively in English and since therefore the divorce from the language of the original was almost complete it was no surprise to learn that some students, especially with the longer and linguistically more demanding texts, such as Dostoyevsky's novels, took the situation to its logical conclusion and read some or all of these works in English translation. This seems to me not a matter for astonishment or even less for disapproval. It is rather to be seen as the natural result of under-estimating the linguistic problems for undergraduate students of foreign literatures.

One might add here the further point that these problems exist to a greater or lesser degree for any foreigner, particularly in the field of poetry. Few, for example, are the English native speakers who can claim, even after many years of study and residence abroad, to have sensitised themselves to Russian language and culture to the extent that their reaction on an emotional and aesthetic level to the poetry of Mandelshtam or Akhmatova approximates to the reaction of the native speaker of Russian. A fortiori, therefore, must this be true of the undergraduate student—and yet the more difficult, emotionally complex and linguistically resonant poets such as Rilke and Pasternak appear with regularity among the authors prescribed for German and Russian first degree courses.

Apart from these more narrowly linguistic difficulties there were also, as I discovered when raising the subjet with fellow undergraduates and later with a number of graduates from different universities, some feelings of dissatisfaction of a more general kind, similar to those which were voiced in departments of English literature. One met frequently an unwillingness on the part of one's teachers to put forward their own value judgements on the literature which one was required to read. Everything was, it appeared, equally good and equally worth reading. Since no value judgements were offered then clearly no criteria were put forward to help the student in his own assessment of the work in question. With this approach went an over-attachment to secondary sources, an over-emphasis on the importance of what other critics had written and on the biographical and historical cir-cumstances of an author's career, rather than an analysis of the value and message of his major works: indeed one felt at times a reluctance to concede that certain works by the same author could be referred to as 'major' or 'minor'. Such an approach is hardly calculated to produce enthusiasts for the cause of literature and literary studies.

The fate of two groups of people in this situation must evoke now a retrospective feeling of sympathy. Even for those of us who flattered ourselves that we did have an interest in literary study the conventional course had deficiencies, but students who were genuinely more interested in language than literature had no other type of course to choose. Within the conventional degree they had to seek refuge in philology/history of the language courses, often linked to the study of medieval texts, or in various background and history courses. And I would even imagine the existence of a smaller group of sufferers, members of university staffs who might also have felt somewhat cramped by the relative subordination of language work. At post-war Cam-bridge it seemed a sad waste of valuable teaching resources that only for one weekly 'prose' class were students exposed to such virtuosos in the field as Trevor Jones in German or L.C. Harmer in French.

I am far from suggesting that the problems of the conventional language and literature degree course were unrecognised or that whatever could be done was not done to improve the situation. However, within the existing format it was difficult to carry out radical reforms since this would have involved a fundamental shift in the balance between language studies and the other parts of the course, particularly the literary component. The only way, it seemed, was to start from scratch and this was precisely the oppor-tunity taken by a number of the new universities set up in the sixties, where language teaching was accorded greater time and status and where the other elements of the degree course offered a greater variety and choice than had hitherto been the case.

The Heriot-Watt course (*B.A. Languages. Interpreting and Translating*), devised and inaugurated by Professor H. Prais, was one of the latest of the new courses to be set up, accepting its first students in 1970. It was at the extreme end of the spectrum, even among the new courses, in the time and emphasis it gave to language training and practice. Together with the various background topics these occupied up to 90% of the teaching time. Like the majority of the other new courses, however, the Heriot-Watt course retained a literary element, in our case small, but not insignificant. In view of the difficulties I have mentioned, which were experienced on conventional courses in the attempt to link language with literary study, this may seem a surprising decision but it was based on the conviction which commands, I would imagine, general support: that the literature of a society is one of the keys to the understanding of its culture and that in this respect it is of as much importance as any other 'background' topic. A further decision was to try to take into account the fact that the literary element has two aspects, linguistic and cultural, and attempt to do something for both. Firstly since the students spent most of their time on economic, political and legal texts, they needed also to acquaint themselves with the sudden change of gear characteristic of language used in a literary context. With this in mind they were required to read works of modern literature, set within each language section, for discussion in the language with the foreign assistant, leading to the writing of essays in the foreign language which could be, but did not need to be, on a subject connected with the work of literature read and discussed.

The Seminars

Having described to some extent the context in which the Heriot-Watt course evolved, the object of the rest of this short paper is to consider in a little more detail the second strand of the literary component of the Heriot-Watt degree, the strand which had the broadly cultural aim of introducing the students to a limited number of works of literature across the four languages taught on the course: French, German, Russian and Spanish. It was for this purpose that Henry Prais proposed the discussion method at 'literary seminars', which from the beginning of the course until 1980, for second and fourth year students and staff, were associated with the residential weekend at Middleton Hall, a country house outside Edinburgh administered by an educational trust for the benefit of pupils and students in the area.

Students on the Heriot-Watt course studied two of the four foreign languages listed above and the seminars, which took place over one weekend each year, discussed books suggested by three of the language sections and read beforehand. In addition all viewed together and discussed a film chosen by the fourth language section which was generally being seen for the first time by most of those present. The participants were divided into small groups, each of which included two or three members of staff, this being found with experience to be the arrangement which encouraged the greatest student participation.

Although the discussion method engaged the enthusiasm of the staff there had to be a realistic assessment of the obstacles to the seminars' success. The first difficulties might be anticipated from the probable attitude of the students to the idea of reading literature. They would be consciously *language* students who had, after all, deliberately chosen a non-literary course. Some were likely to have an anti-literary bent, although the majority claimed this was not the case, saying they enjoyed reading but did not wish to spend their time as students in literary analysis.

Initial doubts were also expressed about the likely student reaction to the weekend seminar, which could in no sense be said to be anything but a minor component, unassessed, and clearly therefore surplus to requirements. These doubts were, I think, rapidly dissipated, paradoxically because this final factor had a liberating effect on the students, subject to continuous assessment in all their language work. If it also happened that they enjoyed the texts they read because their interest was engaged, then the freedom they felt at doing something outside the assessed curriculum became a positive factor.

This made the choice of texts of great importance, especially in the light of the decision to ask all students to read the work, either in the original if they were studying the language or in translation if they were not. There are those who object to the use of translations on modern language courses, considering that they must detract from any work's literary value. This seems to me a standpoint which is both unduly restrictive and unrealistic. Undoubtedly with some works, shall we say those of a poetic or musical nature, where many of the effects rely on the actual sound of the words used, or those where word games are prominent, it may be true that they are less likely to be successful in translation. But even in these areas there are triumphs to record: apart from the well known versions of Shakespeare in German (Schlegel) and in Russian (Pasternak) and such feats as Marshak's transformation of Burns into a popular Russian poet there are continuing successes in what might be considered an impossible task, such as C. Johnson's recent version of Pushkin and N. Demurova's Russian version of Carroll's *Alice In Wonderland* and *Alice Through The Looking Glass*.[5] However, for the vast majority of prose works of European literature English translations can be obtained, not all of them of the quality of those mentioned above, but certainly sufficient to ensure understanding of the substance of the works chosen in spite of an occasional loss of stylistic refinement.[6]

The texts chosen for the seminars were for the most part shorter prose works, either classics (*Candide* or a play by Chekhov) or modern works which had acquired similar status and which might also cast some light on contemporary society or events of the recent past (Camus, Sartre, Böll, Grass). They had also to be appropriate for group discussion by raising either general moral or political issues, not necessarily limited to the culture of the language in which they were written (Gide: *La Porte Etroite*; Kafka: *Metamorphosis*). Not all the works chosen would necessarily be considered 'Literature' with a capital letter but might be chosen because they illuminated an important issue and could lead to a discussion which involved and engaged the students. Such a work was for example *A Week Like Any Other* by Natalya Baranskaya, which was published in the Soviet journal *Novy Mir* in 1969 and caused a stir at that time by detailing very realistically and very openly the difficulties a married professional woman in Leningrad went through in one typical week. The suggestion (from a student) to choose this work came when the English translation was published by the feminist magazine *Spare Rib* and, since the majority of the students were women, the animated discussion which the book stimulated obviously did not limit itself to a consideration of the position of women in the U.S.S.R.—although that was discussed at some length, not least because of the presence and contribution of the Soviet (female) assistant. There was of course a slight extra difficulty in finding suitable contemporary Russian texts: very few Soviet authors who were not dissidents appeared in translation and although we did have one— contentious—discussion on Solzhenitsyn's *One Day in the Life of Ivan Denisovich* it did put the Soviet assistant in a difficult position. One wonders whether an open discussion of the evils of Stalinism would be more feasible today?

I also had the impression that we were slightly hampered in our choice of what would have been desirable texts in Spanish—and to a lesser extent in German—by the absence of suitable translations. In the appendix to this article I list the programmes which I have been able to trace for the seminars betwen 1974 and 1980 to illustrate the range of texts used and the films chosen for discussion by each language section in turn.

The discussions lasted, with an interval, about two hours in all and usually took the form of a short introductory talk either by a member of staff or, in later seminars, by one or more students, to 'present' the book and the 'questions' it raised in their minds which might be interesting to discuss. The meeting was not chaired by the presenter but by a neutral arbiter, who was on occasions required to function in that capacity. The atmosphere of the discussions obviously varied considerably depending not only on the book discussed but on the group of students and staff and how well they knew each other, but quite frequently we achieved the desired lack of inhibition in the expression of views and in the willingness to express bewilderment and puzzlement. With certain books discussions went particularly well: with those where the question was 'what does it mean?' for example, of which Kafka's *Meta-morphosis* or Beckett's *Waiting for Godot* would be instances; or with others which raised moral questions such as Kleist's *Michael Kohlhaas* or Camus' *La Peste*. Particularly good were the discussions on the films, and perhaps here the liveliness of the reaction was due to the immediacy of the common experience and the feeling that everyone in the discussion started from the same point.

Some of the most striking advantages for our course of this method of presenting literature can be seen at once: the reading and discussions were concentrated into a short period and the effect was similar to the dramatic effect of a performance, similar to a visit to the theatre or cinema. The discussion method also fitted well into a course where one of the aims was to develop fluency in the spoken language along with the ability to express oneself coherently in front of an audience. The method brought to this audience in a limited time a number of key issues in four different cultures and reinforced in my mind the benefits of concentrating the arguments on the essential points of one main text, to which all had equal access, rather than on any secondary sources of information. The disadvantages were equally clear: if students were not persuaded that this was a worthwhile enterprise (and this often depended on the success or failure of the first year seminar held in the department without the benefit of a residential weekend) then they might not give sufficient time and attention to the texts provided. The public discussion also favoured the uninhibited extrovert and was counterproductive, it might be said, for the more reticent—often Scottish—students. And of course the staff talked too much. These worries, with hindsight, seem to me to have been excessive. I am not certain that even the silent students were untouched by the discussions: they could be met later in the bar continuing to debate the issues in private conversations.

If I now attempt to isolate the principal lessons of this method of presenting literature the one overwhelming impression I gained in many conversations was the number of converts, half-converts, and possible converts it had made to the cause of literature. Many students, sometimes rather to their surprise, became interested in some if not all of the books, some even enjoyed both the books and the discussion and most judged that they had been present at a worthwhile exercise. It is obviously difficult to gauge the degree of 'success' of such a complex procedure but one did, from the reaction of the audience, sense the liberating effect of open discussion, of witnessing, for example, a passionate disagreement between two members of staff on the basic questions raised by a classic work of literature, and of the realisation that in matters of taste there was not necessarily any one authoritative voice or fixed opinion. At times the force and energy of both attack and defence on a particular point gave everyone a demonstration that for these participants the books and the issues they raised did matter. Often it struck me that the indispensable qualification for speaking about literature is *enthusiasm*: however much one might disagree with the speaker there had to be in the room an advocate for the work chosen, and even if on occasion the poor lecturer responsible was forced on to the defensive, his or her personal commitment to that work was an essential condition for the success of any discussion.

Last, but certainly not least, Middleton Hall itself guaranteed that the weekend would be enjoyable. It provided us with a fine setting, excellent accommodation, occasionally remarkable weather and all the benefits of a residential weekend, particularly the opportunity for closer contact between students of different years and different language sections and between students and staff. To speak about it to those who were there over the first ten years of the Heriot-Watt language course,[7] is immediately to evoke a pleasant recollection. One can only hope that the result has also been that for some of our graduates the attractions of literature have remained in their memory and that in later years they have returned to reading some of the works and authors discussed. However, I would not be surprised if the attractions of literature remain linked in the minds of these former students with the attractions of Middleton Hall.

For the staff on the other hand—while they of course regret the loss of the residential weekend—the benefits of the open, general, seminar discussion method have seemed lasting enough to encourage them to continue the seminars within the Department. As I have attempted to describe, some of these benefits arise naturally from the absence of constraints which are imposed by the format of the traditional language/literature course: the whole group concentrates on a small number of primary texts, carefully chosen; this leads on the more successful occasions to uninhibited discussion with vigorously expressed opinions and value judgements; the use of translated texts means that, usually, narrowly linguistic or aesthetic points are not discussed and that participants concentrate on the main moral and political issues raised by a work. But the greatest benefit of the seminars continues to be the amount of cross-cultural awareness and sheer information conveyed to all the students—whether or not they are studying the language concerned—on some aspects of a foreign culture. In this regard, for the majority of students who study French and German, the contributions of the Spanish and Russian sections are of vital importance, both in widening cultural horizons and in refining perceptions of what is genuinely different in the Spanish or Russian environment and—perhaps more importantly—of what we have in common with these societies.

Notes

1   F G Healey, *Foreign Language Teaching in the Universities*. London 1967, p.23.
2   I have been unable to find any substantial discussion of this issue from the literary side of the modern language degree and it may very well be that this question has unfortunately not attracted hitherto much attention from British specialists in foreign literatures. Professor Healey (op.cit.) and Hawkins (E Hawkins, *Modern Languages in the Curriculum*, Cambridge, 1981) are mainly concerned with their chosen theme of language competence, although they both make a number of valuable comments on the connections with literary studies. However I am obliged to David and Elena Crosbie for drawing my attention to recent works by those specialising in English for Foreigners which have been considering the relationship between language and literature teaching, in particular Brumfit and Carter (eds) *Literature and Language Teaching*, Oxford, 1986; and Quirk and Widdowson (eds) *English in the World*, Cambridge, 1985, especially the article by Professor Widdowson, *The teaching, learning and study of literature*.
3   Healey, op.cit., p. 204.
4   Clearly 'to read' might require more specific definition in any further detailed discussion: the traditional courses seemed to assume not only that one should read fluently but that one should have developed the habit of making an assessment, while reading, for the purposes of literary criticism.
5   This was greeted on its first appearance by an open letter to the translator from Kornei Chukovsky, the doyen of Russian children's literature, printed in the weekly *Literaturnaya Rossiya* of 20 Sept 1968, under the title *Pobediteley ne sudyat* (*Nothing succeeds like success*).
     Professor Demurova described in detail some of the difficulties of translating

Carroll in her article in *Masterstvo Perevoda* (Vol 17, Moscow, 1970) entitled *Golos i Skripka* (*The Voice and the Violin*) which concludes as follows: 'Musicians know very well how music which has been written for one instrument can be arranged and adapted for another. The characteristics of the new instrument have to be taken into account, different, more resonant timbres may need to be used, the pitch may have to be raised or lowered by a tone or a third and so on. As a result the melody may sound a little different but it is still the same melody.

This is what happens with translation: the tessitura may change but the music must remain the same. What the human voice expresses in song so naturally and delicately can also be expressed by the violin.'

6   That there has been an increase in the recognition of the importance of literature in translation is shown by the growing number of university courses incorporating translations in the prescribed literature. The well established Edinburgh University course Russian Studies, of which half consists of literature in translation, continues to attract many students from departments throughout the Unversity.

7   Alas, the residential weekend was one of the first victims of the cuts imposed on the universities in 1981, but I am pleased to say that the seminars have continued since then, although on a slightly reduced scale, within the department.

Appendix

Middleton Hall Seminars 1974-1980
Books and films selected for discussion

		II Year			IV Year
1974	Balzac	*Le Père Goriot*		Aitmatov	*Farewell Gulsary*
	Goethe	*Die Leiden des Jungen Werthers*		Vian	*L'Ecume des Jours*
	Turgenev	*On the Eve*		Hesse	*Der Steppenwolf*
		Film: *Viridiana* (Bunuel)			
1975	Grass	*Katz' und Maus*		Carpentier	*The Lost Steps*
	Rabelais	*Gargantua*		Brecht	*The resistible Rise of Arturo Ui*
	Quevedo	*The Swindler*		Gide	*L'Immoraliste*
		Film: *Nine Days of One Year* (Romm)			
1976	Kafka	*Metamorphosis*		Carpentier	*The Lost Steps*
	Dostoyevsky	*Notes from the Underground*		Hess	*Der Steppenwolf*
	Cervantes	*Exemplary Stories*		Aitmatov	*Farewell Gulsary*
		Film: *Lacombe Lucien* (Malle)			
1977	Borges	*Fictions*		Olesha	*Envy*
	de Nerval	*Selected Writings*		Arenas	*Hallucinations*
	Gorky	*My Childhood*		Camus	*La Chute*
		Film: *The Enigma of Kaspar Hauser* (Herzog)			
1978	Anouilh	*Antigone*		Hesse	*Siddhartha*
	Weiss	*The persecution and assassination of Marat*		Voinovich	*The life and extraordinary adventures of Ivan Chonkin*
	Sinyavsky	*Pkhentz*		Beckett	*En attendant Godot*
		Film: *The spirit of the Beehive* (Erice)			
1979	Lorca	*Yerma*		Kleist	*Über das Marionettentheater*

Malraux	*La Condition Humaine*	Santos	*Time of Silence*
Brecht	*Galileo*	de Beauvoir	*Une mort très douce*
	Film: *Watch your car!* (Ryazanov)		
1980 Quevedo	*The Swindler*	Gogol	*Diary of a Madman*
Aitmatov	*The Ascent of Mount Fuji*	Camus	*L'Exil et le Royaume*
Duras	*Moderato Cantabile*	Fuentes	*The Death of Artemio Cruz*
	Film: *Knife in the Head* (Hauff)		

Coda in Lieu: A Note on the Will for the Deed

Geoff Butler

A contribution from a senior colleague to the *German Life and Letters* 'Special Number for L.W. Forster' (October 1980) began—after a prefatory quotation from Genesis—with the words 'This thing worries me, Leonard'. Frankly, at the time, I thought such public intimacy was a little off-key; and frankly I am still not sure that, despite the changes wrought in and imposed on academic circles in the meantime, it is appropriate to address any 'Jubilar' in print by his first name. In present circumstances, however, I have persuaded myself that the qualm in question deserves to be set aside: they are, after all, exceptional, and arguably unique. And so, of course, is Henry Prais.

The thing that worries *me*, Henry, is that, having been away from the UK academic scene during the decade we are now commemorating, you may find the factors which have led me to write like this unreal. Take it from me, they're real all right. And they have now, in brief, prevented me from penning (outputting?) anything more than a greeting, a bare outline of what I had hoped to work on—and up—in order properly to earn my place in this volume, and a cautious promise to do better later. The factors that are not now exceptional can presumably be taken as read: certainly this isn't the context in which to expatiate on the monstrous treatment being meted out to universities north and south of the border, on what that treatment means to the scholarly and educational values you hold dear, or on the distress currently being experienced and anticipated by the many who share them. Exceptional has been an unanticipated but irresistible and continuing pressure which arose at the very beginning of the period labelled in my diary 'Henry P's *Festschrift*': the present Head of School here fell ill, and I had and have no option but to deputise. Say no more? Gladly, though—for the record—I'd just remind you that, quite apart from the hassles normally associated with such eminence nowadays, we're in the throes of an unprecedented pay dispute which, not least for lifelong members of the AUT thrust into 'managerial' roles, is generating distractions galore. So: though at one time perhaps a fair number of us often found we were too busy for worthwhile words and therefore left undone what we ought to have done, the majority is now busier still, and much of what by rights should receive our keenest attention, subject-related work, has to join a queue—marshalled by accountants, commanded by administrators—that is headed and dominated by tasks related to sheer survival. Oblique it may be, but that, Henry, is my greeting: an amalgam of pleasure—at being able to join the chorus, albeit briefly and ruefully, of those wishing you well—and, yes, of envy, ungrudging and unashamed: long may your retirement continue, long may you enjoy it. 'I could forgive a man for not enjoying Milton';[1] not to enjoy having quit this beleaguered profession of ours would strike me, for one, as unpardonable.

I had hoped to write on Roth. Not on what Roth wrote (so much), but rather on the reception accorded to English versions of it when they first appeared, way back. A colleague of mine, our Deputy Librarian,[2] a Germanist originally, has dug out some old, very short *TLS* reviews which do nothing to dispel a suspicion that, from that day to this, Roth's image in the English-speaking world may have suffered unduly as a consequence of his translators' ... let's say idiosyncrasies. Grist to my mill. Naturally there are plenty of things about German and Austrian literature that your average twentieth-century Anglo-Saxon (let alone, say, the likes of Auberon Waugh) will never have appreciated, been able to appreciate, if only because he or she is ignorant, insular, and often arrogant with it. The interest and enthusiasm you envinced when, years ago, I introduced you to *Perlefter*, and to David Bronsen's mammoth biography of its author, underlines the point: Roth 'wie er liebte und lebte' can appeal immediately, and for—in shorthand—the right reasons, to those who are on his linguistic and cultural wavelength. But what of those who aren't, to whom he can't? It's known that he, or at least his marketability, impressed English and American publishers (advised, I take it, by people who had read him) during his lifetime—enough, at any rate, for them to turn out no fewer than seven of his works in some sort of English between 1930 and 1938.[3] What is not widely known, as far as I can tell, is (a) whether these versions were all as inadequate as the few I've looked at closely of late, and (b) whether—and if so, why—any of them achieved much more than a *succès d'estime*. The *TLS* reviews I've seen so far suggest that in those days, in Britain, in English, Roth's novels may have been just so many lead balloons. If this impression could be confirmed, and matched by cognate data relating to other parts of the English-reading world (notably, of course, the United States), the publishers would have a lot to answer for. For although their recent (re)discovery of Roth has led to an expansion of what the anglophone sees on offer, at the bookshop in Ambridge-or-wherever, they have not, unless I am much mistaken, been improving the translations from the 1930s one whit; they have simply been re-issuing them.

I suppose there's something quixotic about all this. Even if publishers could be made to blush, it's unlikely they'd mend their ways in consequence—not, that is, unless the embarrassment did commercial damage.

But quixotry is thriving these days, Henry. Without a fair measure of it we'd hardly continue battling with the thugs and placemen spawned by Downing Street (and without something akin to it, of course, precious but essentially unquantifiable humanities, a whole range of arts, might have atrophied long since). Naturally I hope I've chosen the wrong word, that reasoned protest at the shortcomings of today's decision-makers will eventually prove persuasive—in publishing as in politics. Teeth-gritting optimism, then, in preference to quixotry. Raabe's 'Dennoch!'.

Which brings me to that promise. It has to be cautious, but some of the straits we're in are necessarily finite, including—I like to think—the worst of mine, as reluctant caretaker. Anyway, the term can't go on for ever (it's my last, incidentally, as a full-timer), and then... Well, then there'll be time to tackle backlogs, eliminate chaff, repair sins of omission. Won't there? No wry answers, please. For Roth's sake, to go no further, let's both assume there will. The lesson to be learned from his 'Anglo-American landfall' is, I'm sure, a lesson to us all.

Notes

1   Charles Lamb, letter to Coleridge, 5.12.1796, as recorded in *The Oxford Dictionary of Quotations*.
2   His name is Keith Jones. Bibliometrists please note.
3   Hamish Ritchie, whom you'll remember, confirmed this for me recently, at a conference on Roth superbly organised (in Leeds) by Helen Chambers. Hamish doesn't, of course, need this sort of acknowledgment; but with so many quantifiers on the loose it's just possible that Helen will find honourable mention useful. Come to think of it, even dishonourable mention is a Good Thing, I'm told, in the eyes of the citation-counters. Hard to credit it, isn't it? It's the only thing that prevents me from revealing the name—you're unlikely to have noticed—of the horse that, to my delight, finished last in the Grand National the other day.

List of Contributors

Janet Altman   A member of AIIC (International Association of Conference Interpreters). She joined the staff of Heriot-Watt's Languages Department (French, German and Italian) in 1983 after working as a freelance interpreter in Brussels and Rome. Her publications include an annotated bibliography on the teaching and practice of interpreting.

Geoff Butler   Professor of German at the University of Bath, he formerly taught at Heidelberg University and University College, London. Particular interests are 19th and 20th century prose narrative and literary translation. Co-editor of *German Life and Letters*. His connection with Henry Prais and Heriot-Watt University go back to 1970 when he was appointed the Department's first external examiner in German.

Elena Crosbie   Born in Leningrad, resident in the UK since 1971. She had close connections with Heriot-Watt University's Languages Department long before her appointment as a full-time member of the Russian section in 1985. Her interests include teaching methodology, neologisms and contemporary Russian literature and theatre.

Jim Halliday   Worked as a researcher in the Foreign and Commonwealth Office before joining the Department of Languages at Heriot-Watt University, where he heads the Russian section. He frequently interprets for official delegations and has a particular interest in the dynamics of Russian political discourse.

David Harron   After secondary schooling in Edinburgh, now a second year student on Heriot-Watt University's undergraduate degree course in translation and interpreting (French and Spanish). He will be spending his third year abroad, at the Universities of Tour and Granada.

Basil Hatim   Born in Iraq and involved with English-Arabic postgraduate translator training at Heriot-Watt University since 1980. He has published widely on text type, text structure and texture, always with an applied linguistic slant towards the didactics of translation. His most recent publication is *Discourse and the Translator*, co-authored with Ian Mason.

Andrew Hunter   Appointed Lecturer in the Department of Languages of Heriot-Watt University in 1970, he gained his PhD on French Marxist literary theory. He is currently editor of Volume IV of the *Greig Duncan Folksong*

186

Collection in collaboration with the School of Scottish Studies, University of Edinburgh, and the University of Aberdeen.

Tom Johnston The first professor of economics at Heriot-Watt University from 1966 to 1976 and as Dean of Humanities closely supported Henry Prais in establishing Heriot-Watt's unique provision of the undergraduate degree course in languages (Interpreting and Translating). He was Principal and Vice-Chancellor of the University from 1981 to 1988.

Hugh Keith A member of the German section of Heriot-Watt's Languages Department since 1976. He founded ILS, the University's translation and interpreting service to industry and commerce and is actively involved in the recently established Institute of Translation and Interpreting.

Rainer Kölmel Born in West Germany, studied history at Heidelberg University. He came to Scotland in 1974 and has been a Lecturer in German and history at Heriot-Watt University since 1978. He has published widely on the history of refugees from Nazi oppression.

Margaret Lang Senior lecturer in French at Heriot-Watt University. Her research interests and publications are in both late medieval and contemporary French languages and literature. She is co-author of *En fin de compte*, a communicative grammar for final year students of French.

Karin McPherson Born and educated in Germany, she has been in Edinburgh since 1959. She is now Senior Lecturer in German at the University of Edinburgh, her interests being post-war German literature, East and West, women's literature, especially the novels of Christa Wolf, and 20th century poetry.

Ian Mason Senior Lecturer in French, linguistics and translation studies in Heriot-Watt University's Department of Languages and currently Head of Department. Co-author of two university-level French language courses and of *Discourse and the Translator* (Longman 1990).

Albrecht Neubert Member of the Academy of Sciences of the GDR and since 1963 Professor of English at the Karl-Marx University in Leipzig. A frequent visitor to the UK, he first met Henry Prais shortly after Heriot-Watt University's Department of Languages was founded. His name is closely associated with the Leipzig school of translation theory.

Stewart Paton A founder member of the Department of Languages at Heriot-Watt University, having been appointed to the then Heriot-Watt College in 1966. He was Senior Lecturer in Russian until 1986 and Head of Department from 1976 to 1981.

Jerry Payne Lecturer in German at Heriot-Watt University. He has built on his experiences gained working as an English-language editor in Budapest and pursues his interests in the country and language by teaching and translating Hungarian.

Mireille Poots   Born in France, she studied in Dublin and since 1967 has been Lecturer in French at Heriot-Watt University, where she has a special interest in French for Special Purposes and, with the support of the French Government, in developing contacts between the University and the engineering 'Grandes Ecoles'.

Hamish Ritchie   Now Head of the. Centre for Exile Studies in Aberdeen University, Professor Ritchie was previously Head of the Department of Germanic Studies in the University of Sheffield. The author, editor or translator of some thirteen books and many articles on German themes, he is an authority on National Socialism.

Anthony Stanforth   He taught German language, linguistics, philology and medieval literature at Manchester, Newcastle and Wisconsin before taking up the Chair of Languages at Heriot-Watt University in 1981. He was Head of Department of Languages until 1989 and is currently Dean of the Faculty of Economic and Social Studies.

Noel Thomas   Professor of German, University of Salford since 1983, Chairman of Modern Languages (1984–1989). Apart from articles on 20th century German literature he has published two books on the novels of Günther Grass and co-edited two further books of translation passages and one on interpreting as a language teaching technique.

Alan Thompson   Economist, Emeritus Professor at Heriot-Watt University, ex-Labour MP and former Chairman of the Broadcasting Council for Scotland and Governor of the BBC.